RUSSIA

SEA OF AZOV

NOVOROSSIYSK

SEA

SOCHI

GEORGIA

BATUMI

SINOP

TRABZON

RIZE

AMASAYA

CAMLIHEMSIN

TOKAT

Y

D0722250

EVERETT PUBLIC LIBRARY
MAY   2019

BLACK SEA

BLACK SEA

Dispatches and Recipes
Through Darkness and Light

CAROLINE EDEN

Publishing Director Sarah Lavelle
Project Editor Susannah Otter
Designer Dave Brown
Food Photography Ola O. Smit
Location Photography Theodore Kaye
Props Stylist Tabitha Hawkins
Food Stylist Pip Spence
Production Director Vincent Smith
Production Controller Nikolaus Ginelli

Published in 2018 by Quadrille, an imprint of Hardie Grant Publishing

QUADRILLE
52–54 Southwark Street
London SE1 1UN
quadrille.com

All rights reserved. No part of this publication may be reproduced, stored in a retrieval system or transmitted in any form by any means, electronic, mechanical, photocopying, recording or otherwise, without the prior written permission of the publishers and copyright holders. The moral rights of the author have been asserted.

Cataloguing in Publication Data: a catalogue record for this book is available from the British Library.

text © Caroline Eden 2018
food photography © Ola O. Smit 2018
location photography © Theodore Kaye 2018
design © Dave Brown 2018

ISBN 9781787131316

Printed in China

'From lands the rising crescent lights:
O blessed ships, from what seas are ye come?'

– Yahya Kemal Beyatlı

'The waters of the world are sovereign Powers.'

– Jan Morris, *Travels*

For Dad, and in memory of Mum, in gratitude.

CONTENTS

PRELUDE AND SETTING

On a map, the Black Sea looks like a lake. Broken only by small islands and thin sandbars, its expanse stretches out to meet the countries that share it: Ukraine, Romania, Bulgaria, Turkey, Georgia and Russia.

On paper, it is easy to picture these places as closely connected, just water between them, not hard-edged at all, a region of connectivity, mobility and interdependence. But just as shared identity, cooperation and cohabitation flow across the water, so do conflict, wariness and division.

Over centuries, the trade of empires large and small has passed across the waves, as has much migration: Russian émigrés, deportees from the Caucasus and refugees from the Balkans. In hope, and in fear, thousands have crossed this sea. This, too, was where Jason, the ancient Greek mythological hero and leader of the Argonauts, came to claim the Golden Fleece and where Xenophon – soldier, historian and student of Socrates – and his army witnessed the ill effects of mind-bending rhododendron honey. It is also where northerly winds blow strong, enormous cherry orchards bloom and where most of the world's hazelnuts are harvested. The Dnieper, Rioni, Southern Bug and Dniester rivers pour into the Black Sea, as does the Danube, which once carried sturgeon and catfish so enormous that fishermen used oxen to drag them ashore.

I first glimpsed the Black Sea through the grubby window of a Turkish bus in 2013. My summer holiday that year was a six-week overland journey, from London to Georgia's capital, Tbilisi. On trains and buses I travelled to Munich, Zagreb, Belgrade, Sofia and Istanbul, then across Turkey's Black Sea coast. Close to the Turkish city of Samsun, a road accident on a sharp bend ahead had shaken us. Once clear of the crash, there was a cautious rush to the bus windows. Mobile phones were taken out and passengers began photographing the waves. The sea's reassuring strength, its sink and rise bleeding out to the farthest reaches of the horizon, lifted the mood and relaxed nerves. Combined with the revolution of the bus wheels, its drift hypnotised.

That simple moment of first seeing the Black Sea, likely intensified by the traffic drama, would become my sharpest memory of the entire trip. Years later, I can remember the scene precisely while only photographs can bring back the details of Munich beer halls, gritty Serbian trains and Georgian cafés. The reoccurring picture in my mind of faces pressed to the grimy windows, and the steady blue-grey waves, triggers the same feeling, then and now: an almost spiritual heaviness. Shortly after I returned home, that same memory started interrupting my thoughts and daydreams, kick-starting a Black Sea obsession, sending me first to libraries and then on trips to Istanbul and Odessa, looking to answer questions by speaking to historians, curators and visiting archives. How can history books claim the Black Sea to be both the 'birthplace of barbarism' and 'the sea that welcomes strangers'? Is anything left of the sea's historic trade routes? What connects its towns and cities today? What lies hidden? And what can its foodways tell us about the back story of the Black Sea's communities and landscape?

For this book, I first thought about circumnavigating the entire coast. But it felt more natural to bookend the journey with two of the Black Sea region's most interesting and lyrical cities: Odessa in southern Ukraine and Trabzon in northeast Turkey. Both mythical, multi-layered places ultimately shaped by their maritime positions. One relatively new (Odessa was established in 1794) and one truly ancient (Trabzon, formerly 'Trapezous' and 'Trebizond', has Greek trading roots dating back to 7th century BC). The third key city in this book, forming a neat centre point, is Istanbul. Not on, but satisfyingly close to the Black Sea, connected to it by the throat of the Bosphorus, just beyond Giant's Grave, a landmark hill for boats coming in from the sea. This multi-layered city, one that can feel like a conservative village one moment and a cosmopolitan megacity the next, is full of people from the Black Sea: cooks, fishermen, hamam owners, bakers, musicians and taxi drivers. It is the ultimate Black Sea diaspora. It is also, arguably, the world's greatest kitchen. Of course, there are plenty of places of interest and remarkable traditions lying between Odessa, Istanbul and Trabzon. Not only cities but also smaller towns and settlements, all with very different atmospheres but connected to one another by the sea. We will stop at many of these, too. During my travels to this trio of cities, including one summer-long journey doing the whole stretch, which is recounted in full within these pages, a curious group portrait of eastern Europe and Anatolia began to form.

Wedged between ocean and land, all of these Black Sea destinations have something of the frontier about them. Something setting them apart from their host countries. Odessa, on the Slavic fringes of the former Soviet Union, is part of Ukraine yet distinct from it, with a cuisine influenced by Jewish and Italian traditions and a spoken language that is often not Ukrainian, but Russian inflected with Yiddish. Constanta, on Romania's Black Sea coast, was Tomis to the ancient Greeks and today is home to one of the Black Sea's largest ports. Varna, Bulgaria's third city, has a glorious Roman baths complex and a grand museum housing the world's oldest gold, while the cuisine of Turkey's huge Black Sea region, I found out, has a geography all of its own, full of smoky and buttery flavours, quite unlike anywhere else. The Black Sea offers waterways and land routes leading east to China; south, to the Middle East and the Mediterranean; west, to eastern Europe, and north, to the Baltic Sea. However you look at the Black Sea on the map, its strategic importance cannot be denied.

This book has been written to be read as a journey, ideally from beginning to end, though some of the essays happily stand alone. Turkey has the biggest slice of the book as it covers the largest swathe of my journey. Odessa, Bessarabia, Romania and Bulgaria, by no means less interesting, have fewer pages accordingly. The chapters are arranged by stops along the coastline, with the narrative driving the recipes.

Just as the location photography showcases the destinations, the recipes are intended to enrich the stories, offering another dimension to the travel writing: a way to 'eat the culture' and taste the journey. Therefore, with this in mind — and because I am a journalist and writer who loves food, not a chef — the recipes included here are simple. Some are spiced with a sprinkling of imagination, though most reflect local ingredients, people I met and flavours that I researched and experienced. Naturally they also echo my own eating habits, which lean heavily towards fish, dairy, pulses, herbs and vegetables and, generally, away from meat. Essentially, my aim in writing this was to produce a transporting and multi-sensory piece of travel writing — one that you can read, see and eat.

— Edinburgh, 2018

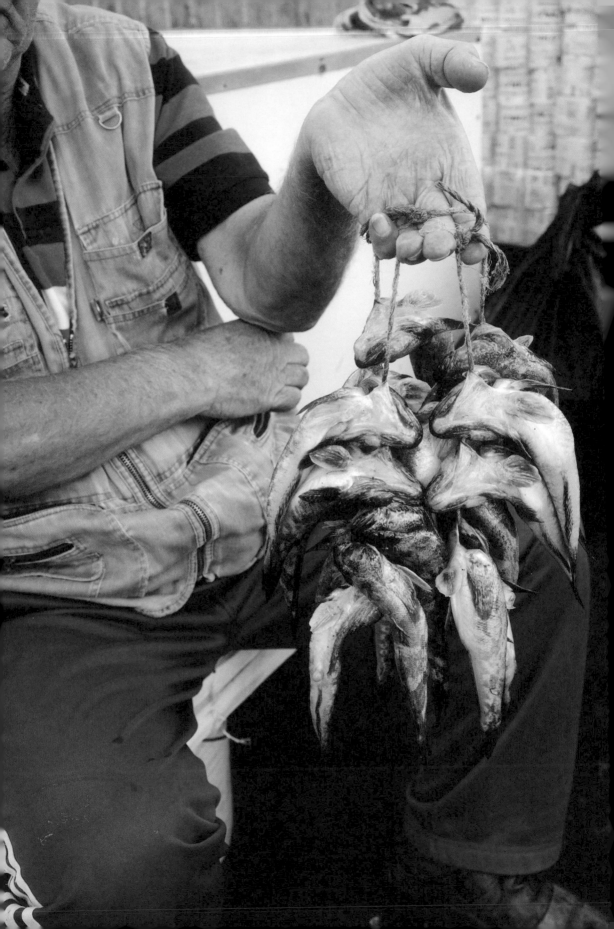

ODESSA

○ ODESSA

○ ISTANBUL

TRABZON ○

A SKETCH OF ODESSA – STEVEDORES, STOWAWAYS AND FABERGÉ EGGS

'No city could match Odessa … with the spirit of jolly buoyancy and light intoxication floating in the air … '

– Vladimir Jabotinsky, *Story of My Life*

Clinging to the Black Sea in southern Ukraine, Odessa has endured much in its short history. Plague, pogroms, the havoc of Communism and the agonies of Capitalism. Yet its mythical status as an important and emotional frontier seaport is as strong today as it was when it was Russia's Eldorado, the fourth largest city in the empire. Greedy, literary and built on the grain trade, this is where Alexander Pushkin was exiled, Anton Chekhov gorged on ice cream made by local Italians, and where Vladimir Jabotinsky, Revisionist Zionist leader, ate Turkish delight in a Greek café while hatching a plan for the state of Israel.

Arriving after-hours, flying up the Black Sea from Istanbul, the silent alleys and badly lit streets gave little away. The summer night had fallen black as pitch and Odessa unfolded in shadowy slow motion. Cars crept. Drunks stumbled. Music spilled out from candlelit basements where struck matches and glowing cigarette tips flashed. A few evening strollers sashayed down Deribasovskaya, a well-lit gaudy pedestrianised thoroughfare, where sad-looking performance horses with love hearts painted on their flanks waited patiently to have their photographs taken. Above it all, pastel-coloured architecture, crumbling and magnificent, rotted in distinguished decay.

Billeted in the hotel's conservatory restaurant, just in time for last orders, I picked the local platter. In Odessa this isn't the usual smorgasbord of cheese and cold cuts, but rather, a disorientating faraway trio of *gobies*, *rapany* and *forshmak*. Something of the city – and the sea – to dive headfirst into.

Each arrived on an individual plate. *Gobies* first. These were easy, little bull-headed fish from the Black Sea; bony, but straightforward. Fried and crispy and unremarkable. Waiting for the next plate, I recalled the warnings at the airport reminding travellers that bribery is illegal (corruption is rampant, this I knew) and wondered about the rumour that once a secret base existed here that trained dolphins for use in military operations. Then, the *rapany*, giant sea snails, arrived. Each shell – the size of a tennis ball – had been flamboyantly restuffed with its snail, chopped and cooked in garlic, cream and white wine.

The glistening mix was disarmingly warm, silky yet chewy, bringing to mind fried mushrooms. It badly needed to be accompanied by strong drinks. As I ate, the world outside shut off and the glass conservatory turned into a mirror reflecting my tired face. Next, *forshmak* for the finale. This is an old-school Jewish pâté of herring and apple, served hot or, in this case, cold. The sweet fishiness was peculiar but the flavours were strangely British, suggesting kipper breakfasts, Bramley apples and school lunchbox sandwich paste. What it required was crisp French breakfast radishes, or maybe a little palate-numbing Tabasco.

Outside, a summer storm brewed. I couldn't see it but I felt it build out there, over the Black Sea, intensifying as it blew in, until it was with me, buzzing in my brain. A waitress cleared the plates. '*Rapany* came to Odessa, stuck to the hulls of trade ships. They eat our mussels, so we eat them,' she said.

That jet-lagged supper — absurdly inexpensive because of Ukraine's faltering economy — stayed with me because it came to symbolise what Odessa is: eccentric, time-warped and strangely familiar, but at the same time really not. A conundrum. Odessa is a young city by European standards, but what it lacks in historical gravitas it makes up for with its splendid architectural bones and worldliness. Cosmopolitan from its inception, its life began when Neapolitan officer General Don José de Ribas seized a Tatar-built fort, Hadji Bey, from the Turks in 1789. His conquest complete, de Ribas asked Catherine the Great if she liked the Grecian name Odessos. She did, but only once she'd feminised it to 'Odessa'.

Sub-par roads connecting Odessa to Moscow played to the city's advantage, with the port offering easier access to Europe, the Mediterranean and Aegean Seas via the Bosphorus and the Dardanelles Strait. From the outset outward-looking, Odessa refused to rely on the empire in the north, instead always looking to the sea for its fortune. This benefited its inhabitants greatly. De Ribas revelled in the world that began to open up, one that allowed small pleasures like drinking European wine and eating mastic-laced sweets.

SALT BEEF AND FURS

De Ribas wanted an upgraded version of his home city of Naples for Odessa but it wasn't until Armand-Emmanuel du Plessis (better known as the duc de Richelieu), a man born into French nobility, became governor of Odessa in 1803 that new roads, schools, theatres and city planning took hold. It took his successor, the Paris-born Count Alexandre de Langeron, to make Odessa the city it became. Under him, in 1817, the city gained free port status, allowing the stockpiling of imported goods without customs duties. Then the fun began.

Ships brought ashore goods as exotic as their origins: bulbous jars of Jamaica rum, oranges from Jerusalem, tins of sardines, bolts of Japanese silks, pots of cayenne pepper, bags of coffee and cocaine, boxes of cigars and tobacco from Virginia. Salt beef and furs left Odessa's docks, while from Constantinople (Istanbul) arrived cargoes of nuts and olives. Silk came from Florence and wine from Spain. Trade ships, from Newcastle, Port Said and Marseille, gathered in the harbour, sometimes three hundred at once. Contraband flooded in, paid for in all manner of currencies, lining the pockets of shipping brokers and filling the stomachs of porters. In Yiddish, 'living like God in Odessa', became slang for having a good time. The city became a vast emporium.

Thriving, and no longer a remote outpost, the city was now a commercial centre full of promise, optimism and opportunity. As Europe's trading partner, Odessa became a Black Sea gateway to the world, attracting hundreds of smugglers and stevedores, netters, dockers and deckhands, all drawn by the sugar-rush of fast cash and the freedom that only a port city can offer. To the workers, the city was 'Odessa mama', as she pleased, fed and provided. Anyone with two hands and the ability to work would be welcomed, no checks required. Everyone mixed.

Bloated with cash, the city's population swelled. French-speaking aristocrats, bohemian nobility and merchants shared dining rooms with Greeks (the first bakers in the city, initially welcomed for their maritime skills and making up 10 per cent of the population by 1795), Bulgarians, Turks, Tatars and Jews. This colourful patchwork population contributed hugely to Odessa's psyche of shrewdness, style and humour. In well-heeled Café Fanconi waiters dressed in frock coats, serving pike caviar smeared on black bread, while in seedier subterranean bars, flagons of beer-like *kvas* poured from metal kegs in cellars serving as underground fridges. Lemon and orange scented the city in the late 1800s as citrus sellers pushed their carts through the streets. Most importantly of all, cargoes of wheat were shipped out in huge quantities from Odessa, making the Russian Empire – for a while at least – Europe's breadbasket.

Journalist and author Aleksandr Kuprin, writing of going out with fishermen to catch mackerel in 1905, almost a century on after Odessa gained free port status, captured the industrious atmosphere:

> Sailors of various nations, fishermen, stokers, merry ships' boys, harbour thieves, machinists, workers, boatmen, dockers, divers, smugglers – they were all young, healthy, and steeped in the strong odor of sea and fish; they understood hard work … and valued above all strength, prowess and the sting of strong language.

Today, decay – in equal measure romantic and tragic – fills the historic centre that hugs Odessa's port. The neoclassical, pseudo-Gothic and Art Nouveau buildings are handsome but threadbare – the stuff of Russian novels – decorated with ornate mouldings, fine arches and columns. Others are too sad for words, crumbling and abandoned, with boarded-up windows, their once grand balconies replaced with cheap plastic. Whatever the state of them, they are all the living history of Odessa. The same can be said of the cafés today that sell 'Jewish food', like forshmak, to non-Jews, a reminder that this was once an intensely Jewish city. A hundred years after the city's formation, Odessa had the second-largest Jewish population in Europe after Warsaw, now much diminished, with Jews making up around a third of the city's population.

In Odessa, a city built on grain and trade, it became obvious that food was the perfect lens for understanding the city's history, psyche and longings. But there was something else here too, a collective sensitivity in the city, something more than nostalgia, more than melody, more than hurt. A self-awareness or melancholy, that stems from the fact that Odessa today somehow fails to live up to its own myths.

A LESSON IN SATIRE

Jerusalem, St Petersburg and Kolkata have in common a certain light, an almost celestial glow, an extra layer of luminosity, a brilliance permeated by the weight of history, environmental bearing and devoutness. Other cities, many more — Bukhara, Marrakech, Reykjavík — fall into the 'atmosphere' camp, because they have weight and heart. But while Odessa has, at times, both radiance and a certain aura, it also has a third quality: imaginative grip. That is, a particularly arresting pull that encourages a craving for something unknown. This can be most keenly felt in the city's historic courtyards, or *dvoriki*. These communal spaces, more than a veranda but less than a terrace, are where the spirit of Odessa — the thing that feeds this 'grip' — hangs most heavily. In the summer, families fill them, spreading out at long food-filled tables, gobbling down cutlets, pouring tea from enamel pots and vodka from decanters while 10-litre bottles of kompot rest with dogs in the shade. This is where the spicy smell of yellow acacia fills the air, tangling up into grape vines and travelling down into the dank, deep-sunk wells and old mazes of catacombs where the souls of long-gone partisans, smugglers and criminals live on.

This discombobulating and addictive grip can be felt in grander quarters too. The light-strewn Passage mall, one of the city's most glorious buildings, doesn't announce itself with window displays — there's no point, the majestic old shops have long gone — but it still dazzles in spirit, in the spaces in between, in what was once there. Golden sunlight floods in through the huge glass atrium. Circling the roof are dozens of baroque statues and sculptures, staring down. Up there, among the ornate plastering and finely chiselled busts, was once one of the finest hotels in the empire. Leagues of wealthy Russian tourists would check into the Passage hotel, then descend down to support a small Fabergé retail store on the ground floor, one of only a handful of such shops worldwide. But this was in the 19th century, and just like the Fabergé shop, now only the dream of what it once was survives. It's true that when old buildings are restored and become too shiny, too present-day, they lose something. But cutting through the usually deserted Passage, little more than a glitzy thoroughfare linking Deribasovskaya and Preobrazhenskaya streets, it's unclear how, despite its abiding soul, a place like this can survive at all. Largely emptied out. Stranded. A ghost.

Getting to know the city, slowly peeling it back, other histories appear. A local magazine, *The Odessa Review,* pointed out that on Marazlievska Street there are two female carved faces decorating the facade of a building. They are eye-catching not for their beauty but because a rope hangs around the neck of each girl. This is a remembrance, of sorts, to the alleged kidnappings of young Odessan women who, in the 19th century, were sold to Turkish harems across the Black Sea. The building that this woeful pair stare out from was allegedly a holding place for these women before they made their grim crossing, and it was here that this young duo chose to hang rather than sail. 'Jewish Street', a typically elegant run-down road, is where the former — and deeply anti-semitic — KGB headquarters was once located. The saying goes that this street is the longest of all, as 'it starts in Odessa and ends in the gulag'. Then there's the myth of the 'Mother-in-Law's' bridge by Vorontsov's Palace. Mihail Sinitsa, a Soviet Communist party official, apparently craved his mother-in-law's perfect pancakes so much he commissioned this narrow bridge so that he could reach her faster.

SUCKING IN THE SMOKE

Silence adds to Odessa's intensity. For a city, it is prize-winningly noiseless. The clamorous world of bigger cities simply doesn't exist. At daybreak, the stillness can feel enormous, with only the echoing foghorns of ships at sea breaking the muffled air. Pootling, rusty trams add a muted vibrational hum. In winter, when cold winds scud off the sea, turning the air to ice, these aged cartoonish streetcars, painted in childish yellows and blues, fill with women dressed in thick black fur coats. In summer, when the city sparkles with possibilities, like too-sweet Crimean *champanski*, the quavering cars swelter and seem to slow down, matching the pace of the city. Easing languidly around bends like slow-moving centipedes, through the heavily scented atmosphere. Dockside, the air smells of rust, tar, salt, brine and diesel. Inland, the fragrance is gentler, of dust, unaired teahouses and perfumy jam. Scents that catalogue memories, unchanged for decades.

Almost every conceivable smell permeates the air at Privoz Market, one of the largest food bazaars in the former Soviet Union, and it was there, in the shadow of giant murals of wheat fields and milk maidens, that I lost an afternoon. Squeezing past tables of curled smoked sausages, earth-rich and bulbous 'Mikado' tomatoes, tables of barnacle-covered flounder and piles of dairy pots, I bartered for jars of *adjika* (a hot and spicy paste known to the Abkhaz as 'salt') and tasted dozens of types of smoked cheese proffered on knife blades by women in frilly purple aprons. The atmosphere was that of a roaring shadow economy, and despite many stalls selling exactly the same meat, vegetable or cheese, everyone has a preferred vendor, with the savvy ringing ahead to get the best stuff put aside. Since 1827, Odessans have shopped here, and according to the historic *Odessa Leaflet* newspaper a thousand 'pairs' of chicken were sold a day in the 1870s.

For lunch, first I'd suck in these smells, breathing in beet-red borscht and inhaling the smoke of fried fish, before following my nose to join office workers in kitsch cafés. Waitresses, dressed like catchpenny bridesmaids in their exaggerated Ukrainian flower-crowns, would bring chicken soup — a dill-heavy broth with matchstick noodles — and sour cherry *vareniki*, all criminally cheap, and usually enough to feed an Olympic team. I'd try to leave room for Odessan Napoleon cake, less dry than the Russian version, with at least ten layers of pastry and lots of custard cream, but usually, I lost.

At night, I'd slump into arty, worn-down cafés or bars that would put their tables outside in summer. And there I'd sit, under the melancholic chirps of caged birds, drinking heavy Cabernet, flicking through menus that offered 'dishes for the company', meaning latkes and pike caviar. All around, heated discussions about music, art and the state of the economy would kick off, tame at first, then, as the dark wood tables topped with white lace filled up with cruets of apple moonshine and pickled herring, the pace would pick up. Politicians — Russian, Ukrainian and even Georgian — would be gossiped about, sending deep belly laughs rippling through the night. Then, usually towards the evening's end, a collective malady, a gloomy ache, would cruise in on the salty sea breeze, dislodging the ambrosial air. When this distemper comes, it absorbs everyone, and everything, slowly seeping in like seawater. It can be felt in cafés, seen on the crumpled faces of diners and in the furrowed brows of waiters. Then, a moment later, it would be gone. A symptom of the Odessa grip. In the morning, all-day dining cafés supply the city with impressive hangover breakfasts: a cup of hot broth, pickles, bruschetta with salt sprats and a shot of vodka.

Geopolitics courses through Odessa's veins. This is a city with a fiercely protected identity that is part of Ukraine, yet distinct of it. Just as some begrudge their dependence on the rest of the country, others resent their disconnection from Russia. Yet, the majority of locals are proud Ukrainians. A little world-weary, but they know exactly who they are. Whatever their background, most will tell you that there is only one nationality in this city and that is 'Odessan'.

Печёночно-
поджелуд...
сбор

Вiтамин
чай

Кр
...

...ёночно...
...желудочный
сбор

Кипрей
иван-чай

Golden Matchstick Soup

I tried a chicken soup similar to this one at Kompot, a famous Odessan café where the upstairs tables allow for excellent people-watching down on to Deribasovskaya Street. With the leftover chicken meat, a bit flavourless after all that boiling, consider using it for a very un-Odessan chicken curry or Asian-style chicken noodle soup – anything heavily spiced to add taste.

SERVES 6

1 celery stick, roughly chopped (plus leaves if there are any)

2 onions, roughly chopped

1 garlic clove, chopped

3 carrots, 2 roughly chopped and 1 grated

3 tablespoons chopped flat-leaf parsley, plus a small bunch of parsley stalks, chopped

2 tablespoons sunflower (or vegetable) oil

1kg/2lb 3oz skinless chicken thighs or drumsticks, or both

2 fresh bay leaves

500ml/generous 2 cups cold chicken stock

1 litre/generous 4 cups water

250g/8¾oz linguine, snapped into matchstick lengths

3 tablespoons finely chopped dill

4 slices of lemon

fine salt and freshly ground black pepper

In a large flameproof casserole over a medium heat, sauté the celery, onions, garlic, chopped carrots and the chopped parsley stalks in the oil for a few minutes until soft and glossy. Season with salt and pepper. Add the chicken and bay leaves, and cover with the stock and water. Bring to the boil and simmer gently, with the lid tightly on, for about 1½–2 hours.

Strain the soup through a fine sieve, discarding the vegetables (keep the chicken for another use, see introduction). Return to the casserole, add the grated carrot and cook over a medium heat for 10 minutes until soft. Add the linguine and cook for 10 minutes or until the pasta is cooked, adding more stock or water if it's too thick. Season to taste, scatter the dill and parsley over, add the lemon slices, then let it rest for 10 minutes before serving.

BABYLON ON THE BLACK SEA –
ODESSA'S JEWISH TABLE

'Odessa is like one of those tricky little snuff boxes — you have to find the catch. Once you know that it opens easily, you can stick your fingers in and take a pinch whenever you want to.'

— Mendele Mocher Sforim, *Fishke the Lame*

Anchoring many Odessan menus, along with Black Sea mussels and borscht, are *tzimmes* and forshmak. They are, as their names suggest, not Russian or Ukrainian, but Jewish. Ukrainian-style forshmak is a simple thing, tasting of what it is: a pâté of soaked chopped herring, mixed with sour cream and apple, served cold on crackers. *Tzimmes*, at its most basic, is a diced stew of root vegetables, sweet with honey or meaty with brisket. In Odessa, these quintessentially Jewish foods are served in non-Jewish restaurants to non-Jewish customers because they have been fully adopted and embraced as Odessan. The city's modern-day Jewish community, hovering around three per cent, is a fraction of what it once was during pre-World War II times but Jewish cuisine remains inseparable from Odessan cuisine.

In downtown Odessa, I sat with Tatiana Zagnitnaya, owner of Sophie Café, to find out more. 'Odessan food is like a mixed fruit kompot. When I was growing up, our Jewish neighbours would share our Easter cakes and eggs together, and for our birthdays we would eat their Jewish gefilte fish,' Zagnitnaya said, leaning her elbows on the table as little plates of cheese scones, hummus and forshmak arrived. Holidays were multicultural in Odessa, Zagnitnaya explained, as were common spaces. In summer, families would gather in courtyards, with the black-and-white television moved outside. 'Fried fish, mackerel and gobies was the smell of my childhood summers. We'd also eat stuffed chicken necks, filled with liver and offal, *tzimmes* with young green onions, sprats and dark rye bread. All Jewish.'

PINK MILK OF SPRING

Escaping the frigid conditions of Yiddish-speaking shtetls (pre-Holocaust all-Jewish towns), where powerful rabbis and Hasidic sages held sway, many Jews who arrived in Godless Odessa in the mid-1800s rebelled. Life was louche. There was fishing in the sea, gambling in dens, operas to attend and feasts of non-kosher food. 'Hello Mr. Lobster, I am coming back to you,' wrote the Odessa-born Jewish author Semyon Yushkevich in his book *Leon Drei*. Being shellfish, lobster is, of course, not kosher. On hearing what misbehaviour their Jewish brethren were up to in Odessa, conservative *shtetl* Jews elsewhere in Europe would wring their hands in despair.

In young Odessa religion didn't count for much. Men were measured on their wealth, ambition and their willingness to graft. The seaport fostered a wild-west atmosphere, bolstered by slack legislation and a sizeable criminal element. Odessa's ability as a city to bootleg and run shady black market dealings was legendary, with much of it taking place under Odessa's streets. Shaded by grapevines, a network of tunnels formed villainous dens and in these hideaways smugglers, gangsters and crooks negotiated and swindled. Unique as Odessa's double-dealing was, it did share a briny grittiness that exists in other great seaport cities, places like New Orleans, Liverpool and Hong Kong.

Into this world was born the city's literary son, Isaac Babel. A famous chronicler of Odessa, he is widely recognised as the greatest prose writer of Russian Jewry, but he is also an unexpected and genius 'food writer', his quick-witted descriptions of mealtimes, meat and vegetables marking him out as one of the greatest. In *Odessa Tales*, a series of complex short stories, Babel reimagines his Odessa as a criminal hub home to a thriving ghetto filled with swanky gangster Jews. Published in 1931 – a decade before Odessa was occupied by the Romanian allies of German Nazis – his masterpiece is a fine snapshot of a lost world where Jews, liberated from claustrophobic shtetls, would fuss, fight and feast. One character is described as looking like a 'pillar of red meat' while other characters get shaken like 'pear trees' or are thwacked over the head with colanders. One man, Jonah, is described as 'a timorous little man' who had developed a taste for wine, 'after all, he had the soul of an Odessan Jew.' In one passage, the black seeds that dot a heavy, dripping red watermelon are described as looking like the 'sly eyes of Chinese women'. Animals are not left out, either. Cows are full with the 'pink milk of spring' and dogs eat well, feasting on jellied veal. In *Odessa Tales* gluttony and food are running leitmotifs, and truth toggles with fiction, much as it does in modern-day Odessa where anecdote, history and myth freely mix.

WATERMELON DOCK AND SORROWFUL APPLES

In Babel's world, heavy-set grocers waddle around, fat on the profits from Turkish olives carried over the Black Sea from Constantinople. These were purchased in *poods* (roughly 36 pounds), a unit long forgotten except for in the old Russian proverb: 'You know a man when you have eaten a *pood* of salt with him.'

Real places, like Watermelon Dock and the Hoehn Factory, whose workshop produced ploughs to work wheat fields, all feature in Babel's stories, as does Café Fanconi, where dandies smoked cigars and slurped ice cream. Inside the famous Baroque opera theatre, Babel describes the sickly light as 'buttery'. The same glow exists today, illuminating the gaudy, neo-Baroque interiors. In Babel's world, during the intermission, theatregoers would gorge themselves on rich liver sausage sandwiches; today, little rounds of bruschetta topped with caviar, preserved lemon and black olives fire out of the kitchen on paper plates.

Babel's streets bloomed with chestnut trees, and on special summer nights life would move outside, just as Tatiana Zagnitnaya of Sophie Café described. Tables, swathed in rich velvet cloth, buckled under the weight of bubbling enamel teapots and samovars. Glamorous and mysterious people arrived by steamship and mingled freely. Muslims walked with their mullahs, their 'striped robes' spilling the 'bronze sweat of the desert' on Odessa's roadways. Even basic *kasha* (groats) is elevated, bringing forth 'carefree childhood memories'. In this freewheeling and outlandish world much eccentric trickery took place, often involving food. Babel describes a cowboy *mohel* (circumciser) who before performing the sensitive rite sniffs a honey cake, downs a stream of vodka and orders the attendant women to 'grind wheat on their bellies' to create more sons and make him all the richer. Men, when tiring of Odessa, would gather, dismiss the world as 'a bordello' and forget it all with rough Bessarabian wine that smelled of 'sunshine and bed bugs'.

As for Isaac Babel's own culinary habits and fondnesses, his grandson, Andrei Malaev-Babel, later told me a little about what his grandfather liked to eat in Odessa. 'His two favourite dishes were scrambled eggs with tomatoes and aubergine caviar "on ice". Ice was a means of keeping it cold, in the good old days. He liked strong tea, and had a sort of a brewing ritual. He also liked to put slices of sorrow-tasting apples in his tea.' These apples were the wintertime Antonovka variety much loved by Russians for their tartness and acidic kick.

A SYNAGOGUE OF LEMON SELLERS

Today, Odessa's Jewish identity owes much to a largely American diaspora who, exploring their eastern European roots, heap collective Jewish memory and love upon it. Touring the sights, full of melancholy, full of nostalgia, they follow a palimpsest of notable Jewish footmarks and shadows long left behind. The Jewish cityscape includes: a memorial plaque at Yevreyskaya Street that marks where Jabotinsky lived, the former home of Chaim Bialik, Israel's national poet, at 9 Malaya Arnautskaya, and on the corner of Rishelyevskaya and Zhukovskaya is a brilliant statue of Babel. He sits, on a sea of wavy bricks, glasses on nose, pen in hand, opposite his old home. The story goes that when

it came to fundraising for Babel's statue the money was raised twice as fast as the funds for a statue of Alexander Pushkin, who made Odessa a temporary home.

But crops, not words, built Odessa and Jews excelled in joining, and outshining, the founding fathers of the city's grain trade. These were wealthy Greek merchants, who also had the monopoly on fruit, wine and vegetables, and Italians who exported wheat to Naples. Jews from Brody in Austrian-controlled Galicia, adept at wheeling and dealing across central and eastern Europe as well as with local producers, led the way from the 1820s. By the early 1900s, Jews owned half of the city's factories. These were ambitious traders, inspired by the work of Moses Mendelssohn whose Jewish enlightenment, or Haskalah, encouraged Jews to modernise, energise and adapt to modern life. Jabotinsky's own father, Yona, was a grain agent who shuttled back and forth to towns along the Dneiper River.

In the late 1800s, there were dozens of small synagogues, some little more than a room, usually named after the owner's trade. As well as the synagogue for tailors, there was a synagogue of lemon sellers and a synagogue of kosher butchers. In 1863, Brody Jews also used the money made in the grain trade to open a spectacular place of prayer: the Brodsky Synagogue, which quickly became more famous for its music than its religious services. One of the few religiously progressive synagogues, serving a fast-growing Jewish population, melodies filled the huge grey stone-clad Gothic building and prayer was accompanied by music. People would travel great distances to hear renowned cantors and choirs perform. When news of this merriment travelled to more conservative Jewish quarters, a saying took hold that that 'seven fires burned around Odessa', in other words, that it was a hotbed of sin. Occupied by the Odessa regional archives since World War II, and during Soviet times operating as a club for shoemakers, when I visited, cracks had formed in the thick walls, some large enough for a child to crawl through. Structurally unsafe, locals joke that it is only the archive's two million or so files and boxes housed in the building that are holding it up.

RAISINS, JUTE, HERRING

Odessa's position as 'breadbasket of Europe' was halted by three factors: the Crimean War (1853–1856), export bans and the surge of the US grain trade, but when this profit-making boomtown was on the up, *kvas* flowed in the city's cafés, Yiddish cabarets were staged and klezmer music filled Odessa's insatiable sloppy bars and halls. As Sholem Aleichem's main character declares in *The Adventures of Menahem-Mendl*: 'If I'm in the mood for bran, there's bran. Flour, salt, feathers, raisins, jute, herring — name it and you have it in Odessa.'

But good times eventually morphed into horror. In 1905, Odessa was the scene of some of the worst pogroms of the Russian Empire, with 2500 Jews murdered in anti-Jewish rioting. Later, Jewish numbers were decimated by pre-war exoduses, massacres by Nazi-allied Romanians, and then later by emigration to Israel and America because of poverty and conflict with Russia. Despite lives lost, and those that would never be, the city's Jewish soul lives on in the bones of Odessa's buildings, in the chapters of books and even in its challah, forshmak and bagels. There are new chapters, too, in the Odessa Jewish story: young chefs are opening restaurants in Odessa inspired by their travels around the Jewish diaspora. One, called Dizyngoff (after former Odessa resident and the first mayor of Tel Aviv, Meir Dizengoff) has Israeli street signs mounted on the walls, hummus on the menu and cocktails with names like 'Purim Spiel'. Its founder, Nika Lozovska, told me that she considers it 'no borders food', representing Odessa's colourful ethnic blanket.

Dark histories and hardship do not mean that Odessa can't be joyous, or hopeful, for when the sun shines on Primorsky Boulevard, by the famous Potemkin Steps, and the mansions glow in the shade of blooming acacias, Odessa feels like a thrilling place. Somewhere, like the foamy port itself, life and opportunity endlessly ebb and flow.

Black Sesame Challah

Maybe only in Odessa would you find Jewish challah — braided bread —
on the menu at an Italian restaurant, but at Bernadazzi, one of Odessa's best
restaurants, I found just that.

MAKES 1 MEDIUM LOAF

500g/3½ cups strong white bread
flour, plus extra for dusting

7g/½oz fast-action dried yeast

2 teaspoons fine salt

50g/2½ tablespoons light brown sugar

160ml/⅔ cup water

50ml/3½ tablespoons vegetable oil,
plus extra for oiling

1 egg, beaten

FOR THE TOP

1 egg, mixed with 1 teaspoon milk

1 tablespoon black sesame seeds

½ teaspoon flaky sea salt

Attach the dough hook/blade to your mixer bowl. Combine all the ingredients
for the dough, initially keeping the salt away from the yeast, in the bowl. Process
gradually until the dough forms a sticky ball. This usually takes a couple of
minutes. Or, to knead by hand, mix the dry ingredients in the bowl and the wet
in a mixing jug. Make a well in the dry mix, pour in the wet ingredients and mix
until you have a shaggy dough, then knead for 5–10 minutes until smooth and
a little sticky. Have a large oiled bowl ready and knead the dough on a floured
surface for 2 minutes, then place inside the bowl, rolling once in the oil,
and cover with a damp cloth or cling film (plastic wrap). Leave for an hour
somewhere warm until doubled in size.

Take the dough and, on a lightly floured surface, split into 3. Using your
hands, roll into 3 oblong pieces around 50cm/20-in long, making sure they
will fit a baking tray. If you find you cannot gain the friction needed to roll
out the ropes, instead of flouring the surface dampen it slightly with a damp
cloth; this can help. Take the 3 pieces and join them, by pinching and tucking
under, at one end, and then plait. It's important not to do this too tightly as
the dough will rise. Pinch and tuck under when you come to the end. Carefully
transfer the plaited loaf to a lightly greased baking tray, cover with a damp cloth
and leave to prove for at least 30 minutes but no longer than an hour.

Preheat the oven to 190°C/375°F/gas mark 5. Brush egg wash over the risen loaf
and scatter over the sesame seeds and sea salt. Bake for around 30 minutes,
keeping a close eye, until golden, then remove from the oven, place on a wire
rack and allow to cool completely before slicing and eating.

Sweet Tzimmes

In Yiddish, *tzimmes* means 'a big fuss' but in the kitchen it is a simple, sweet-ish stew often served during New Year celebrations (Rosh Hashanah), when Jews celebrate the sweetness of life. The carrot coins symbolise hope for a prosperous year and the Yiddish word for carrot, *meren*, also means fruitful. This version, a jumble of vegetables sweetened by cinnamon, nutmeg and dried fruits, is perfect for a light autumn-imbued lunch.

SERVES 6

1 small pumpkin, peeled and cut into 2.5cm/1-in cubes

2 medium carrots, cut into coins about 5mm/¼-in thick

1 medium parsnip, diced

5 dried apricots, chopped

5 dried prunes, chopped

3 tablespoons extra virgin olive oil

¼ teaspoon freshly grated nutmeg

½ teaspoon ground cinnamon

½ teaspoon salt

a few grinds of black pepper

90ml/6 tablespoons vegetable stock

grated zest of 1 orange, plus juice of ½

a few sprigs of fresh thyme, to garnish

Preheat the oven to 200°C/400°F/gas mark 6.

Toss the vegetables and dried fruit in 2 tablespoons of the oil and add the spices, salt and pepper. Toss again, and spread out in a non-stick roasting tray in a single layer. Drizzle the rest of the oil on the top.

Add the stock and the orange zest and juice. Cover the tray with foil or an ovenproof lid.

Roast for 20 minutes, then remove the foil/lid, give the vegetables a stir, place back in the oven, uncovered, and cook until golden brown and caramelised and the liquid has evaporated; this will take around 20 minutes.

Remove from the oven, turn onto a serving platter and scatter the thyme leaves over the top, adding a few whole sprigs for decoration.

One Way with Herring

FORGIVING FORSHMAK

It's a shame that herring is such an unfashionable fish as it's a winner in so many ways: inexpensive, high in omega-3 fatty acids and relatively sustainable. Forshmak (literally 'foretaste' in old German), essentially a herring pâté, has long been popular in the Ashkenazi Jewish world, traditionally eaten as an appetiser or at the Saturday morning Kiddush after synagogue. If you're brave enough to give it a go, here's a jazzed-up version with extra soured cream and a dash of (very inauthentic) spice. The breakfast radishes are essential. It goes well with schnapps.

SERVES 4 AS A SNACK

2 slices of white bread, crusts removed	pinch of sugar
60ml/¼ cup milk	Tabasco, to taste
2 hard-boiled eggs, yolks only	1 teaspoon lemon juice, or to taste
1 Granny Smith apple, peeled, cored and cubed	a few spring onions (scallions) or chives, finely chopped
2 mildly salted herring fillets in oil (see note), drained	small bunch of French radishes, leaves on
200ml/¾ cup soured cream	salt and freshly ground black pepper
1 tablespoon butter	

Soak the bread in the milk for a couple of minutes then add to a food processor with the cooked egg yolks, apple cubes, herring fillets, soured cream, butter and sugar, and process until smooth. Then, with a fork, stir through a few dashes of Tabasco and lemon juice (adding more or less of both to suit), taste and season with salt (if needed) and pepper.

Pour into a serving bowl and garnish with spring onions (scallions) or chives, and serve with the radishes, leaves on, with Matzo, thickly sliced soft white bread or challah.

NOTE:

Salted herring packed in oil can be found in eastern European shops and large supermarkets. Choose a pack that doesn't have additional spices and vinegar.

Another Way with Herring

HERRING AND APPLE SALAD

If forshmak is too far-out for your taste, this salad honours some of the same flavours (apple, herring, egg) but is a little easier going. Go for Matzo, dark rye or toasted challah, to serve.

SERVES 2 AS A SIDE SALAD

2 tablespoons sunflower oil

1 tablespoon white wine vinegar

½ teaspoon caster (superfine) sugar

1 Granny Smith apple, peeled, cored and diced

4 marinated herring fillets, cut into chunks (e.g. Elsinore brand)

juice of ½ lemon

2 eggs

small handful of radishes

freshly ground black pepper

Combine the oil, vinegar, sugar, apple and herring in a large bowl, squeeze the lemon juice over and grind over some pepper. Leave to marinate for at least 2 hours in the fridge.

Boil the eggs for 10 minutes and, when cool, peel and quarter them. Very thinly slice the radishes, using a mandoline or swivel vegetable peeler.

Drain off most, but not all, of the liquid from the herring mix, transfer the salad to a new bowl to serve in, and drizzle over a little of the extra liquid as a dressing. Add the egg quarters to the top of the salad and serve.

AN ICE-CREAM DEBAUCH AND OTHER LITERARY FEASTINGS

'The belly is the belle of his stories, the nose is their beau.'

— Vladimir Nabokov, *Nikolai Gogol*

At the foot of Nekrasova Lane in downtown Odessa, a large mansion sits abandoned. Seeds thrown by Black Sea winds have sprouted into spindly trees, their branches reaching awkwardly out of cracks in the crumbling peach-coloured plaster. Paint curls off wooden window ledges, their panes messily boarded up. In 1850, Ukrainian-born Nikolai Gogol, author of *Taras Bulba* and *Dead Souls*, lived here, in what was his uncle's house. Far from the chill damp of Moscow and St Petersburg, Odessa was a sanctuary of sorts, benefiting from a Mediterranean climate come summertime. On the battered facade, a small plaque shows Gogol's heart-shaped face, his eyes cast downwards, his moustache neat.

Odessa was a literary nerve centre for evacuated intellectuals, and for 19th-century Russian writers such as Gogol, and food was a literary vehicle for ambitious themes — satire, catastrophe, ecstasy and doom. To Gogol, the stomach was 'the noblest organ' and his gastric fixation was as apparent in life as on the page. In Old World Landowners he pays tribute to Ukrainian pastoral life, detailing harvests. Among the pussy willow and pear trees lay apples drying on rugs, downy-soft animals and carts full of melons. Inside the mottled houses stand decanters of yarrow- and sage-infused vodka and jars of gourds and mushrooms, either pickled with thyme, Turkish-style, or stewed in blackcurrant leaves and nutmeg.

BLACK RADISH AND BUTTERY DUMPLINGS

When not writing about food, Gogol obsessed over his stomach. Famously sickly, he complained that his belly, a place where the devil himself sometimes dwelt, was upside down. And in this large house on Nekrasova Lane, he spent the winter nursing himself and struggling to write the ill-fated second part of Dead Souls, a fantastical phantasmagoric poem-novel about a crooked society. 'Dead Souls are not like pancakes,' he once lamented to another writer, 'they cannot be finished in an instant.'

Failing to complete the full work, *Dead Souls* later became the most famous book to remain unfinished. Food in the book, often monstrous and queer,

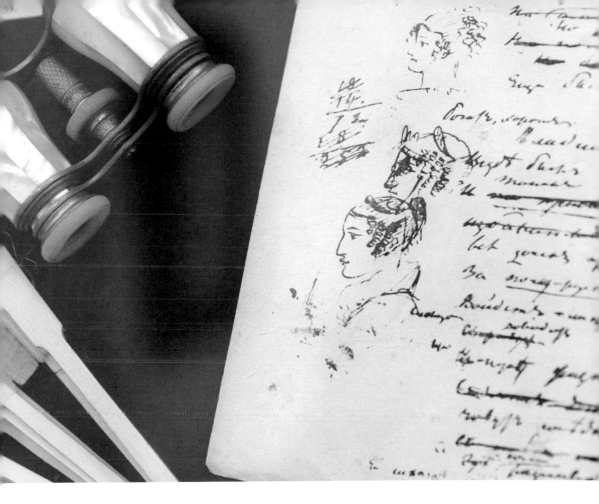

is so prevalent that it pretty much forms the main character. Chichikov, the book's protagonist, enjoying a blowout feast with landowner Sobakevich, gorges on 'a sheep's stomach stuffed with buckwheat groats, brains, and trotters' followed by 'cheesecakes, each much bigger than a plate', before finishing up with unusual preserves including 'black radish, cooked in honey'. Elsewhere in the story, even cockroaches appear 'like prunes', and one pie is stuffed with the cheeks and gristle of a 'nine-*pood*' (325-pound) sturgeon.

His stomach was, eventually, to be the death of him. Gripped with religious mania following a pilgrimage to the Holy Land, he sought spiritual guidance from an ultra-orthodox priest who considered writing to be Devil's work. Shortly after, he declared the second volume of *Dead Souls* a flop, burned it at his Moscow house on Nikitsky Boulevard and slipped into a feverish madness. Fostering an acute eating disorder around the time of Maslenitsa (a sun festival heralding the end of winter before Lent when Russians gorge on bliny, butter, eggs and milk), he had doctors administer all manner of alarming treatments. As well as leeches and boiling baths he tried crackpot cures of cherry-laurel water and rhubarb-laced pills. Shortly after, his self-induced 'holy anorexia' killed him.

While the building on Nekrasova Lane deteriorates more with every passing year, a tribute plays out in the rickety café Gogol Mogol across the street. Locals pack the rainbow-coloured benches for salted herring sandwiches and rough Cabernet, ordered from a menu that comes in a hardback book. In the winter the action moves indoors to the antique-filled dining room, thick with the smell of borscht and buttery dumplings.

IN THESE RED-HOT CLIMATES OF THE EAST

This louche and cosy café scene is the sort that would have appealed to Anton Chekhov, master of the short story. To him, Odessa meant sun-soaked days and easy living, and in his letters he described one particular routine during the hot summer of 1889. At noon, he would take a young debutante out, dining with her at 'Zembrini's for ice cream'. It was Mark Twain, though, who celebrated Odessa's Italian-style ice cream best. Stepping off the Quaker City, a battleship-converted cruiseliner in 1867, he arrived in Odessa at the end of summer, writing about his journey in *Innocents Abroad*: 'It looked just like an American city; fine broad streets … There was not one thing to remind us we were in Russia.' In holiday spirit, he describes sauntering through the markets and finishing the day's entertainment with a full-on ice-cream debauch. 'We do not get ice-cream everywhere, and so, when we do, we are apt to dissipate to excess. We never cared anything about ice-cream at home, but we look upon it with a sort of idolatry now that it is so scarce in these red-hot climates of the East.'

Twain doesn't say where exactly in Odessa he experienced this feast, but Yiddish author Sholem Aleichem placed his ice-cream-eating characters at the white marble tables of Café Fanconi, Odessa's leading coffeehouse: 'I take my seat at Fanconi's … and ask for iced cream. That's our Odessa custom: you sit down and a waiter in a frock coat asks you to ask for iced cream. Well, you can't be a piker,' is how his character Menakhem-Mendl described the scene.

Odessa was a stopping point for many Europe-trotting writers and intellectuals, and their literature, lives and letters line the walls of the city's Literature Museum, a space as eccentric as its founder, Nikita Brygin, a red-haired former KGB officer who had a passion for books. Walking away from the opera house, down towards the sea, large Hollywood-style pavement stars, carved not with the names of actors but with local-born writers and poets, lead the way. Beside Isaac Babel's star is one of the few females represented, Anna Akhmatova, whom Stalin's culture minister referred to as 'half nun and half whore'. Born just outside Odessa, she is one of the 20th century's greatest poets, her work cruelly banned for decades under the Soviets.

Her majestic poem, 'In the Evening', begins:

There was such inexpressible sorrow
in the music in the garden.
The dish of oysters on ice
smelt fresh and sharp of the sea.

Oysters were also a preoccupation of Odessa's famous temporary resident, Alexander Pushkin, who ate them at a restaurant called Cesar Automne. Despite having an entire museum dedicated to him, as well as multiple city statues and busts, he is represented well within the Literature Museum.

Moving a slumbering red dog aside, I walked into the whitewashed galleries, and through the dead air of an eternal afternoon that lingers in museums such as this. Elena Karakina, noted 'Honoured Worker of Ukrainian Culture' and keeper of the museum for 32 years, guided me, reciting Pushkin in Russian as we went.

But we, we band of callow joysters
Unlike those merchants filled with cares,
Have been expecting only oysters...
From Istanbul, the seaside's wares.

Pushkin spent a year of political exile in Odessa in the 1820s, cavorting with Countess Vorontsova, the wife of the governor, while doodling nudes in the margins of his notebook and rewriting the first chapters of *Eugene Onegin*. To Pushkin, Odessa was multicultural and inspiring. He'd sit with his pipe at a restaurant, swim in the sea or drink Turkish coffee. Distinctive with his long fingernails and mutton-chop sideburns, he would walk with an iron stick made from a gun barrel to dine with Charles Sicard, merchant, former French consul and owner of the Hotel du Nord. Today, that hotel, on Pushkinskaya Street, is the Pushkin Museum, where inside, above polished parquet flooring, his eerie white plaster-cast death mask is fixed to the wall. 'Pushkin's Eugene Onegin was the book to read at school if you were hungry,' Karakina said, looking out from under her bowl-cut hair-do and over her spectacles, her eyes wide. 'Imagine! He writes of roast beef, Strasbourg pies, Limburger cheese and golden pineapple.'

GOOD COMPANY AND GALLEY SLAVES

Karakina knows much of these great writers and literati exiles, of their eating habits and souls. She grimaces as she talks of Gogol's hair falling into a plate of spaghetti and talks of famous newspaper editors eating boiled ham and spaghetti on Odessa's beaches. Becoming ever more lyrical, we end with a vivid description of Jabotinsky's face swimming in watermelon juice. 'I shan't tell you more!' she says, wincing with a girlish laugh.

But it wasn't just Russian writers who lusted after Odessa's literary ambience, prosperity and style. Balzac sends his protagonists to trade there. 'Oh! I will go into business again, I will buy wheat in Odessa … That struck me this morning. There is a fine trade to be done in starch,' he writes in *Father Goriot*. Wheat and bakers made an impression on the British journalist Charles William Shirley Brooks – editor of *Punch* and ardent campaigner for (what was then illegal) human cremation. During his travels to Odessa in 1853, he noted the cornucopia of different loaves that appear like 'manna from heaven', the elegant white loaves that would 'do credit to the fancy baker' and then heavy black bread 'which would seem to require the digestion of an ostrich'. But it is in Odessa's monster market, Privoz, where he is really bowled over. There, he finds succulent 'vegetarian idols' in the form of 'millions of onions, dried beans, mushrooms hanging in mighty ropes, pears of a noble juiciness and a sturdy flavour, purple plums of great size and excellence'. He wonders, as many of us do when we visit markets, who on earth is going to eat it all. 'No population, even one of schoolboys let loose with orders to be moderate, could make a perceptible hole in these mighty stores.'

Another wide-eyed British traveller, John Moore, visiting Odessa in the summer of 1824, watched as Russian families stuffed their carriages to the brim with whatever took their fancy from Odessa's port. In his book, *A Journey from London to Odessa*, he describes the scene as a 'grand mart' with Greeks trading imported 'grapes, perfume, shawls and tobacco from the Levant'; Carrarite Jews dealing in 'the best attar of roses and balm of Mecca', while England sold goods from her colonies, Portugal sent Madeira and port, and Spain 'indigo and drugs'. From Odessa's docks went butter, astrakhan pelts, wax, honey and linseed to Constantinople, taking anything between two and ten days in the summer to get there, depending on the winds. Sometimes Odessa's docks would receive 150 vessels from Constantinople in two days. Any suspicious-looking cargo would be picked over by convicts and galley slaves at quarantine. French and Italian was spoken in 'good company' and Russians drank tea, 'substituting milk for brandy', Moore noted.

Today, Odessa's streets are storytelling writ large, even the most touristy among them. Deribasovskaya, named in honour of De Ribas, is a walkway of kompot cafés and chain stores selling cut-price denim. In the summer, families feast on Napoleon cake and sticky meringues. Among the melée, set back slightly, is a golden chair, positioned on a pedestal. It is a salute to

Twelve Chairs, the satirical novel by the Odessan Soviet authors Ilf and Petrov, published in 1928. Its main character, Ostap Bender, is an absurd man, someone that Yiddish speakers of Odessa would probably call a *luftmentsh* (a loafer) who claims to be descended from Turkish Janissaries. His task in the story is to find a missing dining room set, including twelve chairs. It is a bizarre tale, yet it has had a surprisingly wide appeal, being transformed into a Syrian TV series, a Mel Brooks film and two Soviet movies. Odessans could not allow themselves to leave this cultural feat unmarked and queues of people wait to pose with the chair.

Odessa has long greased the imagination of writers, and today its literary nature endures. Every shopkeeper in Odessa stands ready with an anecdote or wisecrack and there are endless plaques dedicated to writers. Something of this bookish dynamism lives on in the food, in the markets and in the cafés, connecting memories of its citizens, too. On the way out of the Literature Museum, we stop in front of a cabinet containing Aleksandr Kuprin's work, and it is his fondness for Bessarabian wine and eating fried mackerel on Odessa's Arcadia beach that brings back early memories to Karakina: 'This I remember from my own childhood, we'd catch them with pillowcases, but now mackerel is gone. Maybe it hated Soviet power and swam away.'

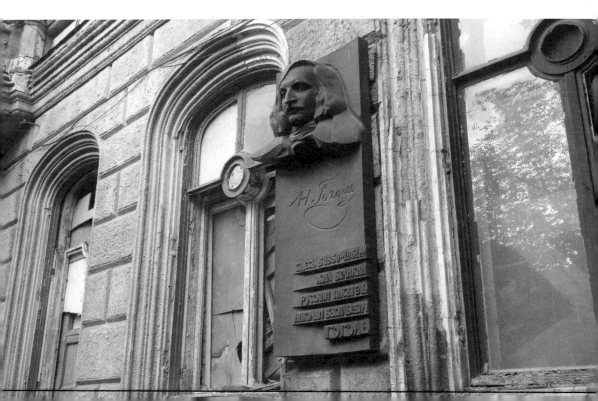

Odessan Coleslaw

If you love hot radishy flavours try to seek out winter's offering of black radishes. Sometimes spherical, sometimes elongated like daikon, they are soot-black but with a white creamy centre and are bolder than regular radishes. Sobakevich, in Gogol's *Dead Souls*, likes his black radishes doused in honey, and this salad reproduces that sweet bitter flavour mix. Across the Black Sea, in Turkey, radishes are called 'turp' and black ones ('kara turp') are often simply grated and soused in vinegar, olive oil and salt.

SERVES 4

FOR THE QUICK PICKLED BLACK RADISHES

200g/7oz black radishes, lightly scrubbed clean

3 tablespoons cider vinegar

2 tablespoons water

1 tablespoon honey

pinch of salt

FOR THE CARROTS

1 teaspoon caraway seeds

2 tablespoons sunflower oil

1 tablespoon honey

1 garlic clove, crushed

1 teaspoon water

½ teaspoon sea salt

good grind of black pepper

250g/8¾oz carrots, peeled and cut into thick coins

Start with the radishes, cutting them into thick matchsticks, keeping the charcoal-coloured skin on (a mandoline with a julienne blade makes quick work of this). Mix the vinegar, water, honey and salt in a small pan. Stir gently over a low heat until the honey dissolves. Remove from the heat and stir the sliced radishes through. Transfer to a bowl and leave to one side while you prepare the carrots.

Begin by heating a dry frying pan and toasting the caraway seeds for 1–2 minutes until fragrant, then lightly bash them using a pestle and mortar, without crushing them entirely, releasing the scent more. Tip into a large bowl and whisk in the oil, honey (if you measure the oil first, then use the same measuring spoon, without washing it, for the honey, the honey will easily slide off, leaving no sticky residue), garlic, water, salt and pepper, then add your prepared carrots, stir to combine and set aside.

Leave both the radishes and the carrots in their separate bowls for a couple of hours at room temperature to let the flavours develop. Keep any juice created by the carrots and toss in. Serve the pickled radish matchsticks, to taste, on top of the carrots.

If you don't want to use all the radishes at once, place in a sterilised jar and keep in the fridge. They will be good for 3 days or so.

Gogol's Marinated Mushrooms

Inspired by the mushrooms described in Gogol's *Old World Landowners*, which are 'Turkish-style', pickled with thyme, these work well on their own, served as an appetiser, or sliced and stirred into stews and salads.

MAKES 1 JAR

FOR THE MARINADE

1 teaspoon fennel seeds

1 teaspoon yellow mustard seeds

100ml/⅓ cup plus 1 tablespoon cider vinegar

150ml/10 tablespoons water

1 bay leaf

1 tablespoon brown sugar

½ teaspoon dried thyme, or 1 teaspoon fresh leaves

¼ teaspoon salt

1 garlic clove, thinly sliced

5 whole black peppercorns

FOR THE MUSHROOMS

200g/7oz chestnut mushrooms, cleaned and quartered, stems left on

1 tablespoon sunflower oil

chopped parsley or dill, to garnish (optional)

salt

Toast the fennel and mustard seeds in a medium pan until they're fragrant and popping, then remove from the heat. Add the rest of the marinade ingredients, bring to a boil, remove from the heat and set aside to cool.

Bring a large pan of salted water to the boil and add the mushrooms. Boil for about 5 minutes until cooked but still firm. Drain and leave to cool, then mix through the sunflower oil.

Once everything is cool, combine the mushrooms and marinade in a large bowl and leave overnight. Then pour everything into a sterilised jar.
To serve, drain the mushrooms and serve sprinkled with herbs. They will keep in the fridge for up to 2 weeks but the oil will solidify, so bring to room temperature before serving.

Mark Twain's Debauched Ice Cream

We don't know what kind of ice cream it was that Mark Twain gorged on in Odessa, but it would most likely have been something simple but decadent. This recipe is for a simple no-churn, rich ice cream jazzed up with a good dash of Caribbean rum. After all, golden-hued 'round-bellied bottles of Jamaican rum' were regularly smuggled ashore in Odessa, if we believe what Isaac Babel says.

MAKES ABOUT 850ML/3½ CUPS

½ a 397g/14oz can sweetened condensed milk

500ml/generous 2 cups double (heavy) cream

2 teaspoons vanilla extract

4 tablespoons dark rum

Put the condensed milk, cream and vanilla into a large bowl and stir in the rum. Using an electric hand mixer, move around the bowl in a slow clockwise direction until it thickens; this will take around 2 minutes. Using a spatula, scrape into a freezer container, cover with lid or cling film (plastic wrap) and freeze until firm, around 6 hours. Eat within a couple of days, as homemade ice cream doesn't have the longevity of shop-bought stuff.

Smugglers (*Kontrabandisty*)

Over fish, under stars,
the little boat races —
three Greeks are aboard,
smuggling goods to Odessa.
Jibing and tacking,
skipping over the waters,
are Yanaki, Stavraki,
and Papa Satyros.
The wind — how it whoops!
How it whistles right past —
sets the nails ringing,
rattles the mast,
and moves with a ripple
neath the hull in the dark:
"Wonderful trade! Excellent work!"
Let the stars sparkle,
let their light pour
on cognac, and stockings,
and condoms galore…
Aye, the Greek sail!
Aye, the Black Sea!
Aye, the Black Sea!..
Thief upon thief

— Eduard Bagritsky's 1927 poem, translated, and reproduced with kind
permission, by Boris Dralyuk.

A BORSCHT REBELLION –
A SHORT MEDITATION ON
THE BATTLESHIP POTEMKIN

Before 1925, the steps leading down to Odessa's docks were simply called the 'Gigantic Staircase' but when Sergei Eisenstein's blockbuster film, *The Battleship Potemkin*, made them the most famous staircase in the world, they became the 'Potemkin Steps'.

Eisenstein's masterpiece - silent, black-and-white, made in just three months - is often tipped as being not the best black and white film ever made, not the best silent film ever made, but simply the best film ever made. His quick cuts and montage techniques are still taught in film classes worldwide. But there are truths and untruths. The Russian battleship Potemkin was real, built for the Imperial Russian Navy's Black Sea Fleet. The crew's rebellion, against the officers in June 1905, also happened and was a flashpoint leading to the events of the 1917 revolution. Its most famous scene, though, the massacre on the Odessa steps, was propaganda.

The film's plot is simple. Life is hard on board Battleship Potemkin. The sailors are downtrodden, tired and fed up with the arrogant officers who freely dish out orders in their white uniforms. Things start really unravelling when maggots are discovered in meat meant for the sailor's borscht. A mutiny erupts and the main sailor protagonist, Grigory Vakulenchuk, later hailed a make-believe hero in Communist lore, is shot dead. The sailors display the body of Vakulenchuk ashore for all to see, and leave a note beside him which reads 'for a spoonful of soup.' Some have said that this film, and its depictions of measly rations, directly contributed to the West's labelling of Russian food as awful. This could indeed be true.

Eisenstein uses the city's steps to great effect in the key scene, when tsarist troops brutally attack the crowd who have gathered in solidarity with the ship's crew. One man falls forward, shot, then another, and another until men fall like dominoes down and down. Others, clutching their throats in horror, watch as adults stampede over children. The most famous scene of all - the pram with a crying baby careening down the steps - is surely one of the most disturbing moments in cinematic history. Almost as harrowing, is the face of the nurse who helplessly looks on, paused in silent scream. Francis Bacon, hardly a stranger to the grotesque, was so inspired by this cinematic moment that he painted his brutal *Study for the Nurse*. It is a crude oil painting of a woman hysterical in an empty room. All context has been stripped away, but it is obvious to anyone who has seen the film who it is.

The steps work in this film, not because they are grand (though they are) but because they offer an optical illusion. The top step is several metres narrower than the bottom one, so from the top, by the Duc de Richelieu statue looking down, the landings are the main view, but from the bottom, looking up, the stairs appear intimidatingly grand and the top looks even further away than it is. The message to those arriving at the port seems to be: 'Look how grand our Odessa is!' Or, to the port docker, way down below: 'Keep on dreaming, keep on grafting, keep looking up. And, remember your place.'

Potemkin Cocktail

This is a twist on the Fireside cocktail, a sour and punchy drink with a hefty wave-slap of Black Sea saltiness.

MAKES 1 COCKTAIL

fine salt

2 ice cubes, crushed

40ml/2½ tablespoons vodka

50ml/3½ tablespoons freshly squeezed grapefruit juice (pink is best)

sprig of rosemary

Lightly rim a chilled tall glass with salt (one way to do this is to dip the glass directly into the squeezed-out grapefruit, give it a wiggle, and then upend the glass on a saucerful of salt). Add the crushed ice and pour over the vodka. Top with the grapefruit juice and stir vigorously. Take the rosemary sprig garnish and light a (long) match, running it along the needles (this will boost the scent), before adding it to the glass.

PORTO-FRANCO – ODESSA'S ITALIAN CONNECTION

'Macaroni boiled in vats of foamy water in front of the shops, sending up steam that melted high in the heavens.'

— Isaac Babel, *Di Grasso*

Alexander Pushkin's character, Eugene Onegin, marvelled at the romance of 'the golden tongue of Italy' that rang out around him in 1820s Odessa. Pushkin himself stayed a while at Odessa's Hotel du Nord on Italian Street, a road as straight as uncooked spaghetti, in that same decade. The surrounding streets, signposted in both Russian and Italian at the time, were spicy with the smell of meatballs and spaghetti, the city's first 'national' dish, because Italians were the first restaurateurs. Some had followed the city's Italian founder, General Don José de Ribas, while others arrived as merchants and stayed on.

Of Odessa's pioneering immigrants, Italians were different. Their dominance, a natural extension of the Italian merchant colonisers whose ships ruled the Black Sea for centuries, lay in architecture, language and trade. Italian architects built the city's showstopper landmarks with Sardinian-born Boffo designing Primorski Boulevard, Vorontsov's Palace and the Odessa steps. Just as Italian was taught in the best schools, it was also the lingua franca of Odessa's commercial harbour, just as it was in Constantinople, across the Black Sea, home to some of the world's oldest trading docks, where the Byzantine Empire had its naval headquarters.

Many clues to Italian trade history in the Black Sea region lie scattered on the sea floor, 2000 metres below. Hidden for centuries, scientists and divers have recently discovered intact masts, rudders and anchors, all preserved by the sea's lack of oxygen below a certain depth. These shipwrecks, 40 or so of them, reveal 2500 years of seafaring history, highlighting the Black Sea's unbroken pattern of trade. Some are Ottoman ships from the 16th to 18th centuries, but others date back further. Among the discoveries is a 14th-century Italian ship, probably belonging to the Venetian empire, an oar-powered Cossack assault vessel, and a Roman shipwreck, its mast still standing, galley tiles and its crew's cooking pots intact. The majority of preserved ships were merchant vessels carrying wine, grain and timber. One, a 2400-year-old ship, was found chock-full of clay storage jars. Remarkably, one still had its contents perfectly preserved, a ship-shape pile of diced-up fish steaks.

Scientists can identify where the ship had sailed from, and when, by examining everything from the anchor to the type of rigging and its cargo.

Most of Odessa's Italian families eventually fled, pushed out by revolution or Stalin or lack of opportunity. But, Odessa's Italian roots live on in the cafés, in the buildings and a curious piece of Odessa's Italian history lives on in that most Italian of songs, 'O Sole Mio'. In 1898, the Napoletano composer Eduardo di Capua arrived to Odessa with his orchestra violinist father. And it was there, inspired by not Naples, but by a Black Sea sunrise, that the hit song was composed. Surprising, but then Odessa has long been a city of virtuoso musicians – and Italians. You could spend a lifetime exploring Odessa's past, and its different communities, but it was time to move on. A bus ride through the backwoods of Bessarabia was next.

Italian Street Polpette

Odessa's very first restaurateurs were Italians and, for a while, their meatballs and spaghetti became the dish of Odessa. This recipe for beef and pork polpette is how I imagine they were eaten back then, on Italian Street. Livened up with fennel seeds and cayenne pepper, a spice sold in Odessa's first shops, these make for a great midweek supper, served with spaghetti or linguine.

MAKES AROUND 25–30 MEATBALLS

FOR THE MEATBALLS

500g/1lb 2oz minced (ground) beef

500g/1lb 2oz minced (ground) pork

1 large egg

½ teaspoon fine salt

75g/2¾oz breadcrumbs

1 large garlic clove, crushed

1 teaspoon fennel seeds, crushed to a powder

FOR THE SAUCE

2 tablespoons extra virgin olive oil

1 medium onion, sliced into half moons

½ teaspoon freshly ground black pepper

½ teaspoon fine salt

1 tablespoon tomato paste

pinch of cayenne pepper, to taste

2 fat garlic cloves, chopped

1 tablespoon dried oregano (or marjoram)

pinch of caster (superfine) sugar

2 x 400g/14oz cans peeled plum tomatoes

200ml/generous ¾ cup chicken stock

TO FINISH

Parmesan

roughly chopped flat-leaf parsley

Start with the sauce. Heat the oil in a flameproof casserole over a medium heat. When warm, add the onion, pepper, salt, tomato paste and cayenne and cook for 2 minutes. Add the garlic and cook for another minute. Add the oregano, sugar, tomatoes (breaking them up with a wooden spoon as you go), and stock, and bring to a boil. Simmer for 30 minutes, then remove from the heat.

For the meatballs, preheat the oven to 220°C/425°F/gas mark 7. Grease a baking tray or line with foil. Add all the ingredients to a large bowl and mix together using your hands. Roll the mixture into around 25–30 golf ball-sized balls. Place on the tray and roast in the oven for 7 minutes, turning the meatballs once, then cook for another 7 minutes, or until browned and cooked through. Remove from the oven and set aside. Meanwhile, blitz the cooled sauce until smooth using a blender. Add the sauce back to its casserole and add the meatballs. Poach gently for 5 minutes, keeping the lid on (or use foil to cover). Then serve on some spaghetti or linguine, topped with freshly grated Parmesan and some parsley.

A WAGON, A BIBLE AND A RIFLE

'The same vine has a different value in different places.'
— Pliny the Elder

Rows of sunflowers, their backs to the road, bobbed in the wind, holding the countryside in rhythm as the last of the sunshine fused out on a satisfyingly bronze note. The darkening sky had injected a sudden urgency to the fields, grey-backed wagtails dipped down, stabbing their beaks into the grubby ploughed farmlands, then lifted up to join their allies in the trees. Children sped home in Wellington boots, zig-zagging along dirt tracks, trailed by their fathers who dragged scythes and dogs behind in the gloaming.

I was Romania-bound, chugging through flat-as-a-pancake Bessarabia, a sort of no man's land that historically covered the space between the rivers Prut and Dniester, but today is divvied up between Moldova and Ukraine. It was the fag-end of a long day and, halfway through the spine-jarring 17-hour journey between Odessa and Constanta on the Black Sea, a late summer pastoral tenderness hummed in the air, reaching in through the windows of the bus. With no sign of a food stop on the horizon, I reclined my seat and shot handfuls of brain-shaped walnut halves into my mouth, fighting off mounting hunger with an airy cream puff bought from an Odessan baker.

In the shadows, our conductor — a wizened Ukrainian with a slicked-back haircut and a crucifix around his neck — sweated, checked tickets and ruffled the mullet hairdos of blonde children. Their glamorous mothers, all glittery hair clips and rainbow-coloured fingernails, constantly and expertly reapplied lipstick in the gloom, despite the washboard road.

This bus ride through Bessarabia was a cinch compared to the one 16-year-old François-David Black endured through these parts in the 1820s. Son of a blacksmith, he had travelled by wagon from French-speaking Switzerland to Chabag, Bessarabia, as part of Louis Tardent's party. Tardent, a 34-year-old botanist, set forth in the summer of 1822, leading eight horse-pulled wagons loaded with rifles and bibles through Bavaria, Austria, and western Ukraine for three months and ten days. His rag-tag caravan of 30 people travelled 1550 miles from the northern shores of Switzerland's crescent-shaped Lake Geneva to the bank of the Dniester Estuary, where the river flows into the Black Sea. Black had been determined to keep a journal for his mother as he went. 'I am writing at midday halt. I have a small board for a desk and a writing case and a bad pen that keeps on running out.'

Settling in Chabag, where the land is very flat and the soil is very rich, what Tardent was met with pleased him greatly: 'If you want to see paradise on Earth, you won't find a better place,' he wrote. Shabo, as the settlement came to be called, would be home to many of the early Swiss colonists for life, although Black, the young diarist, returned to Switzerland in 1825, via the Black Sea aboard an Italian yacht that was almost shaken to bits by the stormy waves.

CHAMPAGNE AND QUAIL PLOV

Black's leader, Tardent, had advanced the charge to develop wineries in Bessarabia. Tsar Alexander I was eager to colonise lands conquered in the Russo-Turkish War (1806–1812) and with nomadic Tatars dispelled, he had taken guidance from his personal teacher, the Swiss scholar Frédéric-César de la Harpe, who had encouraged the idea of moving the Swiss in. On the Tsar's request, de la Harpe put out a call for recognised Swiss farmers to emigrate to this part of Bessarabia to look after vineyards.

Another supporter of the idea was the ambitious governor of Bessarabia, Mikhail Vorontsov. Enlightened, and rich on the successes of land speculation (Pushkin once dismissed him as 'half lord and half merchant'), he was also keen to develop vineyards in Bessarabia. Credited with making Odessa rich, and at times, glittering – his palace at the end of Primorsky Boulevard still stands as a reminder – Vorontsov was, however, busy with his own missions. As well as bringing in steamboats from England for use on rivers and the Black Sea, in Crimea he was busy imitating French wines. There, at the resort of Alupka, south of Yalta, he had enlisted Edward Blore, the British court architect of Queen Victoria who worked on Buckingham Palace, to design a palace on land purchased from local Tatars. A mixture of Mughal pomp and Scottish castle grandeur, it was a triumph in exotic architectural flair, with turrets and fountains carved from a red-veined dove-coloured marble found only in Crimea. Churchill and his party stayed there during the Yalta conference 'drinking buckets of Champagne which would undermine the health of any ordinary man', as one aide later wrote. This was famously soaked up with quail *plov*, a favourite of Stalin's, and chased down with Armenian cognac-style brandy, far stronger than most French varieties. Churchill was reportedly very taken with the palace's lion statues.

LOWER THAN THE VINES

Back across the Black Sea in the settlement of Shabo, the Swiss found themselves to be the latest in a long line of previously settled immigrants who had seen value in the local terroir. Greek colonists had planted the first vineyards there after founding the settlement of 'Tyras' in 600 BC, making

Shabo one of the oldest wine-producing terroirs in Europe. Much later, the Turks recognised that the sandy soil, on the wine latitude, was ideal for grapes, and therefore raisins for their cooking. It was Tardent and his followers, though, who arrived with the necessary wine know-how. In just three years, they had cultivated 100,000 vines and their newly built cellars were packed full of barrels. Even animals seemed in on the success – locals noted in diaries that the oxen trod carefully and knowingly through the vines. Unique grape varieties flourished, like the flowery named Telti-Kuruk, sometimes called 'Turkish fox tail'. Today, the wine produced here under the Shabo label is on the menu at all the best restaurants in Odessa. Drunk there, amongst Odessa's heady atmosphere, it is good (I haven't yet tested whether it travels well).

The Swiss were also following in the footsteps of German settlers. Enticed by interest-free credit, offered by Alexander I after the Napoleonic wars, the Germans built toy villages that looked like they belonged in story books. There were churches with tall pointed spires, so different to the spherical gilt poppy-head domes of the Orthodox churches, and chunky wooden horse stables. In their whitewashed houses, families played pianos and harmoniums and built themselves wine cellars.

Harsh challenges shook the settlers, one after the other. Plague struck in 1830, possibly spread by soldiers returning after the 1829 Russo-Turkish War, but the Swiss settlers managed to hang on and by the 1840s they had enough funds for their own church, decorating it with a bell tower and a cross. In the early 1920s severe famines hit the region and emigration offices were set up locally by shipping companies in towns offering a lifeline of Black Sea opportunity to the desperate. Through it all, the region produced keen and expert winemakers. Louis Tardent's son, Charles, went on to publish *Viticulture et Vinification* in 1854, one of the earliest wine books to be published in Russia and a much-used manual for agricultural schools – highlighting different grapes and winemaking techniques.

But then more horrors followed. A hundred years after the plague, the settlers suffered Stalin's brutal Holodomor, the man-made famine imposed in the early 1930s on Soviet Ukraine and ethnically Ukrainian regions. Then a decade later, following the German-Soviet Pact of 1939, in 1940 the Soviets returned to Shabo, launching a campaign of deportations against minorities. The Swiss mayor, along with his citizens, fled. Properties were collectivised and a *kolkhoz*, a collective farm, was set up. The Swiss days of Shabo were finished.

Today, ordered street layouts aside, little evidence remains of the Swiss settlers, although their trailblazing history is remembered in detail, where they once lived, at the slick Georgian-run Shabo Wine Culture Centre. In a replica kitchen, a display shows how Swiss cookies were made, using a huge manual stamp to place a coat of arms in the centre. Below, in an enormous wine cellar, sits a wooden table displaying a map, a clay qvevri wine jar and a bust of Pushkin, a nod to the poet who came here once to try the wines for himself. This borderland – a wide open steppe-land littered with grasses, wild flowers and migratory birds – greatly appealed to him as a self-proclaimed renegade outlander.

SANATORIUMS, MALLOW AND CLOVER

In the summer, such a pastoral setting, mixed with peace and the fresh air of the Black Sea, draws thousands of holidaymakers – Ukrainian, Belarussian, Moldovan and even Lithuanians – to resorts such as Zatoka down by the Dniester Estuary. Cheap rooms for rent have replaced grander Soviet-era sanatoriums, but the living remains slow and sun-drenched and there's not much to do but swim and eat buckets of berries and fragrant melons sold off the back of trucks.

Only the dreadful roads pose any real challenge today. Just about okay for travel in the summer, lethal and impossible in winter. The churned-up lanes seem a physical expression of the harsh past challenges this particular slice of the Black Sea has seen. A reminder of how tough life was for the Germans, Bulgarians, Swiss, Ukrainians, Russians, Jews, Armenians, Gagauz and Romanians who lived here.

Continuing over ginormous potholes, the driver swerving to miss them when he could, an unreal darkness cloaked the bus, medieval in its density, no electricity breaking it. Rolling deeper into the countryside, a gentle snoring started up, and behind hot, closed eyelids I replayed the day's scenery: a shepherd standing sentinel by his flock with his cloak around his shoulders, belonging to another world. Another driving a herd to a spring where reed, rush and grasses grew. Houses with threshing areas dried out entirely. Barefoot children with dripping watermelon slices and yellow straw hats on their heads, tanned from top to bottom. In the fields, thistle, clover, mallow, daisies and little girls carrying long sticks to thwack down fruit from trees. An utterly beautiful back-of-beyond.

Then, at 4 a.m. sharp, movement in the bus. 'Constanta!' yelled the conductor, giving me, and a couple of other stragglers, the signal to get off, his Brylcreemed hair and crucifix glinting. Over the course of the ride most seats had been occupied multiple times; only a few of us had done the whole hog. Stepping away from the slept-in smell of the bus, and out into the night's cold, salty Black Sea air, I watched as the other passengers dispersed within a minute and I found myself stood on the silent and deserted roadside in Romania's oldest continually inhabited city, the only notable stop on this country's slice of the Black Sea coast. Somewhere out past the railway station, not a good place for this hour, I watched the bus splutter away on to Varna, in Bulgaria, leaving smoke from its exhaust in the wind. Watching it go felt both sad and pleasing.

ROMANIA

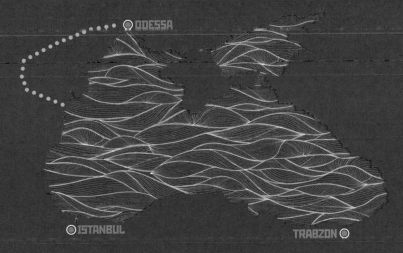

ODESSA

ISTANBUL

TRABZON

GUNSHIPS AND HOLY SPOONS

'All the rivers run into the sea; yet the sea is
not full.'

— Ecclesiastes, 1:7

Constanta, predawn, was dead. I groped through lonely streets until,
guesthouse in sight, I was faced with the red-faced shame of ringing a stranger's
doorbell at 5 a.m. My host, Andrei, a thin man with spiky hair and sunken
cheeks, opened the door and pointed his cigarette in the direction of a
staircase. The room wouldn't be free until later but I could rest in his sitting
room, he said. Grateful, I slumped down on a cream leather sofa. Turning
a huge television to a sports channel, Andrei didn't seem to mind my early
arrival. Ignoring the set, he turned to face me. His Staffordshire Bull Terrier
had died, he said, motioning to a canine portrait on the wall. Then, becoming
lyrically intense, he lit another cigarette and bemoaned politics, worldwide
terrorism and the EU. What did I think about the state of the world, he asked,
twists of smoke rising out of his mouth and whirling out of his nostrils. He
gripped his head in morose sadness. I sympathised. I nodded. I was tempted to
put to use a local saying I'd heard: 'Pull yourself together, it's not like your boat
has sunk in the Black Sea!' But I realised I was stuck. Rudderless, captive, an
indebted audience. I listened until Andrei was half a packet of Kent cigarettes
in, and then fell into a death-like sleep.

Mid-morning, the smell of tobacco signalled Andrei's return. Handing me
a coffee, he ejected me outside onto a small terrace, and onto a plastic chair.
Seagulls, a whole colony, flew in from the direction of the sea. Squawking,
they landed messily on the balcony railing. They were Andrei's friends and
they had arrived for breakfast. As he threw bread crusts into the air, warring
ensued. They flocked closer. Heavier, stronger gulls, knocked into weaker
ones, pecking, flapping and dive bombing. A rookery din. Below, more
gathered, clattering down in search of litter and insects. My host cooed. One
young gull — tracksuit-grey and fluffy-feathered but already hoary-looking and
hunchbacked, vulture-like — Andrei called 'baby'.

BATTLESHIPS IN THE BLACK SEA

Booming gun salutes over the sea announced the start of Constanta's Navy
Day celebrations, sending the birds packing. Faint-hearted, I ejected myself
out onto the sun-baked streets. Crowds of men swayed on the main boulevard.
Dressed in milk-white sailor hats, arms linked and faces ruddy, the better-fed

among them wore their Breton T-shirts high above their guts, exposing beach ball bellies to the August sun. Large women dressed in floral and leopard-print blouses, clung onto the hands of children who, dragging behind, held their melting ice creams out at awkward angles. In between, dazzling like colourful birds, bands of Gypsy girls, all long limbs and longer black plaited hair, swooshed their sequinned velvet skirts, parting the crowds.

Thousands thronged the bunting-lined waterfront. A brass band marched, playing the national anthem, and anchors launched into the sea, in memory to sailors lost. A Romanian flag the size of a cinema screen flapped in front of the Fleet Command building and groups of families gathered there, posing for photographs by phallus-shaped torpedoes. Beyond Constanta's port, one of the Black Sea's largest, the ocean was calm and flat, the horizon broken only by gunmetal-grey battleships, steadfast in the water. Everyone over the age of ten appeared, like Andrei, to be a dedicated smoker of Kent cigarettes.

Drugged by tiredness and grasping for the familiar, I fell into a long queue snaking outside a patisserie. Through the window, bakers paper-bagged up Romanian *covrigi* which looked a lot like Turkish *simit*, or large pretzels. Heavy in the hand, proving its thick apricot content, it delighted. Others fired out of the kitchen filled with sour cherries, cheese and sausages, feeding the hungry and the hungover.

A stone's throw away, one man stood out in the Navy Day crowd. Dressed in a knee-length peasant smock, bound with a thick belt embroidered with purple pansies, and with long wavy brown hair swept carefully behind his shoulders, he looked completely removed from the celebrations. Viorel Marian, or 'Violin', is a socialist-turned-miner-turned-master spoon carver. He had travelled, somewhat optimistically, from an artistic community in the north, with the aim of selling his carefully sculpted spoons to the swaying Constanta masses. A tough call.

One whittling knife and one chisel lay on the table, and above hung dozens of spoons, their long handles and necks carved into detailed owls, crosses, roosters, eagles and angels. I picked them up, turning the cool, smooth willow in my hands. To Violin, spoon carving is a spiritual practice, a way of getting closer to God. But it is an uncertain process, he explained. First comes a heightened sense of joy. Then comes a real fear of losing inspiration. But as he carries on, working and working and clinging on, he suddenly finds himself lost in the craft. This creative energy and emotion is bundled up 'like a knot', finding its way out, into the spoons. The twin spoon, the one I keep hold of as Violin speaks, is the most precious. A holy spoon. It is used just once in a lifetime, on a couple's wedding night as they eat boiled wheat from the same bowl. Two birds represent the lovers, but they don't face one another, they look away in both directions, watching for jealousy and evil. A warrior stance. I bought it but everyone else ignored Violin, passing him by, turned off by his zen vibe and his spoons. Neither were conducive to getting a good Navy Day buzz on.

I took my spoon and climbed 140 steps to the very top of the minaret of Constanta's King's Mosque, where the muezzin gives his echoing call to prayer to the remaining 30,000 or so Turks and Tatars who live here. Far below, yellow container cranes stuck out of the pale blue sea, indicating the port, and closer stood the solemn-looking Lion's House, a grand mansion with palladian columns built to host Freemasons in the 1930s.

A GAMBLE LOST

Steeped in the smell of garlic and wine, a string of restaurants below sold barnacle-clad cloven mussels by the bucket load. At one, the menu was seafaring and eccentric, promising to transport the diner to traditional taverns 'frequented by the dockers, elegant gentlemen and ladies of the night'. Avoiding the 'balls from any animal that is', I ordered a wild mushroom stew with dill and sour cream served on polenta. It was a deeply savoury and umami-tasting, fluffy, moreish pile up. Polenta – or rather cornmeal, as it isn't called polenta until it's cooked – straddles the entire Black Sea region, and in Ukraine and Bessarabia soft cooked cakes of it are cut precisely with a cotton string. Unlike wheat, taxed heavily during the Ottoman Empire, traditionally corn has been a more economical crop.

Lunchtime split the crowds, opening up the boulevard. Fishermen cast their lines into the sea, flipping fishes to patiently waiting cats and standing on manhole covers bearing Constanta's original name, Tomis, in Greek. The covers also bear a picture of the city lighthouse, built in the 14th century by the Genoese who traded at this port and all over the Black Sea. Roma Gypsies spread out on benches playing accordions, laughing and keeping time with a violinist. Children jumped, barefoot, to the music. One musician hooked his instrument up to a speaker and as he played, dozens of small wooden crosses hanging from the cable dangled and danced.

Standing magisterial on the shoreline boulevard was the Casino, symbol of Constanta, partly hidden by a huge flea market. Using the lunchtime lull to spread their goods out further, vendors rearranged ships in bottles, piles of dog-eared postcards and brass menorah candelabras. Oil paintings of horses galloping and bronze nudes were cooed over, while on the ground stood gramophones and silk lampshades and a huge chest of silver cutlery with deer-hoof handles. As I haggled clumsily over a World War II silk map, bright blue waves gently slapped at the Casino, their lull and hue that of the French Riviera.

A tragically dilapidated Art Nouveau beauty, the Casino was opened to the public in 1910. Inside, it is in ruins, with pigeons and cats fighting and fouling under once grand chandeliers, wide staircases and stained glass windows. After hosting invading Red Army officers in 1944, it operated for a while as a restaurant, described in one guidebook as 'a capricious memorial to the age of palm-court orchestras and bath houses', then soon after, its luck ran out and it has been empty ever since. It stands as a grand carcase on a bluff, overlooking the Black Sea, its best days long behind, its one remaining accolade that it is a strong contender for the finest wasted building in the world.

Back at Violin's patch, the patisserie opposite had closed but the bars had taken over, selling beer and pizza to the Navy Day weekenders. Resting in the shade, eyes closed, head tilted back, arms crossed on his chest, it looked as if the only spoon Violin had sold all day was mine. Even so, a genuine, beatific smile spread over his face. Romania has suffered much in recent decades — economic depression, ethnic strife and political repression – so celebrating and having a good time is not taken for granted here. For now, the spoons would have to wait.

BLACK SEA SUPPER FOR THE TSAR

14 June 1914 (1 June in the Orthodox calendar), Constanta. Cossack officers in scarlet uniforms stand sentry on Constanta's pier, guarding the gangway. A volley of guns round off as a banner declaring 'God Save the Tsar' is unfurled in front of the whitewashed Casino. Behind a police cordon an eager crowd gathers, all eyes on the sea. Their king, Carol I, waits, too, surrounded by a retinue of courtiers, men in top hats and medals and journalists with notebooks.

Mid-morning, supported by a battle cruiser, yacht and four destroyers, Russia's Imperial yacht Standart sweeps into the harbour, all shiny mahogany panelling and glittering crystal chandeliers. Slowly, Russia's last Tsar, Emperor Nicholas II, disembarks, followed by his wife Empress Alexandra Fedorovna, in white silk and pearls, Tsarevich Alexei dressed in his sailor suit, and the Grand Duchesses. Filing out to the sound of beating drums that ricochet across the city, they join the Romanian royals at the Casino, Constanta's architectural star, with its enormous shell-shaped windows and views over the sea, as cavalry trumpeters and horse artillery pass by.

Having set sail from Odessa, the Imperial family would stay for the day, allowing the Tsar to spend time with King Carol I. A cathedral visit aside, most of the day would be spent feasting, discussing and plotting. By the end of the 19th century, Imperial Court meals had adopted French cooking techniques, and the menus in Constanta reflected this. After lunch at the Queen's pavilion and afternoon tea aboard the Tsar's yacht, an elaborate gala supper took place. The menu included whole sturgeon baked with vegetables, saddle of deer, 'queen of poultry' Bresse chicken with roasted truffle, and for pudding, peach melba. Mealtimes were lavish, despite historians noting that the Tsar had rather modest dining tastes, preferring borscht and buckwheat to Beluga caviar.

Political discussions aimed at supporting peace in the Balkans took place, but more tantalisingly, there was matchmaking afoot, too. Might the Romanian royal's son, the playboy Prince Carol, be a good fit for the reflective and studious Grand Duchess Olga Nikolaevna? Sadly not. While the idea was supported by the Russian Foreign Minister, Olga struggled to connect with the Romanian Crown Prince – diplomatically claiming that she did not wish to leave her beloved Russia. Of course, it was not to be. The outbreak of World War I was just a month away and Olga, along with her entire family, would be brutally murdered in a cellar in Yekaterinburg, four years later.

TSAR NICHOLAS II'S
IMPERIAL GALA MENU AT CONSTANTA

Potage Princesse

~

Sterlet à la Russe

~

Selle de Chevreuil à la Metternich

~

Mousse à la Weimar

~

Granite au Champagne

~

Poularde de la Bresse truffée rôtie

~

Salade Astruc

~

Fonds d'artichauts Mornay

~

Pêches à la Melba

~

Champagne G.H. Mumm Cordon Rouge 1906

~

Cointreau

Navy Day Covrigi

Covrig (*covrigi* is plural) is very similar to a bagel or an extra-bready pretzel, and an apricot-stuffed one was the very first thing I ate in Constanta. Warm, sticky and doughy, I found it just the thing to start the day. I have baked many of these and every time a little jam has seeped out; don't worry if this happens, the heady dough is so rich that even the bits lacking jam are good (and even more so with a little butter slathered on).

MAKES 2 LARGE COVRIGI/SERVES 2

FOR THE DOUGH

20g/¾oz fresh yeast

100ml/⅓ cup plus 1 tablespoon semi-skimmed milk

300g/2¼ cups plain (all-purpose) flour, plus extra for dusting

10g/2 teaspoons caster (superfine) sugar

4g/½ teaspoon fine salt

35g/2 tablespoons butter, at room temperature

1 egg

FOR THE FILLING AND TO FINISH

about 80g/about 3 tablespoons apricot conserve (I use the Bonne Maman brand), large chunks ousted

1 egg, beaten, for brushing

poppy seeds, for sprinkling

Dissolve the yeast in a little of the milk, then combine all the dough ingredients in your mixer bowl, keeping the yeast and salt separate initially, and, using the dough hook or dough blade, let the machine knead until the dough forms a ball. This tends to take around a minute. Alternatively, combine the ingredients in a large bowl, then turn out and knead by hand on a well-floured surface. Wrap the dough in cling film (plastic wrap) and let it rest in the fridge for an hour.

Preheat the oven to 180°C/350°F/gas mark 4 and line a large baking sheet with baking parchment. Take the dough out and warm it up by kneading it for a couple of minutes on a lightly floured surface. Divide into 2 pieces.

Sprinkle a little water onto a piece of kitchen paper (paper towel) and dampen your work surface just a little. Then roll out one of your pieces of dough into a long thinnish sausage shape about 50cm/20in long and, using a rolling pin, flatten it to around 5cm/2in wide.

Spread half the apricot conserve in the middle along the length of the dough, making sure to leave at least 1cm/⅜in free all the way along the top and bottom edges so you can seal it together, and bring either side up to meet, sealing with your fingers as you go, then pinch the ends to seal. Transfer the covrig to the lined baking sheet, seal side up, then shape into a hoop slightly smaller than a dinner plate, joining the two ends and tucking under, to complete the circle.

Brush generously with egg and sprinkle over some poppy seeds. Do the same with the remaining piece of dough and conserve, to make the second covrig (you might need to give the dough another quick knead as there may have been some rise), placing it on the lined baking sheet (or use 2 baking sheets if they don't fit). Bake for 20–30 minutes or until golden brown. Allow to cool before eating.

Breakfast Polenta

Mamaliga, a close relative of polenta, is, perhaps, the ultimate comfort food – filling, warming and economical. In Ukraine, Bessarabia and Romania it is as common as bread and is eaten in a similar way, with most meals, fresh and warm – a golden dome gleaming like a lantern in the centre of the kitchen table. *Mamaliga* is ancient and can be traced back to the Romans, and later to when the Venetians first traded maize, yellow corn, with Turks in the 16th century, who then introduced it throughout the Ottoman Empire, cementing it further. This recipe is more of a posh umami-laden brunch than a peasant porridge, with the soft, pillowy polenta adopting cheesy flavours, the roasted portobello taking centre stage and the hazelnut crumble adding a lovely nutty crunch. They say in Romania that if cracks form in your golden cupola of *mamaliga* it means a journey is imminent, but this recipe is for soft polenta so we can't rely on this *mamaliga* to predict travel plans.

SERVES 2

FOR THE POLENTA

100ml/⅓ cup plus 1 tablespoon full-fat milk, plus extra if needed

2 tablespoons sour cream

50g/⅓ cup fine cornmeal

50g/1¾oz Parmesan, grated, plus extra to serve

FOR THE MUSHROOM TOPPING

1½ tablespoons olive oil

1 garlic clove, chopped into 3 pieces

2 large portobello mushrooms, stems trimmed

a scattering of pickled mushrooms (see Gogol's Marinated Mushrooms on page 43) or fresh chestnut mushrooms

½ teaspoon lemon juice (if using only fresh mushrooms)

30g/¼ cup blanched hazelnuts, toasted and chopped

small handful of flat-leaf parsley leaves, chopped

1 tablespoon extra virgin olive oil, for the final drizzle

salt and freshly ground black pepper

Warm the milk and sour cream in a large pan and then, stirring continuously, slowly add the cornmeal and mix through the Parmesan. After a couple of minutes, as it starts to really thicken, remove from the heat and clamp a lid on to let the steam finish cooking the polenta.

Meanwhile, heat the olive oil in frying pan and lightly fry the garlic over a medium heat (you don't want to heat it up too fast or it'll not give enough flavour) for a minute or until the oil is scented – golden is fine, but any browner you will get that horrible acrid taste – then remove the garlic, keeping the oil in the pan.

On a high heat, add the portobello mushrooms to the oil, season well with salt and pepper, then cook, turning regularly, until soft and cooked through – this will take up to 10 minutes and they will release liquid, which assists with the frying. If you are frying chestnut mushrooms for the topping, rather than using pickled mushrooms, do that now, adding more olive oil as needed. When the chestnut mushrooms are fried, remove all the mushrooms and squeeze over a little lemon, if you like, to add a hit of acidity (you won't need this if using pickled mushrooms).

At this stage the polenta should have the texture of milky mashed potato, and should not be set; if it has hardened too much, add more milk, over a low heat, and stir vigorously. Don't worry about seasoning the polenta as the Parmesan should add enough saltiness, but do add a good grind of black pepper here.

Divide the polenta between two plates, place a portobello mushroom in the middle of the polenta, drizzle over a little extra virgin olive oil, then scatter over either the pickled mushrooms, or the fried chestnut mushrooms, toasted hazelnuts, parsley and extra grated Parmesan to taste.

Ardei Umpluti

Variations of stuffed peppers – with rice, meat and cheese – exist the world over. Here they are served in a rich, slow-cooked spice-laden sauce, which is how they're eaten in Constanta where they're known as *ardei umpluti* (stuffed peppers). Yellow bell peppers work best here but red work fine too.

SERVES 6

FOR THE PEPPERS

100g/½ cup plus 1 tablespoon basmati rice

6 medium-sized yellow (or red) (bell) peppers

450g/1lb minced (ground) pork

2 shallots, very finely chopped

½ teaspoon caraway seeds

½ teaspoon dill seed

1 tablespoon sweet paprika

1 tablespoon mild chilli powder

1 egg

small handful of dill, chopped

small handful of flat-leaf parsley, chopped

1 teaspoon grated lemon zest, plus 1 tablespoon juice (from 1 lemon)

1½ teaspoons sea salt flakes

½ teaspoon freshly ground black pepper

FOR THE SAUCE

400ml/1⅔ cups passata

300ml/1¼ cups water

120ml/½ cup soured cream

1 tablespoon paprika

1 tablespoon mild chilli powder

salt and freshly ground black pepper

Arrange a shelf in the middle of your oven and preheat it to 190°C/ 375°F/gas mark 5. Soak the rice in a large bowl of water while you prepare the peppers and pork. Cut the tops off the peppers – but reserve them as you'll use them later – and remove and discard any seeds and membranes. To keep the peppers upright, you can shave off a little of the nodules underneath, but avoid making any holes.

Drain the rice and put in a bowl with the remaining ingredients. Using a fork, mix well then stuff each pepper with the mixture, put the tops back on (this helps with steaming) and arrange them upright in an ovenproof dish that will fit them snugly.

To make the sauce, in a bowl whisk together the passata, water, soured cream, spices and some salt and pepper to taste. Pour this around the peppers so that they're submerged about halfway up. Cover the dish with a lid or foil and bake for 1½ hours. Remove the lid or foil and continue baking for another 40 minutes–1 hour, until the tops are slightly golden, the rice is cooked and the peppers are soft and slightly wrinkly. Serve immediately, with the sauce poured around.

Casino Potatoes

The mineral shot of a burst caviar egg on the tongue tends to divide people, but around the Black and Caspian seas there is much love for it. Ovid, who was exiled to Constanta, called the sturgeon a 'pilgrim of the most illustrious waves' and it is in the waters of the Black Sea and Caspian Sea that these ancient fish, said to be older than dinosaurs, live. Russians with deep pockets plump for Sevruga, Beluga and Ossetra varieties (the three most expensive) while some environmentally aware brands are emerging, embracing a method of massaging the eggs out of living sturgeon rather than killing them for their roe. This is less of a recipe and more of a list of three ingredients to combine for when you fancy glitzing up some new potatoes, as I suspect they might have done in the Casino's happier, more freewheeling days.

SERVES 4

200g/7oz baby new potatoes

enough soured cream for each potato

a tin of caviar, on ice

Steam the potatoes for around 5 minutes and then, while warm, add a dollop of soured cream and a little heap of caviar on top of each. Use a horn or mother-of-pearl spoon, as metal spoils caviar.

Constanta Ciorbă

Sour soups (*ciorbă* are a mainstay of Romanian cuisine and are usually meaty, but this rustic version is full of fresh vegetables instead. The sauerkraut can be bought in many supermarkets and adds the key sour element — it is quite punchy but the creaminess of the feta balances it well.

SERVES 6

50g/3 ½ tablespoons butter

1 teaspoon vegetable oil

1 medium onion, diced

½ fennel bulb, finely sliced (keep the fronds)

1 courgette (zucchini), peeled and diced

2 potatoes, peeled and diced

1 teaspoon mild chilli powder

1 teaspoon dill seed

1 teaspoon ground coriander

1 litre/generous 4 cups hot vegetable stock

100g/3 ½oz sauerkraut

2 tablespoons soured cream

salt and freshly ground black pepper

FOR THE GREEN CRUMBLE TOPPING

good chunk of feta, crumbled

small bunch of chives, finely snipped with scissors

finely chopped flat-leaf parsley leaves

reserved fennel fronds

Heat the butter and oil in a large saucepan or flameproof casserole and sauté the onion, fennel, courgette (zucchini) and potato for 5 minutes, stirring occasionally, adding a pinch of salt to help the vegetables soften. Add the chilli powder, dill seed and ground coriander, coating the vegetables. Combine the hot stock with the sauerkraut in a jug and stir, then gradually add it to the pan. Bring to the boil, cover and simmer for 20 minutes or until the vegetables are tender and cooked through. Remove the soup from the heat and, once cool, transfer to a blender and liquidise. Return to the heat, stir through the soured cream and season to taste with salt (go easy as the feta is salty) and black pepper. Pour the soup into bowls, roughly mix the green crumble topping ingredients and scatter it on top. Serve with some warm toast or garlic bread.

Little Ones with Mustard Mujdei

These are *mititei* or *mici*, Romania's famous skinless sausages known locally as 'little ones'. Patrick Leigh Fermor wrote about eating them on the hoof, cold, from a greasy wrapper, but these are best straight from the pan, warm and heavily scented with caraway, a spice that Romanians love.

MAKES AROUND 30

FOR THE MUJDEI (DIP)

2 garlic cloves, crushed to a paste in a mortar with pinch of salt

1 teaspoon sunflower oil

4 tablespoons French mustard

1 tablespoon water

2 tablespoons sour cream

FOR THE MICI (SAUSAGES)

500g/1lb 2oz minced (ground) beef

500g/1lb 2oz minced (ground) lamb

30g/1oz breadcrumbs

1 egg

2 teaspoons coarse salt

1 tablespoon freshly ground black pepper

1 teaspoon caraway seeds, lightly crushed

½ teaspoon smoked paprika

1 teaspoon mild chilli powder

½ teaspoon pul biber (Turkish pepper flakes)

2 large garlic cloves, crushed

neutral oil, for frying

Start with the mujdei: simply combine the dip ingredients in a bowl and lightly whisk together, then set aside.

Next, place all the *mici* ingredients, except the oil, in a large bowl and mix well – but gently – with your hands. Shape the mixture into little stubby sausages, each around 7cm/2¾-in long.

Heat some oil in a wide frying pan and gently fry the *mici*, in batches of around 6–8 at a time, for 8–10 minutes, turning every minute or two, or until cooked through and crispy on the outside. Serve with the mujdei dip in a separate little bowl.

Shepherd's Bulz

Round and made with polenta and cheese, *bulz* are eaten all over Romania. Traditionally shepherd's food, where they are cooked on an open fire out on the pastures and are tennis-ball-sized, this is a baked version using tangy Italian pecorino, a good substitute for the traditional – but hard to find – Romanian Kashkaval cheese. For a good melt that won't collapse the *bulz*, the cheese needs to be mixed with Ossau-Iraty cheese or similar (I tried mozzarella first and it melted so much it took the *bulz* with it). The roasted cherry tomatoes on the vine add essential sweetness and juice; without, the *bulz* are a bit dry. Tomatoes in Romania, fat and earth-rich, are second perhaps only to Bulgaria in these parts, and even in winter (when they are imported from Turkey) they are still good.

MAKES AROUND 25–30 BULZ

300ml/1¼ cups water

250ml/generous 1 cup full-fat milk

knob of butter, plus extra for greasing

270g/1¾ cups fine or medium cornmeal

1½ tablespoons fresh thyme leaves

70g/2½oz pecorino, grated

50g/1¾oz Ossau-Iraty cheese, grated

1 tablespoon olive oil, plus extra for oiling your hands

1 teaspoon paprika

200g/7oz cherry tomatoes on the vine

fine salt and freshly ground black pepper

In a heavy-bottomed pan or flameproof casserole, bring the water to the boil, then add the milk, ½ teaspoon of salt and a few good grinds of pepper. Reduce to a simmer and stir in the knob of butter. Reduce the heat to its lowest setting and immediately start, very slowly, pouring in the cornmeal, all the while stirring with a wooden spoon. Cook until the mixture reaches a thick porridge-like consistency, then remove from the heat but keep stirring for another minute or two. It will thicken very fast and may split and bubble, so keep stirring until it looks more 'set'.

Put the lid on (or use foil) and leave for 5 minutes. Preheat the oven to 180°C/350°F/gas mark 4. Turn out the polenta (cooked cornmeal is called polenta) and, using a spatula, spread it onto a large, clean surface, shaped into a rectangle of about 20 x 30cm/8 x 12in, and leave to cool. It should be firm, springy and not wet.

Meanwhile, butter a baking tray and, in a bowl, mix the thyme leaves and grated cheeses together.

Once the polenta is cool, lightly oil your hands and mould into balls (*bulz*) about the size of a walnut. Using the handle of your wooden spoon, wiggle it to make a hole big enough to stuff some of the cheese and thyme mixture in, and reseal the hole. Spread the paprika out on a plate and dip the *bulz* into it, just covering a quarter or so, and place the *bulz* on the buttered tray. I find keeping an open bottle of oil nearby to keep oiling my hands helps the rolling when you get going and the polenta dries out more.

Bake for 20–25 minutes. At around the 15-minute mark, turn the *bulz* and put the cherry tomatoes into the oven on a separate baking tray to roast, drizzled with the tablespoon of olive oil. By the time the *bulz* are ready, the tomatoes will be, too. Serve together and, if you have any cheese mixture left, scatter it over.

Raspberry Buttermilk Tart

Raspberries are extremely popular in Romania and the tanginess of buttermilk is a classic eastern European flavour. This tart showcases both flavours and is luscious, sourish and light as a clafoutis. It tastes even better after a night chilled in the fridge.

SERVES 6–8

FOR THE PASTRY

200g/1½ cups plain (all-purpose) flour, plus extra for dusting

20g/scant ¼ cup ground almonds

110g/½ cup cold unsalted butter, diced

50g/scant ¼ cup caster (superfine) sugar

1 egg yolk

1 tablespoon cold water

FOR THE BUTTERMILK FILLING

284ml/scant 1¼ cups buttermilk

3 large egg yolks

60g/5 tablespoons soft brown sugar

seeds scraped from 1 vanilla pod

270g/9½oz raspberries

sprig of mint, to garnish (optional)

Preheat the oven to 180°C/350°F/gas mark 4. In the bowl of a food processor combine the flour, ground almonds and diced butter. Process until you have fine crumbs, then add the sugar and mix briefly again.

Next, add the egg yolk and water and pulse until you have something resembling wet sand. Take the mixture and knead gently on a lightly floured surface for 2 minutes, until you have a dough. Then chill it in the fridge, wrapped in cling film (plastic wrap), for at least 30 minutes.

Using a rolling pin, roll out the dough to fit a 23cm/9in loose-based tart tin, leaving at least a spare 2.5cm/1in, in case of shrinkage. (The dough is really delicate, so if you struggle rolling it out, try flouring a sheet of baking paper and rolling out on that and then lifting and lowering the rolled out pastry into the tin that way.) Prick the base with a fork to avoid air bubbles. Line the pastry case with baking parchment and fill with baking beans/dried chickpeas and blind bake for 15 minutes before removing the parchment and beans and cooking for a further 10 minutes or until golden. Once out of the oven, run a sharp knife along the edge, trimming the excess if it didn't fall off on its own during the bake.

For the filling, very gently heat the buttermilk until warm, taking good care that it doesn't boil or it will curdle. Next, quickly whisk the egg yolks, sugar and vanilla with the warm buttermilk. Place your raspberries in the tart and slowly pour the filling over. Bake for around 30–40 minutes until the filling is golden and cooked through. Serve cool, with the fresh mint sprig placed in the centre of the tart, if you like.

SEA COSSACKS AND SHERBET – ROMANIA THROUGH TRAVELLERS' EYES

Only a small retinue of travel writers who've taken themselves off to Romania, at the far reaches of Europe, have put their thoughts successfully to page. But a few of the very best have, and when they did, they revelled not only in Romania's steep hills, river deltas and its royalty, but also in the food.

In his youth in the 1920s, long before the onrush and ease of mass-tourism, Sir Sacheverell Sitwell hatched an ambitious plan to see every 'beautiful place and thing in the world'. Venice took top spot, and Angkor Wat came second, but it was Romania that Sitwell delighted in, viewing it as tantalisingly unspoilt and ripe for exploration. 'At the first mention of going to Romania, a great many people, as I did myself, would take down their atlas and open the map. For Romania, there can be no question, is among the lesser known lands of Europe,' he wrote. Sitwell took eight days to get to Romania, travelling overland from London. Today, that journey takes just two by train.

In Romania, Sitwell would first sharpen his appetite with a glass or two of *tuica* (pronounced 'tsweeka'), a plum moonshine distilled in countryside barns for which the accompanying toast is 'good luck', and then he'd dive into mealtimes, likening them to opening a box of secrets. For him, they were like travel itself: a kind of louche and fascinating reconnaissance into a cuisine that he described as 'distinct as the Russian and offering the same contrast of half-barbaric with sybaritic pleasures'.

Eighty years on since Sitwell published his *Romanian Journey*, the signature flavour notes and dishes he describes remain largely unchanged: little sausages (*mititei*, shortened to *mici*), stuffed peppers (*ardei umpluti*), chicken covered in breadcrumbs served under a mantle of sour cream, the Ottoman import of rice and meat wrapped in leaves (dolma): a cabbage leaf in winter, a vine leaf in summer (*sarmale*), and pilafs of quail. Pudding might be 'fresh peaches and fraises des bois, or wild raspberries' and the art of foraging for these berries is commonplace, then and now. Sitwell also mentions the ubiquitous conserves of cherries and blackberries. Reading his poetic descriptions, it is impossible not to taste the Kashkaval cheese that he finds in round boxes of bark, rich with a 'smoky, acrid, resinous, pinewood taste'. Travelling around the Danube Delta, close to the Black Sea, he is fascinated by the red-bearded men employed in the sturgeon fishing industry whom he describes as a tribe, or 'a kind of sea Cossack'. The crayfish, cooked in saffron or paprika, he considers to possess a better flavour, even, than the 'crayfish or kraftor in Sweden'.

But it is pink-hued sugary things, redolent of the Orient, that inspire Sitwell to let his lyrical tactility rip, saving his most honeyed prose for Ottoman-inspired sherbets:

> As for the sherbet of roses, this is a spoonful of sticky paste, of the colour of pink roses, lying upon a glass saucer. Its taste is delicious, like the scented airs of Kazanlik [in Bulgaria], the valley of roses under the distant Rhodope, where the attar is distilled ... in some old Romanian families a paste used to be made of Lotus petals but this waterlily sherbet seems to have vanished into the past.'

Belonging to a family of literary mavericks, Sitwell was a prolific writer, putting out 40 books on travel, music, art and architecture in his lifetime. He was also, to some extent, following in the family tradition of writing about culinary matters. His father, even more eccentric than his son, spent years locked away in his office, fuelled by strong Egyptian cigarettes, penning an inquiry entitled *A Short History of the Fork*. At night, Sitwell senior would dine simply, enjoying his 'Sitwell Egg', a little disc of smoked meat surrounded by white rice.

After Greece, it was Romania that Patrick Leigh Fermor loved most. Famously, he fell for a Romanian noblewoman, Princess Balasha Cantacuzene, but he found much to admire in the food, too:

> The food in Romania was amazing, a very original native nucleus to which all that was most exciting in Russia, Poland, Turkey, Austria, Hungary and France.

Leigh Fermor's genius lay not only in his travel writer's eye for detail, his wit and his remarkable multilingualism (he spoke Romanian and Bulgarian along with French and German) but in his ability to make his readers just as thirsty for experience, worldliness and wisdom as he. These lines, written in the winter of 1934, capture the lure of the Black Sea, its myriad names and its faraway appeal:

> This was Europe's easternmost rim ... Cherno More, Kara Su, Marea Neagra, the Euxine, the Black Sea ... Constanta, Odessa, Batumi, Trebizond, Constantinople ... the names were intoxicating.

MAP BAIT

Reading Sitwell and Leigh Fermor today is to leap across space and time, to a golden age, a time long gone. Between then and now, Romania was cruelly shrunken by Nicolae Ceausescu's 24-year dictatorship. His rule, a kind of Stalinism presented as something Romanian, riddled the country with menace and paranoia. It was his misguided drive towards independent industrialisation, generating huge foreign loans, that slipped the country into steep decline. Food and medicine became as scarce as electricity, and the Securitate – a network of three million secret police and informers – spread terror and dread, encouraging Romanians not to mix with foreigners and forbidding them to host visitors in their homes. While Romanians could barely afford to eat or heat their houses, Ceausescu exported petrol and traded the country's food for hard currency.

Few books have been published in English about Romania since the fall of Ceausescu in 1989, when, following a quick trial, he and his wife were gunned down on Christmas Day. The exception is William Blacker's *Along the Enchanted Way*. In this beautiful piece of travel writing about the author's years spent with the Roma Gypsies in the bucolic north, Blacker writes of falling in love, experiencing the changing seasons and eating doughnuts filled with bilberry jam.

But, this is far from the shores of the Black Sea. International writers – and tourists – have barely touched upon Romania's 150 or so miles of coastline, or Constanta with its busy port, Genoese-built lighthouse and ancient history, all as essential to Romania as the capital Bucharest and the wooded hillsides of Transylvania. To most of us, it remains a mystery. At the far reach of the country, Constanta is overshadowed by a sad beauty, seeming all too aware of its own neglect. Out of season it is full of hotels busy being lonely, their windows and waiters staring glumly out to sea. The few western visitors Romania does receive tend to head high, walking in Transylvania through Europe's last remaining wild flower meadows, so beloved by Blacker, and bedding down at night in old Saxon guesthouses.

Looking at the map, my finger kept tracing back northwards, over the heart-shaped splodge of birdlife wetlands, freshwater lakes and the reed-covered marshes of the Black Sea delta. Out there exist Russian Old Believer cultures. In a handful of villages the songs the Lipovan people (Old Believers) can still be heard today, 300 years after they fled oppression in Russia after refusing the new rituals introduced to the Christian Orthodox Church – the ripple and stir of the Black Sea's depths the only thing between them and their original homeland. But one of the challenges in a journey like this is to remain on track, not to get distracted by too many mysteries, unseen and unplanned. So the next day I left Andrei, my seagull-loving host, at Constanta's bus station. He had insisted on driving me there in his top-spec black British Jaguar, a car quite at odds with the others on the street. He wished me good luck, and with a gold fang glinting, pumped my hand up and down in an exaggerated goodbye.

Squeezing onto a small wooden bench, waiting for my minibus to fill up, I watched the pell-mell of the bus station unfold. Arrivals to the city bartered for cut flowers while wandering Gypsy women stopped occasionally to look at me, cigarette smoke spiralling out of their mouths. Small, neat cafés ringed the outskirts, selling little more than sweet pastries and instant Nescafé, and a vapour of burning garbage hovered overhead. Constanta continued to puzzle. But when I think back to this trip, Constanta's Casino, Andrei's gulls and Violin's spoons come high up in my league of curious Black Sea memories.

Easing for three slow hours down the coast, the bus passed Black Sea resorts filled with Communist-era apartment blocks, rough scrubland and beaches packed with seal-like sun worshippers. Then, almost too soon, Varna announced itself with a relaxed air. I'd arrived at Bulgaria's Black Sea coast.

BULGARIA

ODESSA

ISTANBUL

TRABZON

OLD GOLD AND DEEP PURPLE

'A dark bowl full of wheat is the sky with stars.'

— Bulgarian proverb

To Bulgarians, the Black Sea is 'Cherno More' and Varna their sea-facing city. Locals cheer on 'The Sailors', their local football team, and it was from here that Dracula's coffin, in Bram Stoker's novel, set sail for England aboard a Russian schooner filled with silver sand. But it wasn't football, silver, or sand, that I wanted to see here in Varna, it was gold.

Varna's Museum of Archaeology, housed in a Renaissance-style former school, was cool and silent. Its snaking corridors and artefact-packed rooms, all deserted. There was no one to admire the statues from Varna's days as a Roman port and no one to see the Thracian tombs. One room, at first, appeared darker and more hushed than all the others. On entering, though, it screamed. Breastplates, bracelets, burial gifts, regal-looking headpieces, figurines and pendants — all gold — shone for attention. This silent Midas room was visually deafening, ringing out with finery, treasure and opulence. And the loudest, biggest treasure of all was also the smallest. Tiny pendant earrings, almost inconceivably old, dating back 6000 years. The might of these little drops practically punched through the glass. This is 'Varna gold', as archaeologists have coined it, and these earrings are the oldest 'worked gold' in the world. They belonged to the first-known culture to craft golden artifacts, and they lived here, on Bulgaria's section of the Black Sea, in what some archaeologists believe to be Europe's oldest prehistoric town. But this mysterious civilisation owed its great wealth to something far more simple and valuable than gold: salt.

A SALTED STATE

In the walled settlement of Solnitsata (literally, 'saltworks'), close to Varna, salt was baked in kilns into bricks from brine, to be traded throughout the Balkans, making the residents who lived there, six millennia ago, very rich. Compared with salt, gold is not anything. Without salt, nerves and muscles can't work, meaning the body seizes up. 'A man would not be unwell if he abstained for an entire year from either the sweet or sour or bitter or hot, but deprive him of salt for a fortnight, and he will be too weak to tie up a chicken…' wrote the 17th-century Chinese scientist Song Yingxing. Gold is luxury but salt is essential. So taken for granted today, this most basic of foodstuffs has shaped — and deeply impacted — trade, taxation, cuisine and empire. The word 'salary' comes from the Latin *salarium* (a Roman soldier's stipend to buy salt). 'Salacious', meaning to be lustful, also stems from the word salt. In Mark Kurlansky's book *Salt*, he points out that this comes from the Romans, who would refer to a man in love as 'salax', meaning he is in a salted state. Varna itself is a salty city with a merchant atmosphere, and a strong sense of history hangs in its briny sea-whipped air. The Romans stayed here for several centuries, and as Stowers Johnson wrote in his 1964 travelogue *Gay Bulgaria*, the port has always attracted outsiders: 'Greek merchant and sailor, Roman, Knight Crusader, Ottoman Turk, sailors of Crimean campaign, fascists of Hitler, red armies of Russia, all walked here where vineyards still press against the city.' Basking in the sun, with sprinklers casting rainbows in the air, it was hard to imagine the grim Turkish barracks that once overshadowed this neighbourhood, full of British troops during the Crimean War suffering with cholera. A particularly malodorous place, it was described by Florence Nightingale as 'a pest hole out of which it was believed no one ever emerged alive'.

A stone's throw from the Museum of Archaeology on Shkorpil Street, I stopped for lunch at a smart restaurant housed in an old herbal pharmacy. On the table sat a little bowl of *sharena sol*, or 'colourful salt', that I sprinkled onto a scrap of bread, unpicking the flavours: definitely paprika, possibly fenugreek. Anchoring the menu was an impressive seafood selection of tiger prawns, caviar and sea bass, making this the most serious carte du jour I'd seen since leaving home. But it was two of the simplest things, found on almost every Bulgarian table that I most clearly remember enjoying in Varna — big pink tomatoes, plump and sweet as sugar, and white, crumbly brined sirene cheese similar to feta. Bulgarian ewe's milk cheese is extraordinarily good, creamy and salty with a distinctly lemony tang. But then Bulgaria is salad country. In the early 1990s Bulgaria exported more fruit and vegetables to Western Europe than anywhere else. Food writer George Lang called Bulgarians 'the Gardeners of Europe' and claimed that they could 'make almost anything bloom'. The Bulgarian Black Sea coast, too, boasts its own impressive local larder of almonds, walnuts, chestnuts, figs and peanuts.

A few streets away, a spice rack in a small hole-in-the-wall shop offered a window into the unsparing Bulgarian pantry. Tins, pots, jars and boxes of paprika, caraway, cumin, fenugreek, mint, basil, rosemary and parsley. There were spices that I had to look up, too: the not so interesting *djodjen* (Bulgarian mint) and the much more curious *samardala*, 'garlic honey nectar'.

CONCRETE ROCK

In a racing green Renault Mégane from the 1990s, I belted up and left Varna for Burgas, detouring first northwards to Kaliakra Bay, where I'd heard it was possible to eat first-rate mussels in a cove that looked like it belonged in a pirate movie. The old car, driven by my fixer and translator, Todor, smelled of diesel, cigarette smoke, dust and sea brine. Spluttering through a town called Kavarna, searching for an unmarked turn-off, we pulled over, lost. Bored children, faceless apartment blocks, the odd Bulgarian red, white and green flag fluttering from a window, gave the town the classic look of an ex-Communist provincial community. Then, looking up, it was clear something was different about Kavarna. Under a huge painted fist was the unmistakable curled lip of Billy Idol's face on the side of a block of flats. A mural, nearly as tall as the seventh floor where his bare chest puffed out. Then, more rock legends that I hadn't thought of in a very long time appeared, too: Alice Cooper, Motorhead's Lemmy, and Deep Purple's Ian Gillan. This unassuming town of 12,000 is, it turns out, known as 'the rock capital of Bulgaria'. Its ex-mayor, Tsonko Tsonev, a self-confessed metalhead, introduced a heavy metal festival and made it his mission to liven up its drear streets with his vision of a rock nirvana.

Skidding down a shrub-lined hill, past sand dunes and moss-covered boulders, finally we came to Dalboka Mussel Farm. From the sea, mid-summer calm, steady and navy blue, men stepped out of small boats, hauling in blue crates overflowing with shells, hand-harvested mussels collected by scuba divers. Under a slung-up hessian canopy attached to trees, sparrows shot back and forth, dipping down to pick up crumbs. In a wooden shack several cooks, all dressed in Breton tops, sweated over huge black cauldrons. The terrace, right above a cove washed by plunging and boiling waves, was packed with Bulgarian holidaymakers in loose summertime moods.

Tatiana Prokopiev and her family have been harvesting mussels in Kaliakra Bay for 25 years, growing them on swinging ropes, in view of the kitchen. It is better, she explained, to have them stationary in a sea farm away from the gritty ocean floor, as 'they're much juicier that way. If they're free to go with the ebb and flow they become tough.' As filter feeders, the mussels feast on phytoplankton and this northerly section of the Black Sea is particularly clean, meaning the mussels are more succulent and flavoursome. Europeans have been collecting mussels for 800 years, and they've been eaten for hundreds more, but their quality varies wildly depending on the environment.

Of the 12 plates of mussels arriving at the table, many reversed things I thought I knew, not only about mussels but also flavour. This being Bulgaria, the mussels came largely stuffed into vegetables rather than cooked in wine and cream, Belgian-style. Packed into cabbage leaves, crammed into aubergines and squeezed into tomatoes with rice, they were all dusted with flecks of dill and served with pickled cucumbers. They were also steamed with bay leaves and allspice, mixed with sweetcorn and peas, dropped into soup and their shells stuffed with rice, as on the streets of Istanbul. Best of all was the spicy sailor's stew full of robust mussels in a velvety tomato and chilli broth. Every time we made ready to leave and travel south to Bulgaria's second largest city on the Black Sea, Burgas, in search of salt, honey and history, another plate arrived. Prokopiev admitted she'd never sampled the mussel dessert, but insisted I try it. Under a cloud of whipped cream, in a little pudding bowl, were crescents of baked apple slices and fat, juicy, orange mussels. There was a slight kick of sea saltiness and a mussel-like texture. But amidst the rich dairy and softly sweet apple, it was plain, inoffensive and mild. If it tasted of anything at all, it tasted like a trick of the mind.

Spicy Dalboka Mussels

This recipe is inspired by the 'sailor's style' mussels, the stand-out dish of the 12 plates of mussels I tried at Dalboka. It is also in honour of Tatiana Prokopiev, her staff and family who are justifiably proud of their connection to the Black Sea and their long-standing enterprise. If anywhere ever deserved the hackneyed travel cliché 'hidden gem', their mussel farm is it.

SERVES 4 AS A STARTER OR 2 AS A MAIN

500g/1lb 2oz mussels

2 tablespoons olive oil

1 large red onion, thinly sliced

3 garlic cloves, crushed

1 teaspoon chilli powder or pul biber (Turkish pepper flakes)

1 teaspoon sweet paprika

10 pink peppercorns, crushed

300ml/1¼ cups vegetable stock

1 tablespoon white wine vinegar

1 x 400g/14oz can chopped tomatoes

good handful of lovage (or spinach if out of season)

¼ teaspoon salt

juice of ½ lemon

small bunch of dill, chopped

small bunch of parsley, chopped

Rinse and scrub the mussels under cold running water and remove the beards by gently pulling them away from the shells.

Heat the oil in a large flameproof casserole, sauté the onion until translucent and then add the garlic, chilli, paprika and peppercorns. Add the stock, vinegar and tomatoes and simmer for 15 minutes.

Increase the heat to high, add the mussels to the pan with the lovage or spinach, and the salt, then cover and steam for 5 minutes or until the mussels open (discard any that do not).

Finally, remove from the heat and add the lemon juice, stir through the dill and parsley and serve in bowls with plenty of crusty white bread.

Bulgur, Grape and Walnut Salad

Bulgarians love both bulgur (cracked wheat) and grapes, and this simple salad combines the two. Bulgaria's grape varieties — jade, purple and magenta coloured and heavy with muscat juices — are excellent, and a third of Bulgaria's wines grow in the Black Sea coastal region of the country.

SERVES 4 AS A SIDE

125g/4½oz coarse bulgur wheat

300ml/1¼ cups water

140g/5oz seedless white grapes, halved

handful of cherry tomatoes, halved

1 tablespoon walnut oil

1 tablespoon olive oil or cold-pressed virgin sunflower oil

1 teaspoon pul biber (Turkish pepper flakes)

30g/1oz walnut pieces

5 tablespoons chopped flat-leaf parsley

a few sprigs of dill, finely chopped

salt

Place the bulgur and water in a medium pan, bring to the boil, then remove from the heat, clamp a lid on and leave to steam-cook for 15–20 minutes.

Put the grapes, tomatoes, oils and pul biber in a large bowl. When the bulgur is almost ready, toast the walnuts in a hot, dry frying pan and set to one side. Then toss the steamed bulgur through the salad, add the walnuts and herbs with salt to taste, stir them through and serve with a bottle of Bulgarian Ugni Blanc (or plain old Sauvignon Blanc).

TRAVELS WITH THE BARD OF POLAND

It was in the Sea Gardens of Bulgaria's other port city, Burgas, behind the brutalist concrete pier where every January for the feast of the Epiphany a priest throws a cross into the icy Black Sea, that I spotted him. Adam Mickiewicz's wide, unmistakable wan face carved into a bas relief, shone out from among the trees, statues of Russian soldiers and Pushkin. It was similar to the one of him I'd spotted in Odessa. Quite by accident, I'd been following him, retracing his Black Sea steps. Poet, raconteur and champion of Polish national freedom, Mickiewicz was exiled to Odessa but he had also camped out here, in Burgas, before spending his final days in Constantinople.

Liberating Poland from Russian control was Mickiewicz's greatest aim in life but he is best known for *Pan Tadeusz*, his epic 12-book tale about the country life antics of Polish and Lithuanian high society. Published in Paris in 1834, along with accounts of revolts and garrisons, are sketches of feasts, hunting parties and wolfish appetites:

> They light a hundred fires,
> roast and boil without pause,
>
> Tables groan under meats,
> like a river drink flows;
>
> The whole night would the gentry drink,
> eat, and sing ...

If an army marches on its stomach the officers' dawn breakfast described in Pan Tadeusz is vigorously, and impressively, boozy: 'That in half an hour twenty-three fillets they munched / And downed half a huge bowl of most excellent punch.' In another passage, a Muscovite general 'puts on a great show, Like a pike cooked in saffron, all glitter and glow.' But Mickiewicz's most flowery prose is given to woodland mushroom foraging: 'In the other hand, tied like a field-flower posy, Carried tree-and-mulch mushrooms, brown, ochre, and rosy.'

Sent to Russia by official order for belonging to the secret 'Philomath' society at the University of Vilnius, Mickiewicz slotted in easily to the salons of St Petersburg and Moscow, both Venus fly traps for brilliant minds. There, he could louche about, speaking French and impressing high society with his poetry recitals. Then in 1825 he left for the Black Sea. He travelled first to Odessa, where he lived a libertine lifestyle, and then to Crimea which, as an impressionable young man and dedicated Romantic, set his inspiration and spiritual vision ablaze. The wild nature of the steppe, dotted with Ottoman palaces, Tatar mosques and Byzantine churches, poured into his mind, and out into his *Crimean Sonnets* cycle. Back in Odessa he gushed: 'I have seen the Orient in miniature.'

And, it was here, in Burgas, much later in 1855, that he tried to raise an army sided with Turkey against the Russians. Sleeping in a military tent, he imagined setting up a Jewish legion within the Ottoman Cossack division. It was to be one of his last missions, as that year he died in wintertime Constantinople. He had existed there a while, in the capital of the Ottoman Empire, at times struggling to find funds for food, yet keeping up a morning routine that would begin with Turkish coffee thick with cream and Cognac, and end with his pipe.

Burgas today, full of holidaying Bulgarians, beach bars and sun loungers, couldn't be further from the miserable tented army camps that Mickiewicz endured. At day's end, I'd join the well-fed sunseekers, feet in the sand, imagining the shipwrecks described in newspapers around the Bulgarian headlands. Emine, 40 miles north of Burgas, is Bulgaria's stormiest cape, but Cape Kaliakra, right by Dalboka Mussel Farm, has the legends: locals say that once, 40 Bulgarian girls tied their hair together above that watery headland and then threw themselves into the Black Sea, rather than be captured by the Ottomans. Then there's 'Maslen Nos' (Oily Cape), named after the shipwrecked Greek boats that spilled their olive oil cargoes in the salty water. It was time to move on. Making a pact to try to find Mickiewicz's house in Istanbul, I left Burgas, watching as a pink moon rose, super-fast, out of the driftwood grey waves, sealing the end of another long, high-summer day.

A Bigos For Adam Mickiewicz

Bigos is Poland's ultimate wintertime stew. Historically, it was made in forest clearings where hunters would drop their game into the pot to add to the pickled fruit and sauerkraut. In *Pan Tadeusz*, Adam Mickiewicz's epic poem, he writes of *bigos*:

> In the pots warmed the *bigos*; mere words cannot tell
> Of its wondrous taste, colour and marvellous smell.

Aromatic *bigos* is mega-meaty and only its rainbow colours, red peppers, yellow carrots, jet-black prunes, pink bacon, match its complex flavours.

SERVES 6

600ml/2½ cups beef or chicken stock

50g/1¾oz dried porcini

a good knob of butter

1 teaspoon vegetable oil

1 onion, sliced into half moons

2 yellow (or orange) carrots, peeled and sliced into coins

1 red (bell) pepper, deseeded and diced

1 teaspoon caraway seeds, lightly crushed

1 teaspoon dried marjoram

2 tablespoons sweet paprika

1 teaspoon sharena sol (see page 107)

2 tablespoons brown sugar

½ white cabbage, shredded

1 apple, peeled and cut into matchsticks (or grated if easier)

250g/8¾oz sauerkraut, drained

1 x 400g/14oz can plum tomatoes

4 slices of smoked bacon, cut into bite-sized pieces

1 fresh bay leaf

100g/3½oz dried prunes, roughly chopped

300g/10½oz smoked kabanos Polish sausage, chopped into bite-sized pieces

salt and freshly ground black pepper

In a medium pan, boil the stock, remove from the heat and add the porcini. Leave to rehydrate for at least 15 minutes.

Heat the butter and oil (which will stop the butter burning) in a large flameproof casserole, add the onion, carrots and pepper and sauté until the onion is translucent. In a bowl, mix together the caraway, marjoram, paprika, sharena sol and brown sugar, then stir in. Add the shredded cabbage, apple, sauerkraut, plum tomatoes (broken apart a bit before adding), bacon, bay leaf and the stock with porcini. Boil then simmer with the lid on, on the lowest heat possible, for 2 hours. Adjust the seasoning, adding salt and pepper to taste, then add the prunes and sausage, increase the heat slightly and simmer again, with the lid on, for 10 minutes.

Serve with decent beer, cold vodka and Polish rye bread. This is all the more delicious reheated the next day.

Blackened Peppers with Feta, Tarragon and Mint

Long red peppers stuffed with cool feta, yogurt, tarragon and mint. Reminiscent of many yogurt- or cheese-laced salad lunches eaten in Burgas.

SERVES 2 AS A STARTER

2 long sweet red peppers

FOR THE FILLING

60g/2oz feta (or ideally Bulgarian sheep's cheese), roughly crumbled into chunks

2 tablespoons thick Greek yogurt

20g/¾oz walnuts, toasted and roughly chopped

1 green chilli, deseeded and finely chopped

small handful of mint, chopped

small handful of tarragon, chopped

good handful of chives, chopped

squeeze of lemon juice

1 tablespoon rapeseed or olive oil

a few grinds of black pepper

Cut the tops off the peppers and scoop out the seeds and membrane. Heat a grill to the max and grill the peppers, turning regularly to get them as wrinkly and blackened as possible. Remove and leave to cool — if you put these in a dish covered with cling film (plastic wrap), or a freezer bag, the steam will make the job of peeling them much easier.

Meanwhile, combine all of the filling ingredients in a bowl. When the peppers are cool, peel the skins off and gently stuff the peppers with the filling. Serve as part of a meze platter, or with salad and bread for lunch.

Caraway and Poppy Seed Sticks

Called *soleni pruchki* in Bulgarian, literally 'salty sticks', these are the perfect partner for a cold beer after a long travel day.

MAKES 16 STICKS

15g/½oz fresh yeast, or 7g/½oz fast-action dried yeast

40ml/2 tablespoons plus 2 teaspoons milk, warmed

125g/1 cup minus 1 tablespoon plain (all-purpose) flour, plus extra for dusting

60g/½ cup rye flour

½ teaspoon salt

1 tablespoon icing (confectioners') sugar

70g/5 tablespoons butter, at room temperature, chopped into cubes

1 tablespoon sunflower oil, for oiling

1 egg, beaten, to glaze

caraway seeds, poppy seeds and flaky sea salt, to sprinkle

In a bowl, vigorously mix the yeast with the warm milk and a tablespoon of the plain (all-purpose) flour. Leave aside until slightly risen and frothy; this takes around 15 minutes for fresh, or more like 5 minutes if using dried.

Next, sift the rest of the flours, salt and icing (confectioners') sugar into a large bowl, add the butter and work with your fingers until the mixture resembles breadcrumbs. Add the frothy yeast mix and bring together to make a ball. Turn onto a floured surface and knead well for 10 minutes until less sticky, slightly stiffer and like a biscuit dough. Let the dough rest for 15 minutes, covered with a tea towel. Lightly oil two baking sheets.

Using a rolling pin, roll the dough out on a floured surface into a rough square shape, then, using your hands, form a 16cm/7in square, about 1cm/⅜in thick (given the texture of the dough, your hands, rather than the the rolling pin, will help to shape this to the desired size). Using a sharp knife, cut into strips, around 1cm/⅜in wide (you should end up with 16 sticks). Brush with the egg wash and carefully lift the sticks onto the oiled baking sheets, keeping space of around 1cm/⅜in between each stick. Sprinkle over a mixture of caraway, poppy seeds and sea salt, and leave to prove in a warm spot for around 20 minutes. Meanwhile, preheat the oven to 200°C/400°F/gas mark 6.

Bake for 10–15 minutes, until golden brown. Keep a close eye as they do bake pretty fast. Leave to cool then store in a airtight container until you want them (they'll keep for up to a week). Ideally, pair with an ice-cold beer.

TO EAT A MAN'S SALT

'A people far from sea explore,
Who ne'er knew salt, or heard
the billows roar'

— Homer, *The Odyssey*

With their backs to the pink- and blue-painted Communist-era apartment blocks, and their faces to the open lake horizon, men and women, young and old, rubbed thick black mud into shoulder blades and over knees, with their hands. The detoxifying gloop highlighted the ache and the whereabouts of the ailment. One woman was gloved and socked by it, another had a stocking's length on just one leg. Younger bodies went for the catch-all approach, covering everywhere but their hair. Once dried and cracked, the goodness absorbed, they'd slide into Lake Pomorie like black-and-white penguins, leaving only straw hats and sun visors above the surface. And there they'd stay for a while, before emerging clean of the ooze. Surrounding them, sparkling in the sun, lay pans of salt. White gold, contrasting sharply with the black mud.

Pomorie's dedicated salt museum, ten miles from Burgas, brought me here. Its displays of old postcards and banknotes perfectly echoed the exact same scene outside: salt pans, next to bathers. One 20-lev banknote from 1928 shows pyramids of salt on one side and, on the reverse, King Boris III dressed in a general's uniform. Pomorie had become rich through the export of salt, with Bulgarians battling over it during the Byzantine period. During Ottoman rule, which Bulgaria was under for 500 years, Pomorie salt was exported and traded all over the Black Sea region, into Turkey and deep into the Caucasus. Today, Bulgaria's production can't keep up with demand and tops up its stocks with imported salt from Israel and Tunisia.

Back outside, the scenery was vivid and animated, in contrast to the hushed museum. The sky, accommodating one of the busiest flyways in Europe, was filled with movement, not of aeroplanes, but migratory birds. At the end of summer, the Via Pontica migration route comes alive with hundreds of storks, pelicans, buzzards and kites. Down below, a colony of rare black and white Sandwich terns nested on a small island, surrounded by the sort of forage-friendly flora that gets chefs excited: marsh samphire, sea holly and sea rocket, divided from the Black Sea by a long sand spit. Despite the grim concrete backdrop, it was a shivery, gorgeous vista, one appreciated by the Roman Empire, whose people had used Pomorie as a health resort. Two thousand years on, its natural charms of sea air, salt, mud and birdlife remain unchanged.

Trundling further down the coast, tracing the migratory birds, I bounced in the Renault towards the Strandja National Park, shared by Bulgaria and Turkey, with its oak houses, gaida (Bulgarian bagpipes) and stories of fire dancing, the Turkish border now only 20 miles away. En route, the smell of grilled bonito in the town of Tsarevo lured us to stop for lunch.

BLACK HONEY AND BORDERLANDS

Bright sunlight raked over the little outdoors harbour café where Yani Shopov, a blue-eyed, third-generation, self-declared 'fisherman's fisherman', brought out scorching fish soup and cold beer from the kitchen. As we sat slurping the bay-infused broth, heavy with snow-white fish flakes, Shopov entertained us with tales of the Black Sea's infamous storms. 'Waves came up to the windows of the seafront houses, the height was terrifying,' he said, his eyes wide as saucers, his arms galloping to show the scale, and speed, of the waves. An older man with a kind face, soft as marshmallow, he had the tell-tale raw-boned hands of a fisherman. His life out there had been a success, partly, he said, because he had survived to tell these tales, adding that there is a good reason why the Black Sea is the colour of mourning. But like all fishermen, salt water of the sea is his lifeblood.

The boozy, salty midday heat sent us back to the road. Relying on instinct, and a map sketched on a napkin, we drove to buy honey from the Todorov family, master beekeepers living in Tsarevo. On the way, the car jogged past colourful monasteries with painted balconies, monastic cells and stalls selling little bottles of holy water. Bulgaria and Turkey, as well as sharing an Ottoman past, trade history and culture (Turks are the largest ethnic minority in Bulgaria), both produce excellent, complex Black Sea honeys. Lice are key to the Todorov's award-winning honey, the son explained as we got there and settled down in his garden. 'Living on oak trees, the lice feed on acorns, their excrement sticks to the leaves and bees feed on this which gives the honey its dark colour.' Batting away sugar-loving wasps, he handed around a jar, dark as maple syrup, sweet and rich as caramel. As the Strandja region, shared with Turkey, is so heavily forested there's little in the way of agriculture (or damaging pesticides) where the beekeepers collect, he explained, hence the complex flavour. I stocked up on the antioxidant-rich honey as the Todorovs told me about Turkey's more famous black honey, known as 'mad honey' (desi bal) found around the Black Sea, a honey infamous for its hallucinatory properties and said to taste of treacle.

Puffing and spluttering, the Renault pressed on towards our last couple of stops in Bulgaria. Within a few minutes, the houses and the shops and the cars were behind us and in front lay the thickly wooded Strandja national park. Little visited, it is a poorly mapped and multi-layered borderland, with valleys full of fables and myths.

Monastery Soup

Near to the salt museum is Pomorie's Monastery Saint George. Founded by Byzantine settlers, and sacked during Ottoman rule, it was once a Thracian sanctuary, as shown on its impressive multi-coloured balconies, bas reliefs and frescoes. This soup is typical of the sort served during Lent in Bulgaria's monasteries. Traditionally, this *bobena* (bean) soup would be cooked in a large earthenware pot. A vegetarian meal in itself, packed full of filling beans, it works well as a middle-of-the-week working lunch.

SERVES 4

2 tablespoons sunflower oil

1 large yellow or red (bell) pepper, deseeded and diced as finely as possible

1 large onion, finely diced

1 parsnip, finely diced

2 carrots, sliced into thick coins

1 teaspoon sweet paprika

good pinch of dried chilli flakes

2 garlic cloves, crushed

700ml/scant 3 cups vegetable stock

200g/1⅓ cups drained, canned haricot (navy) beans, rinsed

240g/1½ cups drained, canned kidney beans, rinsed

salt and freshly ground black pepper

TO SERVE

roughly chopped flat-leaf parsley and mint

1 tablespoon extra virgin olive oil

2 tablespoons soured cream or crème fraîche (optional)

Heat the sunflower oil in a heavy-bottomed pan over a medium heat and cook the pepper, onion, parsnip and carrots, adding a pinch of salt, until the onion is translucent and softened, about 7 minutes.

Add the paprika, chilli flakes, garlic and a few grinds of black pepper and cook for another couple of minutes to release the fragrances. Add the stock and all the beans and turn the heat up. Once the soup has come to the boil, turn the heat down slightly and leave to simmer for about 20 minutes, until the vegetables are cooked through. Remove from the heat and pour into bowls, topping with the fresh herbs, a swirl of olive oil and the soured cream or crème fraîche, if you like.

Sharena Sol

Sharena sol is a colourful salt mix and it is a staple in Bulgarian kitchens. As its name suggests, it is salt pounded with spices, typically paprika, and possibly fenugreek and cumin, and it's sprinkled on bread, fish, chicken and eggs.

20g/¾oz cumin seeds, toasted

1 tablespoon dried fenugreek leaves (also known as kasuri methi)

50g/1¾oz flaky sea salt

1 tablespoon smoked bittersweet paprika (or your preferred paprika)

Bash together the toasted cumin seeds and fenugreek leaves in a pestle and mortar. Once the cumin is lightly crushed, add the salt and paprika to the mixture. Bash a few more times until the sea salt is roughly crushed, but not too fine. Store in an airtight container.

Poached Apricots in Rose Water

Bulgaria's love affair with roses is enduring and nationwide. All over the Black Sea region, petals are packed into everything from breakfast jam to massage oil and *gyulovitsa* (rose petal brandy). Rose petal preserve is for sale all over the Balkans, not just in Bulgaria, and is generally made from the Damask rose. The town of Kazanlak, 120 miles inland at the heart of Bulgaria's Rose Valley, is one of the major producers of attar of roses (essential oil) in the world. This simple rose-scented recipe is super-easy, taking all of around 15 minutes to make.

SERVES 4

50g/¼ cup golden caster (superfine) sugar

150ml/10 tablespoons water

400g/14oz ripe apricots, halved and stoned

a few drops of rose water

TO SERVE

crème fraîche

handful of dried rose petals

handful of pistachios, roughly chopped

Put the sugar and water into a small, heavy-based saucepan. Heat until the sugar dissolves. Place as many apricot halves as you can fit comfortably in the pan, cut-side down, and simmer for 4 minutes. Then flip them over and cook for a further minute or two until perfectly tender. Gently remove from the pan using a slotted spoon, and put them in a wide, shallow dish. Repeat with any remaining apricots. Once they've all been poached, pour over the poaching syrup, add the rose water and leave to cool. Put the apricots, with some of the syrup, into glasses, topped with crème fraîche, rose petals and pistachios.

THE LAST FISHERWOMAN OF BULGARIA

> 'The seas a Theefe, whose liquid Surge, resolves
> The Moone into Salt tears.'

— William Shakespeare, Timon of Athens

Elena's life as a fisherwoman began on a bet. Surely she, a woman and mother to young children, could never catch as many bluefish, goby and bonito as her brawny male neighbours. Born into a family of Black Sea fishermen, she decided to prove them wrong and quickly started to match the men's daily hauls, succeeding time and time again. Today, fewer people are willing to risk their lives fishing out on the Black Sea and Elena believes she is the last fisherwoman left in Bulgaria. From her tiny fishing village, right by the Turkish border, she still takes her small boat out, travelling up the Ropotamo river that flows from the Strandja Mountains to the Black Sea. 'No one wants to do this job any more, people just come and go,' she told me, adding that the pursuit is just as male dominated as it ever was.

I met Elena on the way from Burgas to the Strandja National Park, in a ramshackle little café, where she sometimes helps out, right by the fishing huts. In the gummy sea air, she spoke animatedly of saints and storms, and of praying. 'Fishermen are true believers,' she said, explaining how she held onto a catch when her boat was almost capsized near Sozopol, just up the coast. As she spoke, her eyes widening, she gripped a make-believe bow and pulled an imaginary rope through her hands. Around us burly, cynical seadog men sank beers and a small, scrappy dog cocked his leg.

On fishing trips Elena carries with her bread, and a stove for cooking fish, and she often remains out all night. In the unmatched silence of the open sea, she likes to talk to the seagulls and to the waves, especially when she's night-fishing. And she likes to ignore the rules, too, including the number one rule — rarely ignored by fishermen — that says: 'Never go out alone'.

Bulgarians, Romanians, Ukrainians, Russians and Georgians all call this sea the 'Black Sea' in their respective languages, but the earliest Greek name was 'Pontos Axeinos', meaning 'inhospitable' or 'sombre' sea. Later, it became the 'Euxine', confusingly meaning 'welcoming sea'. Historians think this was either meant as word play to appease its cruelty, or else it was ironic. Whatever its name, it is famously fickle. Wilder and darker in colour than the Mediterranean, it is ringed by perilously high cliffs, meaning no shore, few natural ports and little means of escape from lashing storms. Strong winds galloping down from Russia have regularly bandied Elena's boat about, and when it's really bad, only her faith can comfort her. Not only is life at sea a magnificent calling, she admitted, the rewards and risks are addictive, too, as is the danger of going out alone, which she prefers.

Then, without warning, my chat with Elena began to curve off-course. I could feel it coming. A shift as her gaze changed from excitable to distant. Then, from behind her red-hennaed hair, falling in rings around her soft cheeks, tears started brimming in her eyes. I could see she was struggling with something off-limits, a recent memory or calamity. What was meant to be a light interview suddenly felt darker, almost confessional.

Closing her eyes, she began. Her husband had died when their babies were young, leaving her to get by on her own. He'd be proud if he could see her now, she said, out there on the waves, making an independent living and using her hard-earned skills. This was why she had to fish. She had no choice. It was a case of survival. For the past three decades, just like her tough male equivalents, Elena has lived to tell the tales of shoals, fog and bitter storms, proving that skill, bravery and talent on the open sea matter just as much as muscle. Then, her pale eyes grew distant again and I sensed there was more to come. 'Now, I go out to sea to fish and to think in peace of my daughter, who took her own life,' Elena whispered. It was only out there, among the fathomless sea, a world that Elena had managed to make her own, that she could find the peace and strength needed to heal and take in the loss. Her parting words to me were: 'What the sea can give you, nothing else can.' There was little else to say.

Late Summer Lyutenitsa

When the long Bulgarian summer finally fuses out, winter supplies are prepared. Around the country, lyutenitsa, a simple tomato and pepper relish that marks the end of the summer, is made and heaped into glass jars. Reassuring in its sunniness and simplicity, it is a symbol of Bulgarian cookery. It is very easy to make, especially with a food processor, which does help to get the right consistency.

MAKES 1 MEDIUM JAR

1kg/2lb 3oz red and/or orange (bell) peppers

1 tablespoon rapeseed oil

1 red chilli pepper, deseeded and chopped

1 small red onion, chopped

50ml/3½ tablespoons sunflower oil

pinch of caster (superfine) sugar

100g/3½oz tomato paste

2 garlic cloves, pounded in a pestle and mortar with ½ teaspoon salt

1 tablespoon red wine vinegar

1 tablespoon lemon juice

salt and freshly ground black pepper

First prepare the peppers: place them under a grill on its highest setting and grill, turning frequently, until their skins are blackened. Place in a bowl, cover with cling film (plastic wrap) and leave to steam slightly, before peeling, deseeding and chopping them.

Next, warm the rapeseed oil in a frying pan on a medium–high heat and add the chopped peppers, chilli, onion and a pinch of salt, and cook, stirring regularly, for 10 minutes. As you go, add some freshly ground black pepper.

Once softened and cooked through, add the sunflower oil, sugar, tomato paste and garlic and, turning the heat down slightly, simmer, stirring occasionally, for 10 minutes.

Then take the pan off the heat and allow to cool slightly, before adding the lemon juice and vinegar and transferring to a food processor. Pulse a few times — you're looking to achieve a chunky texture.

Transfer to a glass jar and leave the mixture to cool completely before putting in the fridge where it will keep for around 3 days. Serve it with any kind of bread as a snack — rye or pitta bread, challah or crackers, or as a relish with cheese. It is also a good accompaniment for Romanian Shepherd's Bulz on page 79.

Damask Cocktail

A rose-laced cocktail that works best as an aperitif before a Bulgarian feast.

MAKES 1

50ml/3½ tablespoons gin

15ml/1 tablespoon rose liqueur, such as Briottet Liqueur de Rose

10ml/2 teaspoons elderflower cordial

small dash of Peychaud's Bitters (optional)

a fresh rose petal, to garnish

Shake the gin, rose liqueur and elderflower together in a cocktail shaker filled with ice, and strain into a coupe glass (Champagne saucer). To serve, dot with the bitters, if using, and garnish with the rose petal.

STRANDJA – TO THE TURKISH BORDER

'Leave the beaten track behind occasionally and dive into the woods.'

— Alexander Graham Bell

Straddling Bulgaria and Turkey, stretching between the low-slung central mountains to the Black Sea coast, the Strandja is a primeval stretch of forest, where it is hard to imagine where one country starts and another finishes. 'Strandja' comes from the Old Bulgarian word 'stran', meaning closed and mythical and, in reality, this is fitting. Often, the edges of countries are rooted and fixed — a border crossing, a fence, a sea — here, demarcation is unfathomable. All we had were rustling oak woods as far as the eye could see, shaken by land winds and sea gales, all washed with a slightly Turkish climate and a southern, eastern air. It was a beautiful but befuddling landscape, a 'terra incognita' in our over-mapped world.

Romanticising this kind of scenery is easy, but in reality the first thing we saw approaching the forest in the Renault was black-and-white poverty. Leaving Elena the fisherwoman and her village, Todor and I had ventured off-piste, crawling along a poor lane, more of a gash in the landscape than a road, interrupted by a Gypsy village. It reminded me of those I'd seen years ago in Transylvania. Windows kicked in on the ground floor (where livestock might sleep), rough sleeping quarters above and gaunt horses in fallow fields, their flanks quivering. A very unromantic kind of peasantry and a sharp contrast to the more genteel sunflower scenery of rural Bessarabia, which, though grindingly poor, was hopeful-looking.

THE LADIES OF MALKO TARNOVO

Malko Tarnovo (population 2000), deep in the Strandja, looked a rosier, cheerier village. Solidly rural. Friendly. Todor had arranged a cooking demonstration, of sorts, with a group of local women, not knowing that this would mean eight ladies, all aged 60 and above. Each wore national dress. Gold coins glittered around necks, crimson flowers were pinned to headscarves and deep red aprons hung over hips, decorated with chalky-white stripes. We gathered together in front of a giant, creaking dark wood and stone-built house in the centre of the village where ingredients to make *zelnik*, a filo pie stuffed with greens usually eaten during the holidays, were laid out. The women took it in turns to rip up the dock leaves, brushing the pastry sheets and mixing the yogurt and eggs, demonstrating how the pie is done. Behind me, Todor stood, feverishly translating. Then, out of the house came another woman, dressed the same, who handed around a slice of *zelnik* already baked.

We sat on the ground and ate, the crispy filo showering down crumbs and the greens sticking between our teeth, watching as girlish pleasure spread across the faces of the ladies of Malko Tarnovo. A little white bean and dried mint dip, in a clay pot with a jolly red chilli pepper at its centre, was handed around and we dug spoons in to try it. Usually, indoors, dining room tables would be laid with the traditional appetiser of *bahur* (pork, rice and leeks stuffed into intestines), perhaps some *katchamak varenik* (fried bacon, cornflour and onions), or if it's Christmas in Malko Tarnovo, a pig would be slaughtered and its liver and kidneys mixed with dried chilli. Once we'd eaten, we joined hands and the ladies sang a soulful ditty, forming a chain, dancing the *horo* around the courtyard. Beyond, the myth-heavy meadows and hills vibrated with strong sun, their grasses, wild orchids and trees hiding remnants of Thracian tombs and Greek columns. Crowding around our alfresco lunch, some residents of Malko Tarnovo spoke of a tiny settlement not far away where their ancestors had once lived. A village called Brashlyan that is dissected by the rivers Pantaleyska and Churka. A thin road led us there. Pulverised by Ottoman troops during the Preobrazhenie Uprising of 1903 — and divided up following the Balkan Wars of 1912–1913 when the northern section of the Strandja became part of Bulgaria — it is an obscure and sleepy place today. Historical industries have all but disappeared. Gone are the flax and hemp harvesters who'd carry their wooden swap hooks through the village, and gone, too, are the leagues of sheep farmers who, dressed in thick woollen cloaks, filled the lanes and hillocks with their flocks. No more either are the sacks of charcoal, piled high, ready to be shipped to Constantinople. Today, this is a village full of ghosts and memories with a population of less than a hundred people, almost all septuagenarians. Most working-age villagers have gone to the cities, leaving their parents and grandparents to their beautiful but hardscrabble lives.

Elders here live in perfectly preserved 300-year-old peasant houses, influenced by merchant-style timbered 'Black Sea houses', but frugally decorated with little wood carving, in contrast to their Turkish equivalents. They were built without windows until the late 19th century, not to keep out the biting winter cold, but to keep valuables hidden — for this village, once flourishing with quiet industry, attracted looting *kurdjalii* (Ottoman bandits) and Circassian raiders. In the centre of the village, a church complete with its Russian-hewn bell stands on the grounds of an ancient Thracian sanctuary dedicated to Dionysus, the God of ecstasy and wine. Hanging over Brashlyan, an air of steadfastness lingers on, a reminder of when young, strong villagers took part in the Bulgarian and Greek liberation movements against the Ottoman Empire, very different times, long before the village was sidelined.

Leaving Todor, and the last mountain range of south-east Europe behind, still pleasingly impermeable, I made for Istanbul, the bus putting through the small slither of Turkey that is in Europe, towards Anatolia — 'east' or 'land of sunrise' to the Greeks — the Asian part that makes up 93 per cent. Flying would have been quicker but then I'd have missed all of this. Instead, as is almost always the case, the road had rewarded.

Afternoon Zelnik Pie

When I first recreated this Bulgarian *zelnik* at home my husband, James, and I stood at the kitchen counter eating it warm, mid-afternoon. He said, 'this is a perfect afternoon pie, it could easily take the place of a 3 o'clock tea-time cake.' It was in the afternoon I ate it in Bulgaria too, with the ladies of Malko Tarnovo, hence the name.

SERVES 4

5 tablespoons rapeseed oil

5 shallots, thinly sliced into rings

¼ teaspoon freshly grated nutmeg

200g/7oz rainbow chard (or kale), washed, leaves torn to shreds and stalks cut into matchsticks

200g/7oz spinach, washed

leaves of 2 large sprigs of mint

good handful of lovage (optional, if in season)

1 large egg, lightly beaten, plus an extra egg, beaten, to glaze

300g/10½oz white feta-style sheep's cheese, crumbled

40g/3 tablespoons unsalted butter, melted

270g/9½oz filo pastry

1 tablespoon caraway seeds

salt and freshly ground black pepper

Preheat the oven to 180°C/350°F/gas mark 4. Heat 3 tablespoons of the rapeseed oil in a large saucepan and cook the shallots gently with a pinch of salt until translucent, then add the nutmeg and a generous few grinds of black pepper and stir together, remove to a large mixing bowl and set aside.

In the same pan, add the remaining oil and chard stems, cooking them for 2 minutes. Remove to the mixing bowl then, cooking in batches, gently wilt all the greens (if they're not dry they will spit), including the mint and lovage, if using. Once cooled, if the greens have released water, squeeze this out. Transfer to the mixing bowl and leave to cool completely before adding the egg and cheese. Mix and set aside.

Grease a round 20–23cm/8–9in round tin with some of the melted butter, and cut the filo sheets into rounds to fit the shape of the tin (10–12 sheets in total). Lay 2 filo rounds in the base of the tin, brushing each with melted butter. Sprinkle some caraway seeds over, then add a layer of the greens and cheese and repeat these layers, each time brushing the filo with melted butter. End with a top layer of 2 filo rounds, brushed with plenty of butter, a little beaten egg and with a sprinkling of caraway.

Bake for around 35 minutes, until golden. Leave the pie to cool in the tin for 10 minutes before slicing into it. Serve with a pot of afternoon tea.

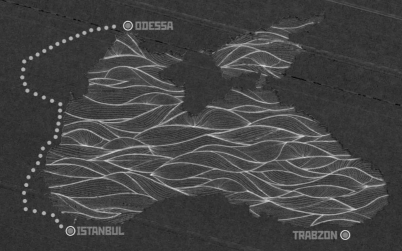

ISTANBUL

ISTANBUL – THE SEA COMES TO THE CITY

'Say Istanbul and a barge comes to mind

Loaded with onions, painted poison-green on coral red,

Sailing in from the Black Sea ports winter and summer'

— Bedri Rahmi Eyuboglu, *The Saga of Istanbul*

'Half the people you meet in Istanbul are from the Black Sea,' said a news bureau chief over meze one night in Istanbul's vine-tangled Cihangir neighbourhood. And, how right he is. Istanbul, straddling both Europe and Asia, is very much a Karadeniz (Black Sea) city, too, connected to it by the throat of the Bosphorus, ever since an earthquake forced a passage from the Mediterranean thousands of years ago.

Today, its neighbourhoods, spread throughout the Asian and European sides of the city, are a soup of Black Sea families, merchants, general stores and restaurants. Busy cafés in Beyoğlu, just off of touristy Istiklal Caddesi, such as Klemuri and Hayvore, sell versions of *hamsi* (anchovy) pilaf, cornbread and buttery chard soups – all quintessentially Black Sea dishes. The mournful strains of *kemençe* – a Black Sea violin – can sometimes be heard around the streets of Kadıköy, replacing Turkish pop and Greek Rebetiko, while Black Sea cultural centres provide solace to the homesick in the form of dances, card games and buffets. At the break of dawn on Sunday mornings, traders start arriving from Black Sea towns and cities, having driven all night, to sell their jam, molasses and nuts, at Istanbul's Kastamonu Market. For centuries, the Bosphorus carried a constant flow of Black Sea-bound traffic, both day and night. Ottoman explorer and travel writer Evliya Çelebi noted in the 17th century that in Istanbul 8000 people were engaged in Black Sea trade, providing the city with rice, salt, honey, butter and leather from the ports of northern Anatolia, Crimea and Europe. So, while the Sea of Marmara is Istanbul's closest and most obvious maritime partner, the Black Sea – not just a coastline but a whole region spreading deep into the interior – permeates Istanbul strongly, seeping deeply into the city's psyche. For visitors, it is easy, with a map and a hit-list, to experience a Karadeniz day in Istanbul, starting on the Asian side of the city, in Kadıköy.

Brushing past a waiter, chef Necla Hanim carried a copper pan of *muhlama* to the table. A trio of cheese, golden cornmeal and butter, it glistened and wobbled as she walked. 'The cheese has a very high fat content. You have to eat it fast or else it sets,' she said, placing it in front of me, and offering a welcome challenge.

Çay Tarlasi (literally 'Tea Field') in the neighbourhood of Kadıköy, is decked out in the style of traditional wooden log houses found around the northeast tea-growing Black Sea region, by the Georgian border. This was where Necla left, with her husband Oğuz Koyuncu, 20 years ago, to open this café here in Istanbul. Newspaper clippings from local restaurant critics (all highly praising the *muhlama*) hang on the walls above encyclopaedias about the Black Sea and black-and-white photographs of submarines. Serving the Black Sea diaspora who want to be reminded of home, local students and Istanbullus who appreciate Necla's cooking, the little café is busy, buzzy and well used.

The stringy cheese twisted around my fork, glistening like stretchy spaghetti, but just as I was about to take a bite, my forkful was interrupted by an intense-looking moustachioed man sitting at an opposite table, who had been listening to our conversation. 'The best ingredients are in there. The best. Trabzon butter, cheese and cornmeal. The best!' he said, pointing at the *muhlama* with his umbrella, a tulip-shaped glass of tea in his other hand. I nodded. Then, finally, with the moustachioed man still watching me (was he the chef's father? A loyal customer? A proud citizen of Trabzon?) I tasted it. The soft, buttery and salty flavours of the *koloti* cheese, also the secret ingredient in Çay Tarlası's *menemen* breakfast, meshed with the rich butter and cornmeal. It was similar to fondue, but so much better than that. I smiled and the moustachioed man smiled back and, satisfied, returned to his newspaper. '*Muhlama* is a poor man's dish back at home, but there we walk it off in the hills. Here, it is a luxurious treat because we don't,' Necla said, folding a napkin. She explained that she has Hemşin (Armenian) heritage, while Oğuz is Laz (ethnic Georgian), both groups found in the far east of Turkey's Black Sea region and in large cities such as Istanbul. The television behind her flickered with images of the war in Syria. Grimacing, she grabbed the remote, and turned it off.

Oğuz, dressed in a lumberjack shirt, hair tied back in a ponytail, heaved his large frame over. 'I'm sorry, I didn't want to shake your hand before because I was eating, not because you're a woman,' he belly laughed as he said this, acknowledging the absurdity. But, there are growing divisions in Istanbul, and people's guards are uncharacteristically up.

'You must try our Laz börek. Even if you have had it before it was not real Laz börek. We don't put syrup on ours,' Oğuz said, disappearing into the kitchen. The Laz are often the butt of jokes in Turkey, drawn as birdbrained highlanders, as the writer Sevan Nisanyan explains in his book on the Black Sea: 'He sports a majestic nose and speaks Turkish with an outrageous accent. His diet consists of *hamsi* (Black Sea anchovies), cooked to the legendary one hundred recipes that include *hamsi* bread and *hamsi* jam … Inevitably the most brilliant Laz jokes are circulated by the Laz themselves.' It's also said that the Laz are fiercely hospitable, and fiery too, choosing, when necessary, to 'talk with the pistol'.

I wonder whether anyone would be brave enough to insult Oğuz who, despite his gentle demeanour, is built like a grizzly bear. Like the *muhlama*, the Laz börek announces itself with an explicit threat to the waistline. It is hedonistic, heavy and irresistible, allowing no possibility whatsoever for seconds. It is different from typical börek because Laz börek is sweet, not savoury. If you imagine a slice of baklava with paper-thin filo, but the size of a deck of cards and crammed with custard instead of nuts, you're somewhere close.

Çay Tarlasi is a classic Istanbul café in that it serves only a handful of dishes and it serves them very well to its loyal, local clientele. Its selling points are simple: time-honoured recipes, good ingredients and family connections. As I leave, my Turkish-speaking friend, Ugur, tells me that Oğuz is the brother of a very famous Laz singer, Kazim Koyuncu, who died tragically young. They look similar, Ugur tells me. Long hair, beards, open faces. I later read that Kazim was an environmental campaigner with concerns about the Black Sea, that he was a singer in a band called The Children of the Sea and that his solo albums were smash hits.

A ten-minute walk away from Çay Tarlasi, is Kadıköy Pazarı, the local bazaar containing a warren of specialist food traders that form a ground zero, of sorts, for lovers of Turkish produce. Glass dispensers of purpley-brown *pekmez* (grape molasses) stand next to piles of *pestil* (fruit leather), canisters of nuts and ginormous plastic tubs of *turşu* (pickles). In the middle of it all, on Güneşli Bahçe Sokak, is the tiny Eta Bal honey shop run by Ahmet Aksoy from the Black Sea tea-centric city of Rize. Reaching over jars of bee milk, pollen and honeycombs, he first hands me his business card, to prove to me that he is, as he claims to be, 'a bee products expert', then dabs different, sticky-sweet honeys onto little wooden strips for tasting. I licked the sticks and squeezed into a corner, making myself as small as possible, to make way for the almost constant stream of customers who pile into his tiny shop to buy his first-rate honeys.

The flavours toggle between chestnutty and floral but it is the Karakovan Balı — black hive honey produced by bees in the wild — that is in a league of its own. Subtle oregano mixes with lavender notes, although it is pretty much indescribable, as it is like no other honey. Honey, like wine, is dependent on its terroir and the green hills of the Black Sea provide beekeepers with high mountain pastures, called *yaylas*, fresh meadows and clean air. Aksoy's honeys are about as far as you can get from the unholy, mass-produced honey found on supermarket shelves back home. Staying on the Asian side of the city, heading five miles north in the direction of the Black Sea, a smoky taxi ride takes me to Trabzon Kültür Derneği (Trabzon Cultural Association) in residential Üsküdar. Ugur, immediately recognising the driver's Black Sea accent, asks him where he's from. 'Rize,' the man replies. We both raise our eyebrows and shrug shoulders at the coincidence.

SALT BOMBS AND MOUNTAIN MILK

If Çay Tarlası, with its wood cabin ambience, suggests Black Sea environs, then the Trabzon Cultural Association in Üsküdar, also on the Asian side of the city, screams it. By an enormous window, I took a seat with Demet from Ordu, a Black Sea port city famous for its hazelnuts. Ordering us some traditional dishes, she began to reminisce. She speaks first of her childhood picking tea leaves, which was a cinch compared with the back-breaking work that goes into picking hazelnuts, and then explained that if there's a food that goes well with walnuts, it will go even better with hazelnuts as they are better with 'everything'. Of course, she misses the food from home. There's the rice pudding made with fresh mountain milk, floral honey and fruit molasses. But most of all she misses the *hamsi* (anchovies). 'Black Sea people love *hamsi* so much that they don't even consider them a fish. It's like comparing humans to animals,' she said, running her hand over the white tablecloth.

Anchovy season in Istanbul, in the winter months, is met with great anticipation. During the season, chefs dish up *hamsi* in all manner of imaginative ways. At Mikla, a top-drawer restaurant in Beyoğlu, during the depths of a cold weathery January, I sat in awe of chef Mehmet Gürs' anchovies. These brackish and plump salt bombs came butterflied and suspended in paper-thin mini olive oil toasts. It was one of the best things I have ever eaten, anywhere. It wasn't the season, so we couldn't order the club's famous *hamsi* pilaf, or the *kaygana*, a quiche-like fritter with anchovies, chard and parsley; instead, we ate crunchy Trabzon börek, filled with rice, sultanas, pine nuts and chard. Around us, birds tweeted and twittered in cages while outside a small funicular ferried people up and down the steep incline, past a traditional Black Sea-style grain store, shipped from Trabzon, and native Black Sea trees, planted to replicate the landscape. It was enough to send me straight back to Trabzon, an unjustly underappreciated city.

An hour later, the Rize-born taxi driver returned to collect us, car stereo on, cigarette smoke lingering. As we settled into the dusty cab, and slowly began slogging through the churning rush-hour traffic, a heartfelt melody came on the radio. With one hand, the driver turned up the volume a fraction, then twisted the dial, tuning in the station until the fuzz and crackling disappeared. 'That man singing on the radio?' Ugur said, turning to face me. 'It's Kazım Koyuncu. Oğuz's brother.' We listened carefully as the driver softly sang along. He knew every single word.

A Laz Börek for Oğuz

Since sampling Oğuz's Laz börek – to my mind the best – I went on to try many more versions, in Istanbul and much further east around the Black Sea. Klemuri, a small Black Sea lokanta on the European side of Istanbul, if you find yourself around there, also produces a great belt-busting version of this milk pudding. The black pepper adds a welcome dab of heat.

SERVES 10

130g/about ½ cup unsalted butter, melted

15 filo pastry sheets

FOR THE CUSTARD

2 large egg yolks

3 tablespoons cornflour (cornstarch)

pinch of black pepper

25g/2 tablespoons caster (superfine) sugar

½ teaspoon vanilla extract

250ml/generous 1 cup full-fat milk

250ml/generous 1 cup double (heavy) cream

Preheat the oven to 190°C/375°F/gas mark 5 and prepare the custard. Place the egg yolks, cornflour (cornstarch), pepper, sugar and vanilla in a medium saucepan and gently whisk together, off the heat, adding a splash of the milk and cream. Then put the pan on the hob over a low heat and slowly pour in the rest of the milk and cream. Cook very gently, stirring constantly, for 5–10 minutes, ensuring it doesn't boil, until the custard is smooth and thick. Remove from the heat and pour the custard into a jug.

Use some of the melted butter to grease a 25 x 30cm/10 x 12-in rectangular dish. Take a filo sheet and place it in the dish, then brush it with melted butter. Repeat the process with another 5 sheets of filo – creating a bottom layer that's 6 sheets thick in total. It's fine if some filo hangs over the edge as it better holds in the custard. When the custard is cool, pour it into the filo-layered dish, and then gently repeat the buttered filo layering process with the remaining 9 layers on top of the custard. Brush the top generously with butter, trim the overhanging edges and very, very gently, with the tip of a sharp knife, score just the top layer into squares — if you go deeper than the top layer the custard will make an appearance, which you don't want.

Bake for 25–35 minutes, or until totally golden. Leave it to cool, covered with a cloth, for around 4 hours and then serve at room temperature, cutting it where you marked the top layer.

Black Sea Börek

A deeply savoury börek filled with rice, sultanas, pine nuts and chard. It is baked as a large pie rather than as small pastries, making it ideal for a lunchtime gathering. The fleshy sultanas give it a lovely sweet note. *Yufka* pastry, often for sale in Turkish/Mediterranean shops, is slightly thicker than filo pastry and usually comes in generously sized sheets; if you can find it, buy it.

SERVES 4 GENEROUSLY

2 tablespoons olive oil

4 shallots, finely diced

100g/½ cup plus 1 tablespoon basmati rice

50g/1¾oz sultanas

200ml/generous ¾ cup chicken stock

6 Swiss chard leaves
(kale works as a substitute)

100g/3½oz feta, crumbled

2 medium eggs, plus 1 extra egg, beaten, to glaze

40g/3 tablespoons unsalted butter, melted, plus extra for greasing

30g/1oz pine nuts

12 sheets of yufka/filo pastry, cut to 18 x 24cm/7 x 9-in rectangles

2 teaspoons nigella or sesame seeds

salt and freshly ground black pepper

Preheat the oven to 200°C/400°F/gas mark 6.

Heat the oil in a large saucepan and gently sauté the shallots with a pinch of salt. When softened and translucent, stir in the rice and add the sultanas, coating it all in the oil, then add the chicken stock. Season with plenty of ground black pepper and bring to a boil. Cover, reduce the heat and simmer gently for 15 minutes, until the liquid has been absorbed and the rice is cooked. Set aside to cool.

While the rice is cooking, cut off the tough tips of the chard but keep the stalks, rinse well and chop into bite-sized pieces. Combine the chard with the cheese and eggs in a bowl, and season with salt and pepper. Add the cooled rice.

Next, thoroughly grease a 20cm/8-in square tin and toast the pine nuts gently in a hot, dry frying pan until golden. Remove and leave to cool slightly before adding to the chard and rice mix.

Layer 4 sheets of yufka/filo in the greased tin to cover the base, with 2 sheets forming a layer one way, another 2 the other way (as your tin is square and the sheets are rectangular), brushing each sheet with a little melted butter as you go. Add half the filling mixture, then add another 4 sheets of pastry in the same way, brushing with melted butter again. Add the remaining filling and, finally, add a top layer of 4 pastry sheets in the same way. Trim the excess, tucking under the corners and edges as you go so you have a neat top.

Brush the top well with the beaten egg and sprinkle over the seeds. Bake for 30–35 minutes or until golden and cooked through. Leave it to rest for 10 minutes before serving.

WHAT WAS SAVED AND WASN'T LOST

It was lunchtime in Beyoğlu and the thin alleyway of Kallavi Sokak was packed with office workers all anticipating a decent lunch. Drifting out of kitchen windows was the remedying smell of baked börek, while firing out of different competing café doorways were waiters — men and women in tight jeans and white shirts — keen to serve, holding plates high, rhythmically and nimbly funnelling in and out of the packed laneway. Waiting silently, watching from under wooden chairs, were Istanbul's bushy-tailed cats, on high alert for fallen scraps. It is a scene played out most days.

Commanding the alley is Ficcin, with the most tables and the quickest turnover. Indoors, and in the alley, diners raised their hands, ordering more salad, cold yogurt soup and shredded Circassian chicken as Ficcin's waiters dished out little heart-shaped china bowls of dried mint, red pepper flakes and sumac, taking down more orders as they went. Inside, on the walls, old paintings of dark forests and ancient forts hinted at the cuisine served: food of the North Caucasus. A nettlesome and guarded region in southern Russia, wedged between the Black Sea and the Caspian. A place of expulsion, shouldering a sad history. At the end of the 19th century, more than a million Muslim highlanders and Tatars were forced out and deported by the Russian Empire. Sent across mountains, and then by ship across the Black Sea from ports around the Caucasus, hundreds of thousands lost their lives, dying of disease, starvation, storms and dehydration on their journeys. Many survivors ended up in Turkey's Black Sea cities — Trabzon, Samsun, Sinop, Varna in Bulgaria, and Istanbul. In memory of their ancestors who perished in the Black Sea, some descendants of the victims refuse to eat fish today.

Leyla Kılıç Karakaynak, one of two sisters who run Ficcin, is a fourth-generation Istanbullu but her family roots are in the North Caucasus, in mountainous North Ossetia, where locals trace their identity back to the Iranian-speaking medieval kingdom of Alania, remaining largely detached from the Russian mainstream today. Despite living here for several generations, she told me that where she's 'from' still very much depends on who she's talking to. In Turkey, the feuding clans and tribes of the North Caucasus tend to be clubbed together under the label 'Circassians', a misleading catch-all term for all Eurasian highlanders, but that's not the case across the Black Sea. 'Here, Ingush, Georgians and Ossetians are all put together, but back there, we are not. We are different,' as Karakaynak put it. It wasn't until she first travelled back to North Ossetia, ten years ago — a long-delayed homecoming of sorts — did she realise what had been saved, and what had been lost.

In North Ossetia, Soviet rule and cultural cleansing had destroyed the habits and culinary traditions that her family had cherished – and closely guarded – in Turkey for the past 150 years. 'You could say we overprotect the culture here,' Karakaynak said, explaining that what she found in North Ossetia was far from an idealised motherland. Instead, it was an experience summed up by one word: extinction. Under Soviet rule, women worked to survive but in Turkey, where the refugees settled, women lived traditional lifestyles of cooking and child rearing, much how their ancestors had done before the arrival of Communism. What had been lost there, had been saved here, retained within Turkey's North Ossetian diaspora, in Turkey's Black Sea cities. Strong traditions of hospitality, beliefs and fables were held onto, kept and were handed down, along with inherited recipes for dishes like Ossetian pies and sour cream porridges. 'We kept our cornbread recipes, sweet and savoury ones, back there it was the folklore food of legends.'

I ordered lunch. The 'Circassian ravioli', as they're listed on the menu, meant 15 or so potato dumplings covering the entire dinner plate, lying partly hidden under a blanket of thick Turkish yogurt laced with orangey-coloured pepper oil. Onto this goes Turkish pepper, sumac and mint, spooned from the heart-shaped bowls. Fiendishly good. It is remarkable, given the manti's primitiveness, that these parcels are capable of hooking you on first bite. But they're addictive. Fresh and thin, the warm potato helps them to melt as they meet teeth and tongue. The signature namesake dish here is *ficcin*. A simple baked pastry filled with ground beef. It takes pride of place at the very top of the menu, which is a printed-out Excel spreadsheet. Robust and offering few frills, ficcin, both the dish and the restaurant, equals the best sort of Istanbul eating there is: unpolished, filling, feel-good food. It may have been the middle of summer, but this would have been the food that got Karakaynak's ancestors through long, bitingly cold winters across the Black Sea in the mountains of the North Ossetia.

That afternoon, across the water in Kadıköy, I found more heirloom recipes from the former Soviet Union at Sayla Manti, a little canteen with a satisfyingly old-school blue and white candy-stripe awning out the front. Operational since the heady days of 1969, the current owner, Fevzi Esen, took the baton from a family whose Tatar grandparents fled the Crimean War, across the Black Sea, arriving at about the same time as Leyla Kılıç Karakaynak's relatives left North Ossetia, 150 years ago. Immaculate in his Pringle-style sweater and clearly proud of his spotless operation, Esen explained that it has taken patience and determination to get the restaurant where it is today. 'I started as a waiter in 1982, and slowly took over the business. I sold my bicycle to buy paintings for the walls, and for meat, I'd buy it on credit from the butcher,' he said as plates of his famous beef manti arrived at surrounding tables. Today, he still uses the same butcher, and still keeps an agreement to pay later, a bit like a bar tab. 'In that way, I am a very typical, loyal Istanbullu,' he said.

I wonder about the name 'sayla', and Esen tells me without a hint of irony that it means 'to choose' in Tatar, then in the same breath adds that the menu contains just two items. But, in typical Turkish style, both dishes are time-honoured, and are exceedingly well practised and executed. The first is çiğ börek, which confusingly translates as raw börek, although it is a fried crescent-shaped mince-filled turnover. It is much loved by Crimean Tatars. And the second is beef manti, coming in four portion sizes and topped with butter from Esen's hometown. He brings in 300 kilos of butter a year just for this purpose and has imported an Italian machine, at great expense, for rolling manti dough out. The food on the menu encompasses 'the Tatar daily diet in Istanbul', Esen added, explaining how he keeps in touch with the relatives of the original owner, including the grandson, who is now 98 years old. As we talk, Sayla Manti fills up with families and well-behaved school children, drinking yogurty Ayran and knowing exactly what to order and expect. This is a place of few surprises, much expectation, and a lot of pride. Esen never intended to change the original menu as he wanted to stay true to the original çiğ börek and manti. His ambition, he told me modestly, was only ever 'to make it a little better'.

Circassian Chicken

Not the prettiest dish in the world, but considered a classic in Istanbul and served widely. It works best as a meze dish, or a lunchtime side, or served on rice for supper.

SERVES 4

400ml/1 ⅔ cups chicken stock

2 large skinless chicken breasts

2 slices of stale bread, crusts removed

80ml/5 tablespoons milk

handful of walnut halves, toasted

1 large garlic clove, crushed to a paste with ½ teaspoon salt

½ teaspoon black pepper

½ teaspoon ground allspice

FOR THE GARNISH

2 tablespoons walnut oil

1 teaspoon sweet paprika

1 teaspoon pul biber (Turkish pepper flakes)

small handful of toasted walnut halves

a few coriander (cilantro) leaves (optional)

Pour the stock into a saucepan with the chicken breasts. Bring to the boil, then simmer and poach for about 10 minutes or until cooked all the way through. Remove the chicken from the stock and, once cool, shred into a bowl, using your hands, pulling the cooked chicken into 2.5cm/1 in-long pieces. Set aside 100ml/generous ⅓ cup of the stock (save the rest for another use).

Put the bread in a dish, pour over the milk and leave it to absorb. Then, in a food processor, blitz the toasted walnuts and garlic paste until you have fine crumbs. Add the milky bread and pulse. Pour in the remaining chicken stock, along with the pepper and allspice, then blend until you have a sauce the consistency of double (heavy) cream.

Pour the walnut sauce over the chicken and toss it through to coat. Before serving, warm the walnut oil in a small pan and add the paprika and pul biber. Set aside. Plate up the chicken mix, scatter over the walnut halves, coriander (cilantro) and pour the pepper paprika oil over the top.

Black Sea Beans

Kuru fasülye, creamy pale beans in thick red buttery gravy, is possibly Turkey's favourite bean dish. It is cooked by bean 'ustas' (masters) as getting it right is harder than it might look. Given the proliferation of excellent *yayla* (mountain pasture) butter accessible to Black Sea cooks, this dish is especially good there.

Butter is key for this recipe so it pays to use rich, creamy farmhouse butter, if possible – your beans will thank you for it.

SERVES 4

300g/1¾ cups dried cannellini beans (dried beans have more texture and flavour)

1 fresh bay leaf

60g/4½ tablespoons good salted butter

1 small onion, grated

3 garlic cloves, very finely chopped

1 teaspoon salt

½ teaspoon freshly ground black pepper

2 tablespoons tomato paste

2 whole dried red chillies, plus 4 extra whole to decorate

1 x 400g/14oz can chopped tomatoes

OPTIONAL ACCOMPANIMENTS AND GARNISHES

lemon wedges

parsley leaves

sliced red onion

hot peppers (guindillas or similar)

Rinse the beans then soak them in a large pot of water for at least 5 hours, preferably overnight, covering the beans by at least a few inches. You want them to have soaking water to cook in so make sure they have enough.

Drain the beans, and reserve the soaking water. Put the beans into a heavy-bottomed pan, such as a flameproof casserole, and add enough soaking water to cover them by 2.5cm/1 in (if you're short, add hot chicken or vegetable stock, or water). Add the bay leaf and bring the beans to a boil, skimming off any froth that comes to the top, then lower the heat, cover and simmer over a low heat until soft but with a little bite, around 1–1½ hours, adding more soaking water as you go, or just fresh water if you're short, if it gets too thick.

Melt the butter in a separate medium-sized pan, add the onion and garlic and sauté for 3–5 minutes on a gentle heat, adding the salt and pepper and stirring often so they soften but don't colour.

Add the tomato paste to the onions and garlic and stir for a few minutes so the mixture thickens slightly and comes together. Then prepare your chillies. Snip off the stems, and using a knife, butterfly open and clear out the seeds. Toast on a high heat, in a dry frying pan, just for a minute or two, to release the heat. Next, tip the canned tomatoes and 2 of the toasted chillies into the onion mixture, stir and simmer for 20–30 minutes. Make sure to stir every now and again so the mixture doesn't catch. Use a blender to mix into a velvety sauce. When your beans are soft, drain and add the tomato mixture. You should have a thick sauce.

Plate up the beans and serve with a whole dried chilli on the top. Lemon wedges, parsley leaves, sliced red onion or guindillas are all nice accompaniments.

Herb-Flecked Cornbread

Cornbread is quintessentially 'Black Sea' in Turkey. It is a dense bread, best served warm. I first tried it with red cabbage soup, in a tiny family-run cafe in Istanbul called Hatice that serves Black Sea food to just 20 or so loyal lunch-breakers. I have added Parmesan and herbs to this recipe as I feel these additions, while not authentic, move it up another level and stop the bread from being quite so dense and dry.

MAKES 1 MEDIUM LOAF

225g/1½ cups fine cornmeal

140g/1 cup strong white bread flour

1 tablespoon caster (superfine) sugar

2 teaspoons baking powder (baking soda)

1½ teaspoons fine salt

50g/3½ tablespoons butter, chilled and cut into small pieces, plus extra for greasing

350ml/1½ cups full-fat milk

juice of ½ lemon

2 eggs

45g/1½oz Parmesan or Grana Padano, grated

2 tablespoons chopped basil

2 tablespoons chopped flat-leaf parsley

1 tablespoon nigella seeds (optional)

Preheat the oven to 220°C/425°F/gas mark 7 and grease a 23cm/9-in round cake tin with butter.

Put the cornmeal, flour, sugar, baking powder (baking soda) and salt in a large mixing bowl and stir together. Add the chilled butter to the mixture and rub it in with your fingers until it resembles breadcrumbs. Mix together the milk, lemon juice and eggs in a separate jug or bowl, then pour over the dry ingredients and stir together until you have a batter. Add the grated cheese and chopped fresh herbs, as well as the nigella seeds, if using, and stir.

Pour the batter into the prepared tin and bake for approximately 35 minutes, or until golden and a skewer inserted in the centre comes out clean. Cool for 10 minutes, then turn out, cut into wedges and serve with plenty of butter to spread on it. Cornbread is not great the next day, but you can refresh it by popping it in the oven for a few minutes to warm back through.

Citrus Cured Mackerel with Gherkins

In recent years, mackerel in Istanbul – filling the famous fish sandwiches (*balik ekmek*) for sale along the Bosphorus – has been more likely to be Norwegian than Turkish due to depleted local stocks. Therefore, I was happy to learn recently of the return of Turkish mackerel at Hayat Cihangir, a fish and meze restaurant run by Tarkan Şahin in the Cihangir neighbourhood. 'We didn't see mackerel since 2009, but now it is back in the Black Sea, and it is better than that of Norway,' the owner assured me. It was wonderful to hear this news as I ate a lively salad, possibly containing the most mackerel-y mackerel I have ever tasted, and listened to Greek Rebetiko music on a hot summer night. This is a version easy to recreate at home.

SERVES 4 AS A MEZE OR SIDE

2 fresh mackerel, gutted and filleted (ask your fishmonger to do this)

1 tablespoon olive oil

FOR THE CITRUS CURE

1 teaspoon black peppercorns

1 teaspoon fennel seeds

25g/2 tablespoons caster (superfine) sugar

50g/3 tablespoons salt

grated zest of 1 lemon

grated zest of 1 lime

FOR THE SALAD

50g/1¾ oz sun-dried tomatoes, halved

80g/3oz gherkins, quartered lengthwise

50ml/3½ tablespoons olive oil

2 tablespoons chopped dill

2 tablespoons chopped flat-leaf parsley

freshly ground black pepper

First, make the citrus cure. Gently toast the peppercorns and fennel seeds in a dry pan, then lightly crush them in a pestle and mortar. Add them to a mixing bowl with the sugar, salt, lemon zest and lime zest and stir together well. Pour the mixture into a tray large enough for the mackerel. Place the fish fillets on the cure, flesh-side down. Cover with cling film (plastic wrap) and refrigerate for 2 hours.

Just before you remove the fish from the fridge, make the salad. Simply combine the ingredients, with pepper to taste, in a large serving bowl.

Rinse the mackerel fillets under cold running water to remove all of the cure, then pat dry with kitchen paper. Heat a griddle pan until very hot.

Lightly rub the mackerel skin with the olive oil, place skin-side down on the griddle and cook for 2 minutes, then remove. Serve the mackerel fillets while still warm, next to the salad.

BOSPHORUS BLUES

'Each villa on the Bosphorus looks a screen

New painted or a pretty opera scene'

– Lord Byron, *Don Juan*

Ship spotting is a habit and art form in Istanbul. To join in, all you have to do is take a pair of binoculars and position yourself at a decent vantage point on the Bosphorus. Connecting the Black Sea to the Aegean, Mediterranean, the Balkans and beyond, the Bosphorus is a 20-mile strait and sea channel upon which a never-ending parade of warships, containers and destroyers navigate.

Watching the Bosphorus is a bit like turning the pages of a newspaper. A snapshot would include: rainbow-coloured goods containers carrying refrigerated lorries of Ukrainian and Georgian produce – cheese, herbs and butter – their captains using the Bosphorus and the Black Sea to get around Russia's closed land borders since the annexation of Crimea. Ferries of Turkish tomato truckers, crossing the Black Sea from Turkey to Ukraine now that Russia has banned their import. Russian ships travelling to Syria from Sevastopol – home to the Kremlin's Black Sea Fleet since Grigory Potemkin, favourite of Catherine the Great, founded it there in 1783 – and northbound Russian Navy fleets returning from the war. This is where Putin exhibits Moscow's naval might, grating the nerves of some Istanbullus, with his missile cruisers and landing ships moving right through the heart of the city. Once a routine sight, during the Cold War era and the Balkans conflict, these hulking war ships are a steady presence once again as the Kremlin reasserts its influence in the Middle East. Istanbul's strategic position, crucial for trade and diplomacy, is as important as it is long. With such drama and unfolding politics, the Bosphorus can make other waterways – even great historic rivers – seem flat and uneventful in comparison.

But this is not to say that it's all war, trade and industry. The Bosphorus is also Istanbul's soul, a vital source ingrained in the life and minds of its residents. Serving as a getaway from the traffic, and the noise and chaos that a city of 15 million, or more, shelters, it is a constant lifeline and, in the height of summer; breathing in cooling salty breezes from a commuter ferry when the city sweats and swelters can be nothing short of sanity saving. It is somewhere to escape to and gaze upon. So much so, that it is almost impossible to think of Istanbul without picturing it.

Ancient legends, myths and superstitions, spooking mariners and fishermen, abound around the Bosphorus, in particular where the strait meets the Black Sea. The most fantastical of all are the disorientating, ship-wrecking Symplegades, mythical clashing rocks that protect the sea from the Godless. These almost defeated Jason – who tricked the rocks by letting a dove fly between them before rowing through – during his fabled Argonaut expedition in search of the magical ram's fleece. Then, there is the giant 12-metre-long grave belonging to saint Yuşa Tepesi, believed by some Muslims to be the tomb of Prophet Joshua, set high on a summit, acting as a haunting nautical landmark marking the mouth of the Bosphorus. Lastly, on the European side, is the Tower of Ovid, in Uskumrukoy ('the village of the mackerel'), a reminder of where, doomed and exiled by Augustus, Ovid was imprisoned before departing for Constanta.

Lord Byron, after visiting in 1810, recognised the malign atmosphere surrounding the entrance of the Black Sea. A canto in Don Juan reads:

The wind swept down the Euxine, and the wave Broke foaming o'er the blue Symplegades;
'Tis a grand sight from off the Giant's Grave
To watch the progress of those rolling seas
Between the Bosphorus, as they lash and lave.

Fishermen have always travelled from Istanbul north to the Black Sea and southwards to the Mediterranean, driven by the seasons, ever since the city's earliest days when Greek fishing villages were scattered along its shores. But, closer to home, micro-trade has flourished, too, on local stretches of the Bosphorus. Wealthy families in the 17th and 18th centuries, especially Ottoman viziers and military pashas, built wooden *yalıs* – summer houses – along the leafy shores, where little boats would pull up to sell the residents fish, fruit and vegetables from baskets. Today, only a handful of the original yalıs, with their red roofs, still stand, but as ever, the seasons can be told by the fish for sale by the water.

Spring means sea bass and summer means mackerel, while autumn heralds the arrival of oily *palamut* (bonito) on their return migration. The bonito migration, as the historian Neal Ascherson points out in his brilliant book, *Black Sea*, was so important to trade that its image appeared on Byzantine coins. Winter means *hamsi* (anchovy) which brings out leagues of solo fishermen onto the city's banks and bridges, throwing lines into the Bosphorus and filling their buckets. 'Nowhere else does the sea come so home to a city,' wrote the English travel writer A.W. Kinglake in 1844, and as Istanbul, a megacity in the truest sense, relentlessly spreads further out, forever stretching its limits, the Black Sea gradually eases closer.

Banker's Fish Soup

One freezing morning in January, I wandered into a tiny fish café in Karaköy. There, I met cousins Muhareen and Muhsin, a chef and waiter, respectively, from the Black Sea city of Ardahan, near the Georgian border. They left their home city over a decade ago to serve the bankers around Bankalar Caddesi — Istanbul's answer to Wall Street and the financial centre of the Ottoman Empire — what they know best: fish. Their café is so popular, and the turnover so fast, that no ice is used for the little fish counter in the window. As it was winter, my soup came with scorpion fish, but for this recipe any firm white-fleshed fish will do. Monkfish works well. Many of the banks have now relocated from here but this *balik corbasi* (fish soup) remains the best fish soup I've ever eaten. It is very hearty and is somewhere between a stew and a soup. Served with warm white crusty bread it makes for a decent lunch.

SERVES 2

2 tablespoons olive oil

½ medium onion, roughly chopped

1 garlic clove, finely chopped

2 carrots, diced

250g/8¾oz celeriac, peeled and diced

500ml/generous 2 cups fish stock

grated zest of ½ lemon

handful of ripe cherry tomatoes, halved

250g/8¾oz monkfish, chopped into bite-sized pieces

salt

TO SERVE

2 tablespoons chopped flat-leaf parsley

white pepper (optional)

lemon wedges

Heat the oil in a pan and gently fry the onion and garlic with a pinch of salt for a couple of minutes until softened. Add the carrots and celeriac and continue cooking for a further 8 minutes.

Pour in the fish stock and bring to a boil. Turn the heat down and simmer with the lid on for around 20 minutes, or until the vegetables are firm but nearly cooked through. Then add the lemon zest, cherry tomatoes and chunks of fish and cook until the fish is cooked through.

Stir in the chopped parsley, dust with a little white pepper, if you like, and serve with the lemon wedges.

TEA AND LONGING IN TSARIGRAD

'Beware nostalgia. You can't run on,
and look back.'

— Mikhail Bulgakov, *Flight*

Swinging incense from a thick, heavy gold chain, the black-clad priest intoned
in Russian to a congregation of three. A tourist, also Russian, paid him no mind,
muttering to himself and searching for a socket to charge his mobile phone.
Dressed in widow's black, an elderly woman pushed open the heavy door and
entered, bringing the number up to four. Spotting the mumbling tourist, and
shooting him a look of disgust, she tucked a few loose strands of hair under her
headscarf before chanting back in Russian to the bearded priest with closed-eyed
conviction. Rays of sunlight streamed in through the large windows, setting off
the saintly frescoes and making the incense smoke dance mid-air amongst the
shimmering flecks of dust. Slowly, the fingers of light softened the old woman's
face. The tourist, his telephone now plugged in, joined in with the recital.

Aya Panteleymon is one of four rooftop Russian churches remaining in this
part of Karaköy, yet when I visited, it was the only one open, proof that there
is no Russian community of note left today. From the outside, the building
looks like just another apartment block. But it was here, in the 19th century,
that Russian pilgrims, en route to Mount Athos in Greece or Jerusalem,
would refresh and worship, bedding down on the lower floors and climbing
up the narrow staircase to pray. It is a steep, knee-creaking, and somewhat
zealous climb up six flights of stairs to reach the top. Below, on the streets of
Karaköy, or Galata as it was before, it is easy to miss it. Satellite dishes and air-
conditioning units dot the unremarkable facade, suggesting nothing of the gold
icons and prayer confined within the top-floor chapel. Down on the street, it
is a busy, industrious scene of people making and selling things. Competing
for space with electrical stores are old-school maritime supply shops with their
coils of thick rope, plastic buoys and buckets, and bakeries puffing out the
comforting scent of baked grain and sesame. One, Galata Simitçisi, founded by
bakers from Tokat in the far interior of Turkey's Black Sea region, provides the
neighbourhood with the finest chewy *simit* of all.

As a break came in the liturgical singing, the Russian tourist unplugged his
telephone. Then, as the melody started up again, he slowly circled the priest,
zooming in and filming the incense and the heavy gold cross around his neck.
The old woman tutted and huffed, her face less beatific now, but the priest,
absorbed and focused, blindly, and utterly, managed to ignore the tourist.

FREEDOM DOCKS

Russian isn't heard in the streets of Karaköy today but just over a hundred years ago it was spoken everywhere. In 1920, thousands of Russian nobility loyal to the Tsar, known generally as white émigrés or White Russians, fled the rise of Bolshevik power and poured into the Galata docks. War-tired, and often empty-handed, they had crossed the Russian steppe, by all possible means, sailing across the Black Sea from the ports of Odessa, Novorossiysk and Crimea, arriving in Constantinople. They made up the latest wave of mass immigration to the city, following in the footsteps of the tens of thousands of Jews who fled the Spanish Inquisition and found a home here and, much later, Muslim refugees fleeing the Balkans, Crimea and the Caucasus. On Heybeliada (one of Istanbul's Princes Islands) enormous makeshift canteens and soup kitchens were set up, supported by the Red Cross and the Red Crescent. At Aya Panteleymon, the tiny cells swelled with dozens of people, looked after by priests in floor-length black robes and stiff cylindrical kamilavka hats. If anything, the sight of Galata's rooftop Orthodox golden crosses must have been a familiar and reassuring one as the boats came in.

JAZZ AND RUSSIAN LACE

New arrivals found a country facing up to the Turks' defeat in the World War I, and a Constantinople occupied by British, French and Italian Allied forces. By October 1923 the last allies had left, and by the end of that month 600 years of Ottoman rule was over and the Turkish Republic was established with Ankara as its capital. Bursting forth was also the city's decadent jazz age, in which the White Russians would play a significant part, with cabaret shows, acrobatic performances and casinos. Aristocracy, count-generals and dukes of the Tsar's White Army, who'd been defeated along with their Army of Volunteers, settled in Galata, Beyoğlu, Karaköy. Folkish balalaika music could be heard in the salons of the Pera Palace hotel, where the Kiev-born variety singer Alexandre Vertinsky took a room, while outside, on the streets, Russian chauffeurs — fluent in Russian, French and Turkish — lined up waiting for business. During the holidays, Russians queued at pastry shops called 'Petrograd' and 'Moscow' to secure their orders of Easter and Christmas cakes, while young Russian women dressed in pinafores sold flowers and lottery tickets in the Cité de Péra (today the Çiçek Pasajı or Flower Passage). Others improvised, using what skills they had carried with them, working as fur merchants, stonemasons and musicians.

Rumours began circulating in Constantinople about the affairs and decadence going on in newly opened Russian restaurants around the Grand Rue de Pera. Gossips hinted that fallen Russian baronesses were working as coatroom attendants, looking after the furs of other blonde, blue-eyed women, who were dining with officers dressed in their medals. Sturgeon, Olivier salad and steak tartare were said to be prepared by former bureaucrats, with their dishes washed by Russian nobility. Memoirs of the time noted that divorces rose sharply in Constantinople as local men fell in love with Russian women dressed in European fashions of velvet and lace. 'White Russian ladies were faithful customers of Necip Bey lipsticks. Some say it was the White Russians who invented the fashion of false beauty spots and a sprinkling of a few drops of perfume on handkerchiefs trimmed with lace,' wrote historian and author Jak Deleon, himself a descendant of White Russians.

It was an era captured by Mikhail Bulgakov in his novella *Flight*, which paints an absurd picture of desperate refugees, striking glamour, Cossack colonels and cockroach racing. In Bulgakov's Turkish bazaar exiled Russians sell what they can: 'lemonade — lovely, fresh lemonade!' And, 'boots, boots, boots for sale. Army boots. Russian boots. Good and strong.' Of course it wasn't all chaos, bootlegging and absurdity. Many White Russians went on to remarkable things. One particularly shrewd businessman and adept musician, called Vladimir Smirnov, fled Russia when the Bolsheviks destroyed his family's vodka distilleries. Using Constantinople as an escape route, he then moved to France, taking with him the recipe for his triple-distilled vodka, so beloved by the Tsar. And, changing the name slightly to Smirnoff, there he worked on developing one of the world's most famous drinks brands.

The most celebrated White Russian restaurant of all was opened in the 1920s by two White Russians and a Crimean Turk, all women, who called their city not Constantinople, but 'Tsarigrad' in the Slavic way, and their restaurant, Rejans. Missing the fashions and food from home, and eager to recreate a slice of the society they'd left behind, they opened the wood-panelled restaurant at the end of a small pasaj (passage) just off the Rue de Pera. Here, the first ever woman waitress in Istanbul worked — and if you believe the rumours, so too did a Grand Duchess — serving lemon-infused vodka and chicken kiev to spies, bohemians and politicians. On a good night, high-calibre diners — Greta Garbo, Agatha Christie, Mustafa Kemal Atatürk or the King of Spain — would be entertained by a ten-strong balalaika orchestra, dressed in white satin, complemented by dancers, accordion players and performers in full Gypsy outfits. Sometimes the band would be joined by Baroness Valentine Taskin on the piano who, having fled Russia aboard her uncle's private train in the winter of 1920, called Istanbul home until she died in 1992.

Lemon or 'yellow' vodka oiled conversation and romances and was poured from chilled decanters by all Russian restaurateurs. To keep a tab, pencil marks would line the bottles, showing where the drinker began, and where they finished. The recipe for yellow vodka was simple: a litre of good Russian vodka, the rind of a whole lemon, a few peppercorns, left to infuse for a day or two, then served nitrogen-cold at mealtimes to enhance the borscht and beef stroganoff.

Rebranded as '1924', today Rejans is less about the food — although it is good enough, featuring crab *pelmeni*, Circassian chicken and Osietra caviar — and more about imagining a bygone era. All night, bow-tied waiters steer the trundling vodka trolley around the high-ceilinged room, its wheels going full-tilt, its vodka bottles juddering, each home-infused and wedged loosely in a bed of gleaming crushed ice. Peeling labels hint at the different infusions: 'cinnamon', 'lemon', 'cherry' and, curiously, 'salmon'. Each as lethal as the next. The drinks trolley pauses at each white linen-topped table except one, the best one, tucked in the corner with a panoramic view of the mirrored dining room and reserved for eternity, as a little plaque suggests, for Turkey's secularising founder, Atatürk.

GALAS TO GHOSTS

Just as refugees and Russian exiles found a home in Istanbul, so before them did Adam Mickiewicz. I had found his statues easily enough in Odessa and Burgas, but finding the house, now a museum, where he lived out his final days, proved harder. It is very centrally located, just a ten-minute walk in a straight line from the shiny shops of Istiklal Caddesi but there is no website, my phone calls went unanswered and taxi drivers claimed not to know the address. It stands in Tarlabaşı, deep inside Istanbul's oldest slum, a predominately Kurdish neighbourhood but home to many other minorities, including Gypsies and Syrian migrants. The neighbourhood, while clearly very run down, doesn't feel particularly unsafe, at least during the day, despite the pall of hardship hanging over the streets and the aggressive political graffiti. Mickiewicz came to Constantinople in September of 1855, continuing his political activism and his life's ambition to liberate Poland, which had been under imperial Russian control since before his birth. As in Burgas, he was supporting regiments consisting of Poles and Cossacks who could fight alongside Turkish forces against the Russians. The Ottomans' support for Mickiewicz's liberation movement was aroused by their own territorial battles with the Russian Empire, which grew more persistent over the course of the 19th century.

Finally, I located the museum and a security guard carefully unbolted the door. Inside, a giant replica Ottoman-style tent which Mickiewicz — forever the Romantic — liked to sleep in, stood beside a trunk that he used as a writing table. He died here, in this house, of cholera in November 1855, and a plaque marks the spot where he was laid before his body was shipped to Paris by steamer. It is a small, unusual museum, nicely done. It was also empty. No one ever comes to visit the museum, the guard told me. Stuck to one wall are dozens of Mickiewicz's books, their pages for visitors to tear off as mementos. Only a couple had been taken away. I took a page of *Pan Tadeusz*, translated into Turkish, Polish and English. 'A crowd of rabbits sprang up all around Like white narcissi blooming from the ground. Their long ears gleamed; their eyes like rubies...' the page read. It is an underused museum, the opposite to where Mickiewicz's body lies today, in the Gothic Wawel Cathedral in Kraków, next to grand Polish monarchs. Thanking the security guard, I left Tarlabaşı, walking past partly demolished houses and ongoing building projects, all earmarked for transformation, and headed for Taksim and one of the other last remaining White Russian restaurants in Istanbul, Ayaspasa Rus Lokantasi.

Opened in the early 1940s by Judith Krischanovsky, a White Russian emigré known for sporting a black ostrich feather in her hair, today the restaurant offers Russian piano music on weekends, and a menu that delivers on the restaurant's promise of 'unchanged flavours from 1943'. Madame Krischanovsky, a fixture at the restaurant, continued to greet each diner arriving for her borscht, Vienna schnitzel and 'chicken chickenski', right up until she died in the 1980s. Today it is run by a cheerful Turk with a passion for Moscow, but when I sat for lunch only a couple of other diners came and left. A sense of suspended animation hung in the air, and the atmosphere, and service, felt muted. Restaurants like these are particularly vulnerable to developers, rent hikes and passing fashions. Rejans, or 1924 as it is now, has closed and reopened countless times, most notably when a fire ripped through tailors above and water flooded the floors below in the 1970s. But for now it hangs on, trading on its nostalgia but offering good food and a fun night out too, right in the middle of the city's most expensive real estate. It is impossible to know how much longer Istanbul's remaining White Russian restaurants – perhaps precious, perhaps pointless – will hang on, but what is for certain is that every time an old classic closes, with all of its memories, folklores and ghosts, the culture of Istanbul is interrupted. Permanently, and inexorably.

Yellow Vodka

Lemon or 'yellow' vodka was served in all White Russian restaurants, and you can still order it today in the city's few remaining Russian restaurants.

SERVES 2

1 litre/generous 4 cups Russian vodka

peeled rind of 1 whole, unwaxed lemon

5 black peppercorns

Combine the ingredients. Leave at room temperature for 2–3 days to infuse. Return the infusion to its original bottle. Serve very cold, with food.

Nessi's Orient Vert

In their heyday, wealthier White Russians propped up the bar at the Pera Palace Hotel which today is under the watchful eye of Nessi Behar. When I told Nessi about this book, he kindly offered to create a cocktail. I agree with my friend, Kate Ferry, who when trying the cocktail with me on the Pera Palace terrace one night, said that this drink is a bit like an After Eight mint, best served small, after supper.

MAKES 1

40ml/2 tablespoons plus 2 teaspoons Crème de Menthe

20ml/1 tablespoon plus 1 teaspoon Kahlúa

40ml/2 tablespoons plus 2 teaspoons milk (to be shaken and used as froth on top*)

1 mint sprig

Add the Crème de Menthe and Kahlúa to a cocktail shaker with ice and shake well. Strain into a Champagne coupe glass, add the milk froth and garnish with the mint leaf.

*Froth milk using an electric frother, or transfer to a glass jar, add a couple of ice cubes, seal, and shake as hard as you can for 30 seconds.

TURKEY'S BLACK SEA REGION

SAFRANBOLU / AMASRA / KASTAMONU
SINOP / AMASYA / TOKAT

SAFRANBOLU – MOON CHORUSES IN THE CITY OF SAFFRON

'Moonlight is sculpture,
sunlight is painting.'

— Nathaniel Hawthorne, *Notebook*

Morning had broken, and then just as quickly, had deserted Istanbul. A swirling duvet of clouds blotted out the sun, hiding the Golden Horn's procession of sky-piercing minarets. Booming thunder rolled, shaking the city and vibrating solid bricks and mortar as zig-zags of forked lightning collided mid-air, momentarily revealing the bulky mosques, just for a few seconds, before low swollen clouds, mist and spray blotted them out again. On the street, slow-moving cars, their hazard lights flashing, gave up and pulled over. News reporters on the television pointed to a torrent of water rushing through a flooded Istanbul Metro station where a train ought to be. This was no ordinary summer storm. No day to travel. My bus, due to depart for Safranbolu, the Black Sea's 'city of saffron' in the next hour, seemed improbable. The concierge, however, didn't share my concerns. 'No problem. The storm is passing,' he said. 'I'll get you a taxi to the bus station. You have a waterproof jacket, yes?' Wincing, I checked out, half believing him and half wondering if I was mad to even try.

Steadying myself with a bus station bowl of lentil soup, and some rich tomato 'breakfast' paste on bread, I boarded the bus. We gingerly eased out towards the city limits as the weather slowly began clearing, allowing Istanbul's metallic swarm of bumper-to-bumper traffic to return. Inconvenienced commuters, piling into yellow honking taxis and belching buses, reappeared as suddenly as the sun which, ringed by a dazzling crown of light, looked apocalyptic, as though the hand of God might punch out from it any moment.

Then we broke free, chugging along unremarkable motorways, outrunning the weather, leaving the clogged lanes behind. Every so often an attendant walked down the aisle, doling out sickly lemon-scented cologne from a faux-crystal bottle, freshening hands and perfuming the bus. Travelling eastwards, we skirted tantalisingly close to Sapanca, positioned on the Baghdad Railroad, linking the Gulf of Izmit with the Black Sea. There, orchards are full of ancient cherry, quince and hazelnut trees and its people, descendants of the Caucasus who were expelled by the Imperial Russian Army in the 19th century, live long lives existing on a Black Sea-centric diet of cheese, maize and black cabbage. Six hours later, the bus arrived, with the punctuality of a Swiss train, at a station just outside Safranbolu. Looking at a map, the scale told me that we'd travelled no further than a matchbox-sized section of this huge country.

Eerily quiet in the dusk, only the black-timbered, white-painted Ottoman mansions — called *konaks* — announced Safranbolu's old town. The backstreets, tangled and cobbled, had a noticeably medieval look, designed to be wider at approach points to allow animals to turn, and with street corners purposefully rounded to stop carts crashing. The *eski cami* (old mosque), *eski hamam* (old bath house) and Medresse of Süleyman Pasha, all date back to the 1320s. I sloped up a steep lane to a tiny family-run restaurant with views, and ancestral portraits on the walls. Out on the vine-covered terrace, washed by air cleaned by surrounding pine forests, I ordered small glassfuls of vitamin C-packed Cornelian cherry sherbet and watched night fall. Out from the galley kitchen next came a hissing plate of lamb kebab, carrying with it a waft of fatty, meaty smoke, and a bowl of Turkey's go-to soup, *tarhana*. Turks like to say *tarhana* is the world's first instant soup and I imagine this to be true. Crushed wheat, parsley, basil, tomatoes, red pepper and mint are all thoroughly dried out in the sun, then the lot is crumbled, decanted into a jar, and later cooked and rehydrated. A kind of slow-to-make, highly portable convenience food that lasts for ages. 'Once it's ready, you can forget it at the back of the cupboard for many years,' one cook told me.

WILD STRAWBERRIES

Sitting at the junction of caravan routes, connecting central Anatolia with the Black Sea, Safranbolu has the finest selection of preserved Ottoman mansions in Turkey, despite losing many of its grand timber konaks through fire. These handsome konaks, perfectly square with tiled roofs and overhanging second storeys, are crucial in understanding the city, and one couple in particular are key in unlocking them: Gül and Ibrahim Canbulat. Their painstaking project, Gülevi Safranbolu, now run as a hotel, is three neighbouring authentically restored 18th-century Ottoman mansions. Each once belonged to a family whose trade and business were fundamental to the city's success: one family was in textiles, another, timber, while the other, the Betenler Mansion, is named after a man who served as a judge in Jerusalem.

Storing my belongings in the wall niches, I organised myself in the traditional way, much as has been done for centuries inside these konaks. I pulled back the covers of the bed, which, snug to the window, practically overhung the cobblestone lane below, and washed, standing on thin slats of wood, in a traditional concealed 'cupboard' bathroom, or bathing cabinet. Reclining on the divan bed, with moonlight lighting the room, my eyes fixed on the eight-pointed star at the centre of the elaborately carved wooden ceiling, where we'd usually expect a lampshade to be. It is simple yet complex domestic architecture as with konaks, where decoration is primarily indoors. At the front of the mansion, the only real adornment is the elaborate wrought-iron lock to the main door, heavy, geometric and floral. As the night grew cooler and later, the night-time breeze blew stronger, pouring in through the wooden lattice windows. It carried with it the sound of dogs crooning their night choruses to the moon. Then, a few hours later, dawn arrived with the songful early-morning call to prayer, 'haya 'alas-salaah, haya 'alal falaah' ('make haste to prayer, make haste to salvation').

The next day, by a procession of mulberry trees, stood Ibrahim and his wife, Gül, dressed for the outdoors in British Barbour jackets. 'We're all going on a picnic, hope you can join us?' Ibrahim said, his eyes twinkling. We set off, through drizzly weather in a convoy of three cars filled with friends and family, towards the Küre Dağları, a forested mountain chain rising above the Black Sea coast, famously adept at trapping the moist maritime air and mist. Unpacking the kit in fine rain, the scene appeared more British autumn than Turkish summer, but Ibrahim was well prepared.

Under a giant fir tree, as the heavens opened, a makeshift kitchen was quickly set up and a blow-torch used to ignite the picnic fire. It was flaming within seconds. Satisfied, Ibrahim straightened his thick-rimmed spectacles, and spiked two whole chickens — pre-marinated in oregano, garlic paste, black pepper, salt, honey and lemon — settling them into two old bread-bin-sized tins, once used to hold 18 kilos of briny *peynir* cheese, then put them above the fire. Cigarettes were smoked, beer was drunk (despite it being 11 a.m.) while Gül nimbly assembled a trestle table big enough for us all by the lake, laying out a tablecloth, coffee mugs and flowers. A natural, easy scene, despite the spectacular effort, but such is the way in Turkey where hospitality is generous and uncomplicated, and food is taken seriously, but not too seriously.

Wafts of smoky, charred roast chicken rose up, melding and mixing with the clean, damp forest air, signalling that lunch was ready. Tearing into the chicken, einkorn, an ancient grain popular in these parts, and bulgur, Ibrahim explained that in Safranbolu, despite the name, it is almost impossible to find any saffron-infused dishes on restaurant menus. Locals use it in *zerde* — rice pudding — and *aşure*, a labour-intensive dessert of dried fruits, legumes and wheat sweetened with sugar and fruit juices, but that's it. In the tourist cafés the usual trio of dolma, manti and shashlik is served, not utilising the locally produced saffron, some of the world's finest. Just as wheat contributed greatly to Odessa's wealth, and salt brought riches to Bulgaria, golden saffron not only gave this town its name but also its early affluence.

Returning from foraging, Gül took my hand and delicately placed there five tiny wild strawberries the size of TicTacs. Concentrated and super sweet, there was not a single hit of acidic tartness despite their paleness. We lost hours in the shadow of the Kure Mountains, relaxing, making friends and marvelling at Ibrahim's art of picnicking. The lake was silent and mist-shrouded, while beyond, the primeval fir forests, thick with moss and home to bears and boars, exuded a noticeable air of romance and mystery.

SHOES FIT FOR THE BATTLEFRONT

Picnicking families are well served at Safranbolu's food market where nearly everything is sourced and harvested locally. Some traders specialise: a basket of chestnuts, a box of borage, a bag of walnuts. Others colour-coordinate, laying out cucumbers, courgettes, green chillies, parsley, green peppers, spring onions, runner beans, marrows, lettuce and spinach — every single hue of green. Others spread a rainbow-coloured variety out on cotton sheets: nettle, honey, bee pollen, eggs, oyster mushrooms, chard, purslane, mulberries, peaches, pears, various peppers. Prized 'Kastamonu' garlic heads were held up by their straggly necks by sellers, while melons arrived by the truck load. One woman, her leather handbag neatly placed on her lap, sold only okra which she had laid out neatly on a little rug at her feet. Everything displayed with the utmost care and pride.

Çarşı, Safranbolu's old town market, is a contrast with its boxed sweets, labelled spices and plastic-wrapped tea. The trades that gave their names to the lanes, Tanners Street, Butchers Street, Ironmongers Street, are now mainly long gone — and in their place, inside the wooden, single-storey shops, souvenirs, *lokum* (Turkish delight) and antiques. On Shoemakers Street, sitting on a thick woven kilim cushion under a tangle of vines, I watched as young boys shot like darts, ferrying tulip glasses of tea back and forth to tourists browsing rows of red and black leather slippers called *yemenis*, flat-soled and hand-stitched. Today, these slippers are made by just one man, Erhan Başkaya, who toils all day in an impossibly small and hot wooden store. He is the last yemeni-maker of Safranbolu, practising a craft that began here in 1661, and his shop the last of 48 workshops that once crowded the lane here, one next to the other. Inside, at his desk, he squinted through his glasses, stitching the butter-soft shoes by hand, his crutches leaning on a table next to him. Outside, a sign read: 'The tanneries and cobblers of Safranbolu provided soldiers with shoes during the War of Independence.' The message being: if they were good enough for the battlefield, they're good enough for you.

In contrast, the SafranTat factory, just a few miles away, employs dozens of workers whose job it is to quality-check the little chewy squares of lokum, dusting each one with icing sugar by hand. On a good day they produce 1500 kilos of saffron and pistachio lokum, with many of the boxes heading to the narrow lanes of the old town market. The lokum is very, very good, yet, despite its global appeal, the freshness of SafranTat lokum means that it is never exported. To try it, you have to eat it here.

Around the cobblers and the lokum sellers stand old coffee shops, built to serve the tradesmen who worked here before tea became the Turkish drink of choice, ancient wood-panelled shops selling *salep*, a drink made with the flour from the tubers of wild orchids, and cast-iron ladles hand-beaten by ironmongers. Most active are the saffron sellers touting the silky and golden bulbs, piled up in wooden crates. They have laminated photographs to present to local tourists, showing harvesters sorting the stamens in the saffron fields five miles or so outside the city. But, Ibrahim was right: none of the restaurants I stopped in used saffron in their cooking. Therefore, it was a special treat to try it at Ibrahim and Gül's own Ottoman mansion that night. Starting with a white onion soup, we moved on to chicken livers ('we Turks like to eat innards,' Ibrahim teased), roasted duck, then saffron-laced *zerde*, a very light but gelatinous rice pudding — wobbly and translucent but dotted with raisins and pine nuts, suspended in the saffron yellow. High-quality saffron does encourage a calm and happy mood. There was a saying in 16th-century England: a jolly person was said to appear as though they had 'slept in a bag of saffron'.

After this generous meal, I walked back to my room under a midnight moon, stepping on splatted mulberries and fat fallen figs that littered the path, their cloying aroma mixing with the greenness of summer leaves. Billeted in the window-bed once again, the breeze blew stronger that night, steadily flowing in through the filigree windows. The whistling wind hushed the street dogs, putting an end to their bedtime baying and, well fed and relaxed, I slept straight through the call to prayer.

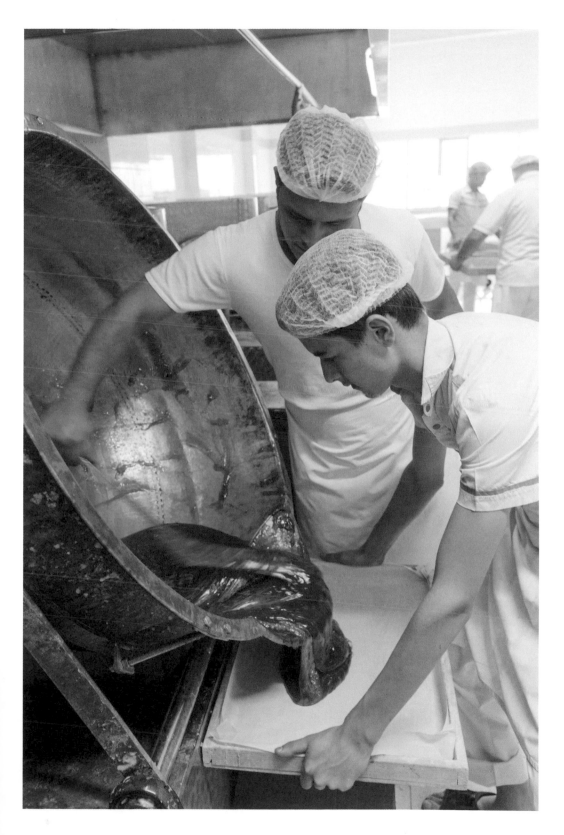

Bus Station Breakfast Paste

Admittedly more common in the Marmara region than the Black Sea, this is a recipe for the breakfast paste I enjoyed on the bus to Safranbolu. It is especially good on dark rye bread.

MAKES ! JAR

280g/10oz sun-dried tomatoes in oil, drained

½ teaspoon sweet paprika

½ teaspoon cumin seeds, toasted

1 garlic clove crushed

small handful of parsley leaves

50g/1¾oz walnuts, toasted and their skins rubbed off

½ teaspoon lemon juice

2 tablespoons walnut oil

Combine all the ingredients in a food processor and blitz until you have a thick paste. Decant into an airtight jar (it'll keep for a couple of weeks). Serve with thick crackers, challah, caraway sticks or cornbread.

Sacred Onion Soup

Ibrahim and Gül Canbulat are impeccable hosts and I was honoured to be invited for supper at their Ottoman konak in the heart of Safranbolu's Old Town for supper. Over dinner, Ibrahim kindly gave me the recipe for our starter, onion soup, and I have attempted to recreate it here. It is a Christian dish called *sogan salmasi*, which in Byzantine times was called *kutsal corba* (sacred soup). It is a very good sick-bed soup. I must add that if there are any errors here, they are most definitely mine, and not Ibrahim's.

SERVES 4

12 small round shallots

500ml/generous 2 cups vegetable stock

500ml/generous 2 cups full-fat milk

80g/3oz short-grain white rice, rinsed

5 sprigs of thyme

½ tablespoon salt

15g/1 tablespoon salted butter, melted

freshly ground black pepper

Keeping the shallots whole, top and tail them, then peel off the papery golden skin. Soak them in iced water for 10 minutes (to temper the powerful flavour slightly), then drain and set aside.

In a flameproof casserole, slowly bring the vegetable stock to the boil, then add the milk, shallots, rice, thyme sprigs, salt, and black pepper to taste, return to the boil and reduce the heat to medium so that it's simmering well.

Stirring regularly, to avoid skin forming, cook for around 20 minutes until the rice is soft, keeping the lid off as you want the liquid to reduce a bit. When the rice is cooked, and the onions are soft, stir through the melted butter. Serve the soup, with 3 shallots in the middle of each bowl.

Red, Hot and Cool Strawberries

The tiny pea-sized strawberries that grow in the Kure Mountains close to Safranbolu are so much more flavourful than the plastic-looking strawberries ten times their size that supermarkets favour. They reminded me of an unusual strawberry pudding we'd enjoyed in summertime Istanbul. It was simple, thick yogurt with a chilli strawberry compote on top — sweet, hot and cool.

SERVES 4

1 dried árbol chilli, or similar

200g/7oz strawberries, rinsed, hulled and chopped into 1–2cm/½–¾ in pieces

50g/¼ cup caster (superfine) sugar

squeeze of lemon juice (optional)

150g/generous ⅔ cup thick yogurt

150g/⅔ cup cream cheese

a few mint leaves, to decorate

First, cut open the chilli, taking off the stem and discarding the seeds. Toast the chilli, opened flat out, in a hot, dry pan until the nutty aroma is released, then place the chilli in a mortar and crush it with a pestle.

Next, place the hulled strawberries in a heavy-bottomed pan. Add the chilli, leaving out any larger uncrushed pieces, to the strawberries along with the sugar, and stir to combine. Heat the mixture over a fairly high heat until the sugar melts and starts to bubble. Bring to the boil, then reduce the heat and simmer for 15 minutes, stirring occasionally and keeping an eye on it — be ready to remove the mixture sooner if the strawberries start collapsing. You want the strawberries to roughly keep their shape. Remove from the heat and allow to cool. If it's too sweet, add a little squeeze of lemon to counter excessive sweetness.

While the strawberries are cooking, whisk together the yogurt and cream cheese in a mixing bowl until smooth. Then cover the bowl and place in the fridge to chill.

When the strawberries are cool and you're ready to serve, fill 4 tumblers or small bowls with the yogurt mixture and spoon over the chilli-strawberries. Top with some whole mint leaves.

JAM ON A ROMAN ROAD

In Ibrahim's garden, filled with morning bird song and piped-in opera arias, I met Timur, a Tatar and retired Black Sea captain. I'd arranged that he would drive me out to Amasra, an ancient Greek coastal city on the Black Sea, but just as we began planning, I lost him. He'd returned to the Black Sea of the mind, casting his thoughts back to storms, sea missions and raki sessions. 'Black Sea is big storms, no harbours, and no escape. You have to sail. No choice,' he said, eyes sparkling. 'If you've fish, but no raki, then sailors cannot eat. Without raki, we would say "my fish is crying"!' Stroking his grey beard, and peering at me from under thick, bushy eyebrows, he continued: 'On our little boats there was very little radio coverage, we'd often lose contact for hours. There would often be trouble.' Timur, clearly a man more at home at sea than on land, had on his head a navy blue cap with an anchor and '1967', stitched in gold on it, the year he joined military high school. We finished our thick coffee, swapping the china cups for a glass of cornelian cherry brandy.

'I call it corncello,' Ibrahim said in a mock-Italian accent. 'It's light, just 10 per cent alcohol, stored for two years.' Perfect for mid-morning, then. 'None for me. I am driving,' Timur said, faux-sobbing into his handkerchief. The laws of the road, we all agreed, are different to those of the sea.

Packing into a rattly and hot two-door Renault, Timur turned the ignition, puffed out his chest and cheeks, and then we were gone, passing slow-moving tractors steered by farmers in straw cowboy hats and overtaken by spluttering, belching Kartals, Turkish versions of old Fiats, the feeble stream of air-conditioning doing what it could against the mid-summer heat. Villages appeared deserted. 'Now empty,' said Timur, pointing at one settlement. 'Anyone of working age is at the local steel factory.' The iron and steel factory, one of Turkey's first major factories, built on rice fields close to Safranbolu, had proved the death-knell for much trade and local agriculture, the 84 or so local tanneries in operation since the end of the 19th century included. Eerily, but as is the way in Anatolia, graveyards marked the approach of the orphaned villages. 'This is to remind us of two things. Firstly, that time is not finite and, secondly, that you should remember to pay your respect to your ancestors,' Timur said firmly. The round turbans sitting atop the Ottoman gravestones signalled that a man of God is buried here, or a Hajji, someone who'd gone on the pilgrimage to Mecca. Surrounding the villages are deep and dark forests, kept damp by Black Sea mists, packing tightly against the lanes. I heard that in the autumn these woodlands fill with varieties of mushrooms so precious that they fetch more than meat in local markets.

Travelling northwards, we stopped for chai on the brow of a steep hill. Timur, ordering three tulip glasses of clear golden tea, one after the other, slurped strongly, declaring the 'shiny, fresh village water' the best there is. Under the sun, we sweated out the tea at the same speed we drank it. Then, passing through a police checkpoint (the result of a state of emergency, following the coup d'état attempt in 2016), we drove extra slowly along a lane crowned by a densely packed canopy of bright green oak leaves. A vivid, glowing neon-green tunnel stretching for ten miles.

Then, almost in shooting distance of the coast, Timur pulled over at the small city Bartin, keen to show me the unusual all-female market. This rare sort of bazaar was first signalled by a mosque-sized wall mural depicting four women surrounded by a carpet of melons, beans and tomatoes; and then, as we turned a corner, there was the scene played out in real life. The market, as promised, was exclusively run by women. The vendors, some very young, some very old, all wore an unspoken uniform. A floral headscarf, a plain coloured top and a peasant-style floral skirt, with few exceptions, making the market look like a living Liberty fabric. Some women sat shelling beans into their laps, skilfully flipping their aprons or skirts to empty the pods, while others sliced off strips of thick, springy pancake-like *saj* bread for tastings. Extraordinary, blazingly bright, produce spilled everywhere. White purslane, red cornelian cherries, massive tomatoes, orb-like and pink.

Just like in hamams across the Muslim world, this was once where local women used to matchmake for their daughters and nieces while the men worked in the fields. Today, women still trade their produce but, as far as I could tell, men have swapped sickles for suits, sitting around the edges of the market in small cafés smoking, reading newspapers, drinking tea and playing backgammon. Some were clearly on their lunch breaks; others looked grizzled, permanent and set-in, a part of the furniture. At the far reaches of the market, bakeries pumped out hundreds of *simit* rings and sticky buns next to classical Ottoman mansions.

TWO HARBOURS AND BIRD'S ROCK

Packing a melon, we drove on, winding down all the windows and letting in the fresh, salt-smacked air. When the Black Sea's bright cobalt-blue waves, interrupted only by Amasra's double harbour, came into sight, glee spread across Timur's face. A Greek colony in the 6th century BC, and mentioned by Homer in the *Iliad* as Sesamos, Amasra was likely settled even earlier than that.

'Now, we are on an ancient Roman road,' Timur said, stopping the car on a hairpin bend, steering me out into the sun, and through the burping, smoggy traffic. Crossing the hot and sticky tarmac, we frogmarched up a hundred or so steep steps on the road's cliffside, until, stopping on a concrete platform covered with dense mossy foliage, Timur pointed skywards to two giant symmetrical spread wings carved into the rock face, next to a headless human statue, visible through a clearing, right above us. Built by order of Claudius on the Roman roadside, the interlocking wing feathers and plumage of Bird's Rock still clearly defined, its epitaph reads: 'For peace and friendship between the states and for the memory of the Emperor Germanicus, Gaius Julius Aquila cracked this mountain and built this resort with funds granted to him.' A little trickle of local tourists sloped past us on the stairs, everyone looking up, their cars parked below.

Back down below, on the Roman-built road, Timur introduced me to Hatice, a local jam maker. Guaranteed passing trade, she'd set up under a sunshade canopy with her back to the Black Sea, facing the Bird's Rock tourists, waiting patiently for their trade. On the glass jars were written the different flavours in marker pen. Timur read them out, picking them up one after the other: chestnut, green fig, orange, strawberry, rose, pine cone ('don't eat the pine cones, just for flavour'), acacia, aubergine, plum, oregano seed, and oregano flower. The fruits and seeds, and peels and flowers glowed, suspended in the jars, backlit by the sun. We packed one rose jam and opened another, a strawberry one, there and then. The berries, both deep crimson and dusty blush pink, were heavily perfumed, bringing to mind the Latin word for strawberry, fragaria. Hatice, wrapped up warm in a maroon velour jumper, despite the heat, explained her process: first she boils the fruit, then she adds lemon then water, and after cooling it, she re-boils it again, this time with sugar. 'Green fig is the hardest one to get right,' she said, as we waved her goodbye.

Atatürk watches over Amasra, his unmistakable profile cast in a cinema screen-sized wire frame, on a hill above the two vivid harbours. 'He lights up at night,' Timur advised, as we watched young headscarved women traipsing up a hillock to pose next to him. Below, on the sun-baked streets, fishmongers yelled out the names of their Black Sea catches: 'Karadeniz uskumru! Karadeniz sardalya! Karadeniz somon!' (Black Sea mackerel! Black Sea sardines! Black Sea salmon!'). No wonder people have always come to Amasra, with its harbours, hills and Black Sea catches. After the Greeks and Romans it was part of the Byzantine Pontic kingdom. The Genoese had a port here in the 14th century, too, until the multilingual Mehmed II (fluent in Turkish, Serbian, Arabic, Persian, Greek and Latin) conquered it for the Ottomans. He also converted the little Byzantine church into Fatih Mosque, when he took the city in 1460. In his honour, the sermon during noon prayers on a Friday still begins with the drawing of the sword. Big seagulls and other unidentifiable seabirds squalled, flapped and swooped around the mosque. Timur stood watching the gulls intently, his eyes following where they went, as I circled the mosque looking at its minaret and latticed windows. I remembered that I had heard somewhere that seafaring men believe gulls carry with them the souls of dead sailors.

The surf barely lapped the shore, making the Black Sea look a solid block of blue, glittering as though someone had thrown a tumbler of diamonds across its glossy surface. On pontoons along the shoreline, men in T-shirts and sandals, and a couple in chef's hats, cleaned fish for seaside restaurants while ducks, comedic with their quacking and flapping, fed on fallen scraps. We settled into a café right on the water and waiters brought out more food than we could eat. Baked sea bass and grilled bream, Russian-style salad with mayonnaise and a glass of raki, pleasingly cold. But it was the warm halva, recommended by Timur, that was best. 'After fish, people drink raki and then they have warm baked halva. Remember that, if you've fish, but no raki, then sailors cannot eat. But this doesn't apply if they are driving,' Timur said glumly as his beloved baseball cap blew off in a sea breeze, sending him running after it, arms waving. The clay-pot halva, rich with sesame, had hazelnuts scattered on the top and Timur, returning with cap in hand, gave it a good squeeze of lemon to cut the sweetness. Another glass of raki was sent over, on the house. Timur grew strangely silent, and it wasn't until we slid back into the Renault to return to Safranbolu, that he let me know that it wasn't almost losing his special nautical baseball cap that had made him sad. Gripping the steering wheel, eyeing me in the rearview mirror, he said in a sing-song voice: 'My fish is crying. My fish is crying! No raki. No raki, for me.'

Baked Sesame Halva

A baked halva pudding for Timur, which just as he told me, is perfect after a fish and raki supper.

SERVES 2

150g/5 ¼ oz block of plain or vanilla halva

1 tablespoon date syrup

100ml/⅓ cup plus 1 tablespoon milk

small pinch of salt

5g/scant ¼ oz pistachio kernels, finely chopped

a few edible rose petals (optional)

1 teaspoon lemon juice

Preheat the oven to 180°C/350°F/gas mark 4 and have ready two 10cm/4in ramekins.

In a large bowl, break up and smash the halva until you have something akin to breadcrumbs. Add the date syrup, milk and salt and then transfer to a food processor and blend until creamy and smooth. Pour the mixture into the ramekins and bake for 10 minutes or until the top is bubbling and golden brown. Remove from the oven and allow to cool for a few minutes, then sprinkle over the crushed nuts, and rose petals if you fancy them, and top each ramekin with just a few drops of lemon juice. Serve warm, in the ramekins.

A REVOLUTION ON THE HEAD

You smell Kastamonu before you see it. Silently seasoning the streets with its smell, the heady aroma drifts on the wind, spilling through neighbourhoods. Sulphurous, savoury and vaguely familiar, a clue to its source lies in a trio of open-sided farm sheds, the size of aircraft hangars, just outside the city limits. There, piled inside, are not hay bales, tools or tractors, but millions of ivory-white garlic bulbs, stacked floor-to-ceiling, warming and humming in the sun, waiting to go to market. Kastamonu's super-strength *beyaz altın* (white gold) is famous for being up to ten times more pungent than regular garlic.

I'd only travelled 60 miles from Safranbolu, but Kastamonu couldn't have been more different to that postcard-perfect, UNESCO-listed city. Gone are quaint cobbled lanes, souvenir stands and slick salesmen, here instead are garages greasy with oil, locksmiths bursting with rusty tools and workaday *lokanatas*, unchanged in decades, crowded with backgammon-playing men slamming down their pieces with nicotine-stained hands. Without tourism dollars to fall back on, it is a grafting and toiling city where, also unlike Safranbolu, many of its Ottoman konaks lie in disrepair, abandoned and decaying behind peeling facades, simply rotting away. The most dilapidated of them, little more than burned-out skeletons, are hopelessly gone, blackened with soot. Behind the walls of the cared-for ones are comfortable, deeply settled rooms, laid with floorboards polished by decades of footsteps, lined with threadbare kilims. Homes handed down through generations.

But for all of this, Kastamonu is a city with a clear identity and a strong underdog appeal. Located on one of the old branches of the Silk Road (to Tabriz in modern-day Iran) its bygone trading atmosphere can still be keenly felt in the Kursunluhan caravanserai, a place that once provided rooms and stables to merchants carrying flax, mohair and linseed destined for the Black Sea and borders beyond the Ottoman Empire. It is a city that remembers its more recent past, too, as the only section of the Black Sea region to be left unoccupied by foreign forces after the Ottoman empire fell. The city had spirit and I liked it on sight.

On that first morning, standing under the arches of the Nasrullah mosque, its 16th-century brickwork gradually reworked over centuries, I was distracted by the new spectacles and signs that greeted me. Opposite fluttered posters of serious, unsmiling men, high above a string of shops. Faces from eras long gone, they are the founding fathers of Kastamonu's beef pastirma (pastrami) business, providing life-sized proof of long, successful legacies, taking on the newer, nearby competitors. Quite literally promoting their shops from the grave. Above

Ellezler, founded in 1870, are printed headshots of four generations, their eyes steely, their mouths sage, the images softly faded by years of sunshine. Next door at Fatih, founded 50 years later, are portraits of two neatly moustachioed men, one in a trilby-style hat. Further into the old *bedestan* (market), crammed with hardware shops, cobwebs of cables and barbershops, is Tabakoglu, one of the most famous *pastirma* shops, its interior walls lined with photographs of men tending to cows, next to yet more sober family portraits. Below, piled onto shelves, are little pyramids of Kastamonu garlic and jars of rose and cherry jam, their crimson hue matching the maroon slices of air-dried beef, sliced paper-thin hanging in strips from the ceiling. Women with neat floral headscarves queued patiently as the butchers packed the pastirma into glossy scarlet-and-gold boxes, tying them neatly with the sort of red ribbons and bows usually reserved for baked fancies or cakes. A hand reached out from behind the counter, beckoning me to try a slice. It melted on impact with my tongue and I stood silently, picking out the flavours in the çemen, the heavily spiced wrapper surrounding the marbled beef: fenugreek, garlic and paprika. Potent yet light. Excellent, I imagined, in the morning with fried eggs on top, in the Kastamonu way.

In the market's other specialist delis, small, select boxes of black garlic are sold for higher prices in contrast to the sprawling mounds of white garlic which carpet the city's outdoor areas, tumbling freely out of wicker baskets and rolling into the street. Leaving the bedestan, I followed a trickle of local tourists up to Kastamonu castle, crunching a few bulbs underfoot, past women selling Persil-white lace and crochet and battered old konaks with grand carved wooden doors and elaborate iron locks. A few stands sold Black Sea nuts, bags of hazelnuts and walnuts. Both good, but neither as popular as the small, mellow, earthy chestnuts, harvested from Kastamonu's virgin forests, available in the cooler months. These are highly prized. Cherished when in season, and dreamt about when not, they go into pilafs, ice cream, cabbage leaves, soups and halva, as well as being candied and boiled. At the top, by the castle's bastions, families posed by giant red Turkish flags, spreading out on the grass, picnicking on pastirma, sipping tea and tearing at bread. In the distance, the far-off blue-hued Ilgaz Mountains hovered in the heat, while directly below the city sprawled out, serene at a distance but up close, a metallic and industrious churn.

IF YOU WANT TO GET AHEAD, GET A HAT

Only at night did the city centre cool off, bringing out bats silently zooming overhead, and kittens mewling for their mothers in dark corners. Traffic eased and traders piled their hillocks of garlic into sacks, throwing them into pick-up trucks, while women swept the blankets of white paperlike peelings from doorways. In the city centre the 16th-century Nasrullah bridge, with its arches and Silk Road legacy, offers a concise history of Kastamonu. Photographs taken of the hunchback arches in the 1920s show men crossing, commuting to work, dressed in European-style suits, fedoras and Oxford-style bowler hats. Back then there were five arches but now, to make space for added traffic lanes — modern Turkey means more cars and more people — it only has two. But it is those hats, as seen on the pastirma portraits and in these old photographs that matter, as it was here that Atatürk introduced his Hat Law, famously banning the fez in 1925. Appearing on Hittite frescoes, the fez is both an ancient and politically charged headwear. Atatürk, preferring the astrakhan kalpak, considered the fez to be a symbol of opposition to Turkish nationalism, claiming that their religious overtones made them unsuitable for modern Turks. Banning the fez was both symbolic and a shock.

Later, in the liberal 1970s, the humpbacked bridge was bookended by Efes Pilsner billboards, something increasingly rare now as the dehydrated pall of conservatism marches on in Anatolia. Finding an Efes lager in certain Black Sea towns can be almost as hard as finding a fez, worn nowadays only by tourist-touting ice-cream sellers. The following day, I left Kastamonu much the same way I came in: chugging on to the ancient seaside city of Sinop in an empty bus, keeping pace, for a while, with a slow-moving tractor piled high with thousands upon thousands of wobbling, snow-white garlic bulbs.

Chestnut and Sage Pilaf

In the Black Sea region of Turkey there are at least a dozen varieties of chestnut trees growing, and an annual harvest of several thousand tons of chestnuts. This very simple, comforting and buttery pilaf has brown polished flat-sided chestnuts as the star ingredient. Full-flavoured, it works just fine on its own as a simple supper but traditionally it is served as a side with partridge.

SERVES 4, GENEROUSLY

350g/2 cups basmati rice

15g/1 tablespoon salted butter

3 tablespoons olive oil

handful of fresh sage leaves, a few finely chopped, the rest kept whole

180–200g/6½–7oz cooked whole roast chestnuts

2 strips of unwaxed lemon zest

500ml/generous 2 cups vegetable stock

flaky sea salt and freshly ground black pepper

TO SERVE

knob of salted butter, melted

2 tablespoons Greek yogurt

Put the rice in a large bowl and cover with cold water to soak for a few minutes while you cook the sage.

Heat the butter and olive oil in a heavy-bottomed pan, such as a flameproof casserole, add the chopped sage and the whole sage leaves and cook, sprinkling on a few sea salt flakes as you go, just for a couple of minutes to release the scent and to make them slightly crispy. Remove the whole leaves and set aside for the garnish, leaving the chopped sage in the pan.

Drain and rinse the rice and add it to the pan, along with the chestnuts and the strips of lemon zest. Stir, coating well with the oil, and season generously with salt and pepper.

Pour in the stock and bring to the boil. Cover with a lid or tight-fitting foil, turn the heat down and simmer for 6 minutes.

Remove the pan from the heat, take the lid off and, using the handle of a wooden spoon, make several holes in the rice mixture to let the steam escape. Then put the lid back on and leave to steam for a further 10 minutes. Serve drizzled with the melted butter, topped with the whole fried sage leaves and with a little Greek yogurt on the side.

Cornershop Pilaf

This recipe is based on a garden-green bulgur pilaf made in Kastamonu with the ancient grain, einkorn. I found instructions on how to make it pasted to the window of a shop specialising in the grain, although I've swapped hard-to-source einkorn here for coarse bulgur. A one-pot meal in itself, conjured up in no time, and you can probably get most of the ingredients at your own cornershop.

SERVES 4 AS A SIDE DISH

generous knob of butter

3 spring onions (scallions), thinly sliced on the diagonal

400ml/1⅔ cups vegetable or chicken stock

170g/6oz coarse bulgur

1 scant tablespoon pul biber (Turkish pepper flakes)

100g/3½oz baby spinach leaves, stems removed, cut into strips

12 or so cherry tomatoes on the vine

1 tablespoon olive oil

juice of ½ lemon

2 tablespoons chopped flat-leaf parsley

2 tablespoons chopped dill

2 tablespoons chopped mint

salt and freshly ground black pepper

Gently heat the butter in a pan and cook the spring onions (scallions) for just for a couple of minutes to soften them. Then pour the stock into the pan and bring to the boil. Pour in the bulgur, seasoning generously with salt and pepper, and top with the pul biber. Clamp on a lid, reduce to the lowest heat and cook for 5 minutes, then add the spinach, stirring it through the bulgur, so that it will wilt. Remove from the heat, cover, and let it steam-cook for another 20 minutes or so, until the bulgur is cooked but retains a little bite.

Preheat the oven to 200°C/400°F/gas mark 6.

Put the cherry tomatoes, still on the vine, in a small baking tray, drizzle over the olive oil and roast for 8–10 minutes.

When the bulgur is cool, add the lemon juice, fold in the herbs and tip out onto a serving platter, placing the vine tomatoes on the top.

Bedtime Pudding with Tahini Cream

During hot summer nights Kastamonu collectively gorges on ice cream but during the winter, locals switch to seasonal *kabak tatlısı*, candied pumpkin with walnuts, a warming, comforting bedtime treat. This recipe requires the pumpkin to sit overnight, so is ideal if you're making a pudding ahead.

SERVES 4

1kg/2lb 3oz pumpkin, peeled, deseeded and cut into matchbox-sized rectangles, about 5 x 3.5cm/2 x 1¼in and 1.5cm/½-in thick (butternut squash can be used as an alternative)

250g/1¼ cups caster (superfine) sugar

juice of 1 lemon

1 tablespoon tahini

4 tablespoons Turkish kaymak, crème fraîche or clotted cream

225g/2¼ cups walnuts, toasted and roughly crushed, to serve

Spread the pumpkin out evenly in a high-sided roasting dish. Pour over the sugar, toss the pumpkin to coat it evenly, then add the lemon juice and toss again. Cover the dish with a tea towel and let it rest overnight.

The following day, the sugar should have dissolved and the pumpkin should have released its juices, leaving a good amount of liquid in the tray. Preheat the oven to 180°C/350°F/gas mark 4, uncover the tray and toss the pumpkin thoroughly in the liquid so it is evenly coated.

Bake for 1 hour, regularly spooning over the juices so the pieces are evenly candied. Remove from the oven and allow to cool, then, using a slotted spoon, remove the pumpkin and spread it out on a plate, allowing it to cool completely before placing in a large serving bowl.

In a separate bowl, stir the tahini through the cream. Serve the candied pumpkin in bowls and top with spoonfuls of the tahini cream, with crushed walnuts scattered on top.

RAIDERS AND AMAZONS ON THE EUXINE

'And Thou, vast Ocean!
On whose awful face

Time's iron feet can
print no ruin trace.'

— Robert Montgomery, *The Omnipresence of the Deity*

The blue backwash and frothy spill of the Black Sea terminates the road from Kastamonu to Sinop, its surging swell contrasting with the parched scenery that leads to Turkey's northernmost peninsula. It had been a slow journey to the coast, with the bus puffing along at a sluggish and steady pace, its gradual advance turning the landscape into a vivid cinematic photoplay of sorts, shot through a dusty window. Rising grounds of velvety hills, bosomy and pale as sand dunes, met the scrubby Anatolian badlands, quasi-biblical and wide-angled — its repetitiveness as soothing on the eyes as the sea.

Sinop's natural harbour means it is a famously sheltered spot, reliable and steady. 'The Black Sea has three safe harbours — July, August and Sinop,' the saying goes. Yet this jolly adage conveniently forgets the terrifying bandit raids that regularly plagued Sinop, and surrounding towns, 400 years ago. Back then, sheepskin-wearing Cossacks would criss-cross the Black Sea on their *chaikas* (long boats), attacking, pillaging and kidnapping, coming in from the direction of the setting sun, obscured and hidden. In the 1600s Sinop was viciously sacked, as was Varna, up the coast in Bulgaria. Trabzon, too, suffered a massive assault when a Cossack fleet of several hundred plundered and burned the city. The boldest looters even penetrated Constantinople, sailing into the Bosphorus from the Black Sea, targeting Greek merchant ships. English ambassador Thomas Roe wrote about the raids and torched villages, observing that 'all the villages on the Bosphorus, to the gates of Constantinople tremble … the city is not without fear … Twenty galleys keep [a look out at] the mouth of the channel.'

During the journey, I wondered who, in a hypothetical battle, could take on the much mythologised Cossack raiders and win. Perhaps only a Black Sea people more glamourised than the Cossacks themselves, the legendary Amazons. Described by Homer as *antianerai* (manlike), they were fine horsewomen, tailoring trousers for their bowed legs, training eagles and going into combat with axes. Their graves, found on the Pontic Steppe during archaeological digs, contain their bones and weapons, enough proof to some that their existence was real. Surely, with their riding and archery skills, they could see the Cossack raiders off? After all, according to legend, it was the Amazons who named the city for their queen, Sinova.

PRISON BLUES AND WOODEN BOATS

With three millennia of outward-facing trade, shifting goods and people, standing in the grim confines of Sinop Prison is particularly gut-wrenching. Closed in the late 1990s, the jail is now a museum drawing in holidaying Turks, and sometimes American archaeologists who dig around the periphery, uncovering Sinop's layers of empires and conquests. Inside a stuffy room, rusty bars framed the cape in the distance, its sea waves, gunmetal grey with just a little white spume on the breakers, taunting and promising escape. Surely, there cannot be a crueller view in the world for the incarcerated than the sea?

For westerners, this sinister prison brings to mind the classic 1970s drug-smuggling movie *Midnight Express* — where a young American is jailed in Turkey for attempting to smuggle hash — but for Turks the jail looms larger in the collective psyche as a place of confinement for writers locked up on political charges. Down one thin arm of a corridor, I elbowed my way into a group of local visitors jostling for space around one particular steel door. Heads close together, we peered into the tiny cell through the bars, only to see a room empty except for a small bed and a long-necked Ottoman lute hanging on the wall above. One dewy-eyed man, ushering his children forward, told me that it was here that Sabahattin Ali — whose 1940s novella *Madonna in a Fur Coat* is one of Turkey's bestselling books ever — was locked up. His five-poem *Hapishane Şarkısı* (Prison Song) includes these lines:

Hold your face up
Even though you can't see the sea;
The sky is like a sea;
Never mind, heart, never mind…
When your problems rear up
Throw a curse on God…

It was within this grim prison that 150 years ago two Russian convicts taught their Turkish cellmates how to make model ships, little figures of freedom, to occupy the hands and mind as the wasted months and years slipped by. Today, these boats, once handed out as gifts from the city to arriving VIP ships, have become the unofficial symbol of Sinop, and are made in their thousands. Workshops surrounding the touristy, cobbled old town square are filled with miniature sails, masts and rudders. The artisans who make them peer over spectacles, carefully painting and carving the hulls, decks and sterns of toy boats,

setting them onto stands or magicking them into bottles. All visitors to Sinop seem to leave with one.

A mild and relaxing antidote to Sinop's grim prison is Pervane Madrassah, built by Seljuk grand vizier Süleyman Pervane in the 13th century. Now geared more towards tourists than seminary students, only the gentle click-clack of a weaving loom interrupted the silence between the cool, thick walls. Inside, Nurfer Tosun worked on an embroidered tablecloth, surrounded by completed linens stitched in purples, pinks, reds and greens, all for sale. In perfect English she asked how I liked Sinop and we exchanged thoughts on its climate, museums and wooden boats. Then, steering me onto a little kilim-topped stool, she poured out muddy Turkish coffee into two pewter cups, reminding me of the heartfelt Turkish maxim, 'If we drink coffee together, we will remember each other for forty years.' I paid for one of her embroideries, a table runner that had taken three days of close work, with a green, orange and gold, almost Aztec design, complimenting her skills as she wrapped it. 'Thank you. I have just a little talent,' she said modestly, then, lightly putting her hand on my arm, added, 'I almost forgot, you have to have lunch at Ornek Manti. It is famous. They top their manti with half yogurt and half walnuts. It is special. Really, don't miss it.' Within 30 minutes, I was there.

IN A NUTSHELL

Above Ornek Manti, laundry-filled balconies billowed, puffing like sails next to blue-and-red sketches of boats painted directly onto the brickwork. Inside the restaurant below, despite its being an in-between hour – too late for lunch, too early for supper – the space was packed. Tables spilled out into a little front terrace from indoors. Squeezing in, I did as Tosun said and ordered the half-and-half manti, eating each one individually, tasting each bite. It was a simple force of flavours and textures: toggling between smooth, silky and yogurty and then crunchy, nutty and chewy. Endless glasses of tea ('no charge, you are our guest') kept coming as I slowly reduced the gigantic mound.

Finally whisking the plate away, the waiter handed me a little marzipan-style sweet ('a gift, you are our guest') topped with half a walnut. A thick paste made of roasted finely ground hazelnuts, walnuts and icing sugar, it was sweet but not cloyingly so, the handiwork of master confectioner Mehmet Gürbüz, whose shop opposite, now run by his son, looked busy. The son told me that as a boy in the 1940s, Gürbüz chose not to go into the family tailoring business, deciding instead to create what he craved most, the candies in the local sweet-shop window. There, in his hometown of Boyabat, an hour inland, Gürbüz still runs his original wood-panelled shop. The next day, I travelled there to meet him, discovering that very little had changed since he opened it in the 1960s.

It was a throwback to a lost world. Between thin white wooden window frames shone a row of old-school cookie jars packed with golden and pink hard-boiled sweets. Inside, Gürbüz's neat shop is filled with creaky old wooden apothecary-style chests and more sweetie jars. Unscrewing one, I dipped my hand in and took out a glowing honey-flavoured sweet. 'Don't chew!' Gürbüz advised. Glistening and super sweet, as the boiled sweet slowly reduced, its tiny chewy honeycomb nuggets were released. Opposite the shop, a minibus parked on the roadside, windows open, was filled to the roof with straggly Kastamonu garlic, while next door, a butcher with lacy net curtains displayed just one hunk of unidentifiable meat hanging from a mean-looking hook, its juice slowly dripping into the window ledge. Boyabat is a quiet, unassuming town, dominated, like so many Turkish towns, by an enormous castle. Back at the Sinop outpost, Şekerci Mehmet Gürbüz, Mehmet's son, told me that just like SafranTat in Safranbolu, the sweets don't have additives or preservatives, so are not exported. To taste them you have to do so here. 'Even so, we are a name in Istanbul. People know us,' he said, smiling, as I paid for a box to take to my next stop, Amasya.

After sundown, as the navy-blue sea slapped the front a little harder, a familiar ritual unfolded, much as it does in Odessa, in Constanta and in Burgas. Families of three, maybe four generations, walked along the boulevard, linking arms, eating mastic, milk or cherry ice cream, weighed out on scales in old-fashioned cafés. The elders, women cloaked head to toe in black çarşafs, nibbled on corn-on-the-cobs while their husbands, smoking, and drinking sweet tea, managed the grandchildren. In the water, bobbing in the harbour, little boats with names like Masallah and Ali Yavuz flew Turkish flags, displaying photographs of Atatürk. It is a charming, slow-paced and civilised scene. One that appealed to Atatürk himself, who once said of his new capital, 'I wish Ankara had half of Sinop's beauty.'

Half and Half Manti

Sinop's famous manti tend to be large and soft, half topped with melted butter and chopped walnuts, and half with thick, silky yogurt. Sinop's manti makers wouldn't dream of cheating, but manti makes for such a good weeknight supper that this lazy version — using ready-made gyoza wrappers — makes them a cinch. These are for sale in Chinese and Far Eastern supermarkets and you can buy them online. I had hesitated at this cheat but I then spotted that gyoza wrappers feature in two Turkish cookery books I have at home, one being the masterly *Turquoise: A Chef's Travels in Turkey* by Greg and Lucy Malouf, so I'll stand by the substitute.

MAKES ENOUGH TO FILL 25 ROUND GYOZA WRAPPERS

25 Gyoza wrappers

FOR THE FILLING

300g/10½oz minced (ground) lamb

1 onion, finely grated

3 tablespoons finely chopped flat-leaf parsley

½ teaspoon salt

½ teaspoon black pepper

FOR THE YOGURT SAUCE AND TOPPING

2 garlic cloves

1 teaspoon flaky sea salt

1½ tablespoons extra virgin olive oil

300g/scant 1½ cups Greek yogurt

1 tablespoon lemon juice

30g/2 tablespoons butter

½ teaspoon pul biber (Turkish pepper flakes)

15g/½oz walnuts, crushed

If your wrappers are frozen, the first thing to do is to let them defrost thoroughly. Then combine the filling ingredients in a bowl, cover and set aside in the fridge.

Next, prepare the yogurt sauce. Use a pestle and mortar to grind the garlic with the salt until you have a paste. Heat the olive oil in a pan over a low heat, add the salty garlic and sizzle until barely coloured. Transfer to a small bowl, whisk in the yogurt and lemon juice and set aside. Heat the butter in a small pan and stir through the pul biber, then set aside.

Lay out your wrappers on a clean surface with plenty of room to work.

Place a scant teaspoon of filling in the centre of each wrapper, taking care to keep the edges clean and free of filling, otherwise they won't seal properly. Don't be too generous with the filling — it can prevent you sealing the dumplings properly, and they might pop open during cooking.

With damp fingers, fold them into half moons, taking care to make sure there is no trapped air in the filling pocket, which can cause them to pop. Continue until the filling is used up.

Bring a large pan of salted water to the boil. Lower in the manti with a slotted spoon and cook until they rise to the top and are cooked through; this should take 4–6 minutes. Drain and serve, topping half the manti with the yogurt sauce, and half with the crushed walnuts, pouring over the pul biber butter.

Sinop Sea Bass Stew

Up on the rooftop terrace, opposite a mosque, Turkish pop music plays at Mert Kanal's seafood restaurant, Okyanus Balik Evi. Below, at street level, the fishmongers clear away the unsold fish for the day. Around us, people drink beer, Turkish Kayra rosé, and smoke cigars and cigarettes. But mainly, everyone drinks raki. Summertime season is in full swing and fireworks shoot up over the Black Sea. Suddenly the call-to-prayer belts out of a dozen mosque tannoys, all a stone's throw away, and it battles with the disco music, which continues. At Kanal's restaurant I ate an excellent sea bass stew that relies on little more than good, fresh ingredients. Kanal serves it with classic Black Sea cornbread and a side of pickles. He also talked me through the recipe, which is below. Do as the Turks do and have a bottle of raki on the table for this dish. To serve it, fill a small tumbler with one third raki, and top up with ice-cold water.

SERVES 2

4 tablespoons olive oil

150g/5¼oz Sweet Bite peppers, stalks removed and deseeded,
or long sweet red peppers

2 shallots, finely sliced

3 garlic cloves, finely sliced

2 teaspoons dill seed

1 x 400g/14oz can chopped tomatoes

½ teaspoon pul biber (Turkish pepper flakes)

1 teaspoon sweet paprika

100ml/generous ⅓ cup water

1 tablespoon white wine vinegar

2–3 sea bass fillets, skin removed (get your fishmonger to do it), chopped into bite-sized pieces

1 x 400g/14oz can butter beans or broad (fava) beans, drained and rinsed

sea salt and freshly ground black pepper

TO FINISH

chopped flat-leaf parsley

about 1 tablespoon finely chopped dill

lemon wedges (optional)

In a flameproof casserole, heat half the olive oil until it is almost smoking, and quickly fry the peppers until their skin is wrinkled and blackened, taking care as the pan will spit. Take the casserole off the heat and remove the peppers so they cool, then peel and quarter them.

Put the casserole back on a medium heat and add the remaining olive oil and the shallots, and cook until softened and golden. Add the garlic and dill seed and briefly cook, taking care not to burn the garlic. Next, add the chopped tomatoes, pul biber and paprika and cook for a couple of minutes, then add the water and leave, with the lid off, to bubble and thicken, for 5 minutes.

Add the vinegar and stir through, then add the fish and put the lid back on. Cook the stew over a low–medium heat for 5 minutes, until the fish is cooked through. Then finally add the beans and cook for a minute or two more until they're heated through. Taste and adjust the seasoning (giving it a particularly good grind of black pepper), then serve, sprinkled with parsley and dill, and with a few lemon wedges on the side if you like.

Walnut Candies

Mehmet Gürbüz's walnut paste — similar to a marzipan or sweetmeat — in the city of Sinop, makes for a perfect post-supper sweetener or a mid-morning coffee accompaniment. This is an easy version to try at home.

MAKES 15

75g/¾ cup walnut halves, plus an extra 15 to serve

75g/¾ cup ground almonds

1 teaspoon ground cinnamon

100g/scant ¾ cup icing (confectioners') sugar

1 tablespoon cold water

½ teaspoon vanilla extract

Preheat the oven to 180°C/350°F/gas mark 4 and spread the walnut halves out on a baking sheet. Toast in the oven until fragrant (about 10 minutes), then leave them to cool and rub off the skins the best you can (putting them in a tea towel and rolling them gently works well). Leave the oven on.

Place the walnuts, ground almonds and cinnamon in a food processor but don't switch it on yet.

Put the icing (confectioners') sugar in a small saucepan with the water and heat gently until it melts, then remove from the heat and stir in the vanilla. Next, transfer the icing sugar mixture to the food processor and process until you have a mixture that resembles wet sand. Tip the crumbly mixture onto a clean work surface and bring it together with your hands.

Next, gently roll out the mixture into a fat sausage, 15cm/6-in long, then wrap in foil and leave at room temperature for an hour to rest. While the paste rests, toast the extra 15 walnut halves on the same baking tray you used before, and at the same oven temperature, for around 10 minutes, or until fragrant. Set them aside to cool, but don't try and rub off the skins as this will cause them to break.

Finally, to make the candies, slice the sausage of paste into 15 rounds, each 1cm/⅜ in wide, using your fingers to press and shape them into neat rounds. Put a walnut half on top of each one for decoration and serve with tea or coffee. They will keep for a couple of days in an airtight container but may dry out a little; if they do, re-work them with your hands then replace the walnut half on top.

ROCK TOMBS AND A BACKWARDS-RUNNING RIVER

If, as Atatürk said, Sinop is beautiful, then Amasya is strikingly so. Surrounded by orchards full of glossy red apples, giving the city a relaxed feel, it lies wedged in the mid-Black Sea region, 70 miles from the shore. Heaped at the side of the river, creating a steep gorge, is a jumbly escarpment of pigeon-grey limestone stacks forming Mount Harşena, which, at almost the height of the Eiffel Tower, looks as though it has been thrown down from heaven, landing in a bundle at the riverbank.

I started at Amasya's museum. Inside one of the main galleries, no bigger than a tennis court, a dozen Turkish tourists rotated slowly, like the hands of a clock, around eight coffin-shaped display cases. Stopping and pointing, eyes wide, looking downwards, they muttered and grimaced. Some, the less squeamish ones, brought out cameras and shot, flash off, into the glass cabinets. Inside, slow decay, bit by bit, piece by piece, serially ate away at the Seljuk nobles, who once ruled the city of Amasya but were now encased within. Dead for 800 years or more, but memorialised as mummies, they are the remains of ministers, governors and their children, some with vital organs still inside their shrunken bronze-coloured bodies. Unearthed in the 1920s from tombs under local mosques, they are now, somewhat cruelly, returned back to the world once more, naked, and with faces sneered and contorted, mirroring the tourists' expressions. The information panel, in English and delightfully matter-of-fact, informs of the grim and long-winded traditional Turkish mummification process. First, the brain is removed. Using an iron bar it is pulled in pieces through the nostrils after being liquefied. Then, after most of the organs are removed, mimosa, bilberry and other sweet-smelling spices are poured into the cavity. Finally, after laying in tar for 70 days, the body is wrapped in cotton and handed back to the family. Quite the homecoming. Mummification was an honour and, just like the sultans who ruled before him, the secularising Father of the Turks, Atatürk, was embalmed, too, his body now in a casket of mahogany and walnut wood at the monumental memorial tomb Anıtkabir, in Ankara.

Beyond the museum walls, Amasya's personality is subdued, and like many other Turkish cities in the Black Sea region it feels immune not just to western influence, but Ankara and Istanbul, too. It has a quiet assurance, and a stilted atmosphere. A bit like ageing wine left in a cellar; promising, still and heavy. The roads and surrounding scenery leading to it hint of the city's stilted, curious air: zig-zags of pine-scented lanes and dirt tracks are edged by signposts warning of boars and gazelles; floodplains and fields of sunflowers are sheltered by parched hills. Glinting in the sun, iron-topped mosques stand squat and bulky, serving tiny hamlets virtually unchanged by time, and the odd villager, in the shade of weeping willow trees, slumbers on a tiny wooden stool, fingers running methodically over prayer beads.

Host to more than a dozen civilizations, including the Persians and Romans, Amasya was captured by the Ottoman Sultan Bayezid I, aka The Thunderbolt, in 1392, whose conflict with the nomadic conqueror Tamerlane was to be the death of him. But it is only by looking up, and walking eastwards up the Yeshil Irmak (Green River) past the six bridges, some as old as the mummies and others with pleasing names such as the Bridge of Birds, that you'll see what matters most here in Amasya, the tombs of the kings of Pontus. Overhanging the water, high above the half-timbered Ottoman villas, they are rock-cut, weather-worn and smooth, dominating the town, lighting up a garish neon blue at night, a reminder of when, in the 3rd century BC, Persian governors established the Pontic Kingdom, choosing Amaseia (Amasya) as the capital city. When he defeated this kingdom, Julius Caesar debriefed the Roman senate with his renowned saying, 'veni, vidi, vici' (I came, I saw, I conquered).

These were the tombs that Strabo, the world's first geographer, born here
in 64 BC, would have seen. Believing the city to have been founded by the
Amazon queen Amasis, he wrote, 'My native town is situated in a deep and
large valley ... There is a lofty and perpendicular rock which overhangs the
river ... and the tombs of the kings.' He wrote in detail about the Black Sea
(referring to it simply as 'the Sea'), and of fishing for bonito in the Golden
Horn. He died here, too, but lives on, in a way, cast in bronze in statue form,
clutching a book and standing next to a globe, on Amasya's riverbank. The
cityscape, of valley, rock and river, inhabited for more than 5000 years, is
easily identifiable from Strabo's description today.

Above the tombs, there is a ruined castle that, some say, stood strong against
the armies of Tamerlane for half a year, quite a feat given that his men were
capable of beheading 10,000 Hindus in an hour when they sacked Delhi.
Some locals claim that the Ottoman troops, stuck up there, with no chance of
descent, had to tunnel down, through the rocks, to the river that slices the city
in two, to gather water. And the river has stories of its own, as well. According
to a British journalist visiting in the 1960s, when the southern-flowing Ters
Akan Nehir joins the Yeshil, previously known as the Iris River, it then changes
direction, flowing north on a weird parallel course.

CANDY OF THE MIND

Almost everything of interest in Amasya surrounds the river. The touristy
north bank, with its tombs, hotels and English-menu cafés, is the polar
opposite to the working side of the city where people sell things and attend
school and mosques. On the modern side, walking towards Atatürk Street,
passing the Mongol-built lunatic asylum (which, despite sounding truly
alarming, actually pioneered the use of music therapy) and the handsome
Mehmet Paşa Mosque, with its vaulted rooms for travelling dervishes, I found
Amasya Çörekcisi. Baking Amasya's famous buns since 1925, the bakers achieve
sweet rolls that are as flaky as they are soft, studded with walnuts, poppy seeds
and hazelnuts. Inside, as quickly as bakers pull their trays out of the fiery ovens,
assistants pull down elaborately decorated boxes covered with postcard images
of the city, that stand stacked floor to ceiling ready to be filled.

Crossing the river, in a restaurant housed in a restored Ottoman mansion
filled with old wirelesses, typewriters and portraits of Atatürk wearing his black
astrakhan hat, I found another local delicacy, white *toyga* soup. I shuffled into
a window seat, the tea in my hand glowing like amber resin in its tulip glass,
and dug my spoon into the soup, thick with chickpeas, wheat and yogurt,
topped with melted butter. Outside, young couples paraded on the bridges.
Shy headscarved women, and boys with stubble dressed in pressed white shirts,

took photographs of each other and ate ice cream. On the other side of the water, some dressed up as sultans in costumes loaned by photographers, posing with swords, velvet tunics and fur-lined silk robes slung over their shoulders. Thoroughly spruced up for domestic tourists, in Amasya you can marvel at the tombs and the mummies, eat the special apples, upon which compliments have been heaped since the Romans, and you can search out the local okra, which Mehmet the Conqueror's horsemen would dry out and wear as ornamental beads. All of these easy pleasures are here, and they are enjoyable enough. But you might, as I did while sitting and watching the dressed-up lovers and the flowing river, conclude that Amasya feels a little like an out-of-whack time machine, a popular place of easy wonder with its ice-cream vendors and kitsch sultan statues, but perhaps a show that has seen better days.

I left Amasya travelling eastwards again, past carpet hawkers not selling antique Anatolian kilims but rugs with the faces of Erdogan, Atatürk and various sultans printed on them. Following the flowing Yeshil Irmak towards the road that would take me to Tokat, two hours inland at the very fringe of Turkey's mid-Black Sea region, I was reminded of a local saying warning of the water, 'Tokat dumps in it, Amasya drinks it', but as the sun hit the clear-running river, and it reflected the huge limestone cliffs and clouds hovering over their tops, it felt an unfair proverb. As far as the city was concerned, I wasn't sure whether I was leaving too soon, or if I had Amasya, so encrusted by centuries of sagas and empires, right in my mind at all.

Toyga Soup

Toyga soup is a speciality of Amasya, made with yogurt, chickpeas and wheat topped with a little dried mint. It is comforting, simple and this version makes for a decent lunch.

SERVES 4

FOR THE SOUP

70g/⅓ cup pearl barley

250g/1¼ cups Greek yogurt

1 tablespoon cornflour (cornstarch)

1 egg yolk

1 garlic clove, mashed to a paste with a good pinch of fine salt

700ml/scant 3 cups water

1 x 400g/14oz can chickpeas, drained and rinsed

1 tablespoon thyme leaves

small bunch of spinach (optional)

½ teaspoon salt

freshly ground black pepper

FOR THE TOPPING

30g/2 tablespoons salted butter

1 teaspoon dried mint

1 tablespoon lemon juice

pul biber (Turkish pepper flakes), to taste (optional)

Rinse the pearl barley and tip into a large pan of salted, boiling water. Cook according to the packet instructions until tender, but still with a bit of bite.

When the pearl barley has about 10–15 minutes to go, put the yogurt, cornflour (cornstarch), egg yolk and garlic paste in a bowl and whisk until no lumps remain. Whisk in the water then pour it all into another large pan. Bring the liquid to a boil then simmer for 10 minutes, stirring occasionally.

Add the drained pearl barley to the soup, along with the chickpeas, thyme, spinach, if you're adding it, salt and some pepper. Bring back to the boil, then cover and simmer for a couple of minutes. Set aside.

While the soup is simmering for the final time, make the minted butter for the topping. Melt the butter and add the dried mint, then, off the heat, add the lemon juice.

To serve, ladle the soup into bowls and drizzle the minty lemon butter over the top. You can sprinkle some pul biber over the top, if you'd like.

TOKAT KEBAB – MEALS ON WHEELS

'Mountain, Slap' read the slip of paper. An address, of sorts, for a restaurant, scribbled on the back of a hotel card and put into my hands by a concierge in the off-lying city of Tokat, deep in the mid-Black Sea region, 140 miles from the coast. The hotel staff seemed as surprised by me as I was by their new, highly polished business hotel with its empty lobby and vacant bedrooms complete with new prayer rugs in the wardrobes. I handed the taxi driver the card. Moving his spectacles up his huge nose, he pointed at it with his other hand, and then looked at the concierge for assurance. He nodded. Nicotine had stained the interior of the yellow cab a sallow buttermilk beige and as we drove down the main drag, past the city's brand-new mosque, built to hold 3000, the engraved ornament dangling from the rearview mirror bounced, blurring the words of the Prophet.

We drove on in the dark, not leaving the city limits but climbing up a very steep hill, presumably the 'mountain', round and round and up and up, until we got to the top, and I was faced with what looked disappointingly like a conference centre. I had only one night in Tokat, enough just to catch something of the atmosphere and the local museum, before returning to the coast and heading to Trabzon. I hoped for an interesting experience.

Stepping inside, there was still higher to go. Hauling myself up three flights of stairs, I finally met a waiter, dressed in a bow-tie and starched white shirt, at the top. He led the way down a corridor, and then stopped to slowly open a dark, wooden door. A whoosh of cigarette smoke, with a top note of smoky lamb, filled the hallway. Inside, the dining room, perfectly circular with floor-to-ceiling windows, had its tables and chairs tight to the edges of the room, for unobstructed views over Tokat during the day, or your own reflection at night. The ring-shaped room looked like one of those gimmicky revolving restaurants found at the top of trophy Chinese skyscrapers in the 1980s, with their Lazy Susan rotating tables and express business lunches.

High up, out of sight and away from the more conservative citizens of Tokat, a scene of heavy R&R unfolded. On each table were the same three things: a bottle of raki, a couple of cartons of cigarettes and a heap of Tokat kebab. Following the same recipe for centuries, six-month-old Karakaya lamb, cooked with aubergine, tomato, a scattering of garlic cloves and peppers, served on paper-thin lavash bread, it is so far above everyday kebabs that it is capable of sending many a Turk misty-eyed at the mere mention of its name.

Collectively, the restaurant reclined on scalloped faux-suede chairs, butter-soft and designed to encourage Sultan-style lounging. Everybody, children aside, sucked on cigarettes, their tips fizzing red-yellow between index and middle fingers. With its ruffled and swag-tasselled curtains, Brylcreemed waiters and polished white tiled floor, this was certainly no hidden-away den of depravity, though, more of a date place, if anything. It is also one of the few restaurants in Tokat serving alcohol. Bottle after bottle of raki arrived hard and fast to diners, wheeled on trolleys across the shiny, slippery tiles, pushed by slick, but surely dizzy, waiters who wheeled round and round, orbiting for hours.

Halfway through demolishing a plate of Tokat kebab and chargrilled vegetables, I spotted that at the foot of each table stood an unexplained oddity. A plywood chest of drawers, also suspended on little wheels. Each table had one and every half hour or so, these too would go on a journey around the restaurant, zooming past the kebab and raki trolleys, disappearing for a while, before returning. But, returning with what? More cigarettes? Bootlegged booze? Playing cards? I never did find out. Nor did I find out whether the centre of the restaurant would transform into a dance floor, as its layout suggested, once the raki soaked in and the clock marched towards midnight. But just being inside this restaurant was a refreshing shot in the arm, an antitoxin to synthetic touristy cafés, somewhere offering up the chance to peer through a keyhole, to see how secular, middle-class Turks in provincial cities like to relax and socialise.

Outside, in the smoke-free night-time air, I waited for a taxi, reading up on Tokat. Twinned with Mogadishu, it counts old Seljuk caravanserais, calico artisans and orchards of wild pear trees among its unorthodox attractions, and there are a few impressive historical quirks, too, such as the fact that it hosted Vlad the Impaler (Count Dracula) in its castle dungeon for seven years. Not an unimpressive roll-call, and that's before we even get to the kebab. Eventually a young driver, all clipped beard and pointy, shiny shoes, arrived and opened the taxi door for me. His English was good. I showed him the hotel card and he nodded. Then I turned the little card over and asked what 'Slap' meant. 'Oh, it's quite simple,' he said. 'It's English for Tokat.'

Trolley Kebab

The people of Tokat are justifiably proud of their local kebab and it would be disrespectful and foolhardy to try to recreate it here. Without the special clay oven, Karakaya lamb and the tail fat, it can't be done. But I do want to put something down on paper in memory of the meat feast high above the city as described in the essay above. I am calling this little homage to that night 'trolley kebab' for reasons obvious in the essay.

SERVES 4

500g/1lb 2oz lamb leg, fat trimmed, cut into 4cm/1½-in pieces

2 small onions, finely

1 teaspoon cumin seeds, toasted and crushed

60ml/¼ cup vegetable oil

1 whole garlic bulb

2 tablespoons olive oil

1 aubergine (eggplant), chopped into 4cm/1½-in pieces

1 green (bell) pepper, cut into chunky finger-sized slices

2 large, ripe tomatoes, quartered

salt

TO SERVE

spicy Turkish peppers

4 lavash bread, or similar

Place the meat in a large bowl, sprinkling over a couple of pinches of salt. Add the grated onion (squeezing out as much liquid as possible to remove), crushed cumin seeds and vegetable oil to the lamb. Toss and leave to marinate for 2 hours.

Preheat the oven to 200°C/400°F/gas mark 6. Discard the outer layers of the garlic bulb, leaving intact the skins of the individual cloves, and slice 1.5cm/½ in off the top. Drizzle 1 tablespoon of the olive oil over the exposed head and wrap the bulb in foil. Bake for 30 minutes, or until the cloves are soft. Leave aside to cool, then pop out each of the whole cloves.

Preheat the grill to a hot setting. Rub the kebab skewers with a little oil (if you use bamboo skewers just soak them in water first). Thread the meat onto them, alternating with the vegetables, brushed with the remaining 1 tablespoon of olive oil. With the aubergine (eggplant), keep the cut side facing the meat so that it soaks up the flavour of the lamb.

Cook the skewers under the grill for 15–20 minutes, turning occasionally. Remove from the grill and leave to rest for 2–3 minutes. You may need to work in two batches; if so, tent the first batch in foil to keep them warm.

Finally, remove the lamb and vegetables from the skewers and serve with spicy peppers, on grilled lavash bread, sprinkling over the squeezed-out garlic cloves.

TRABZON
AND
ENVIRONS

ODESSA

ISTANBUL

TRABZON

TRABZON – BYZANTINE OUTLIER AND PORT OF PERSIA

'Then, between sleeping and waking, there rose before me a vision of Trebizond: not Trebizond as I had seen it, but the Trebizond of the world's dreams, of my own dreams.'

– Rose Macaulay, *The Towers of Trebizond*

Standing with their backs to the wind, under a statue of Mustafa Kemal Atatürk, a group of ecstatic men struck flares, one after the other, sending volleys of red smoke up into the night sky above Trabzon's main square. Car horns blasted and the crowd, dressed in the Turkish working-class uniform of blue stonewashed jeans and black leather jackets, bellowed in return. They roared as more flares were lit, shooting up in red zigzags. Trabzonspor, their football club, had just beaten a Spanish team, 2–0, and from the roof of the Şişman Efes pub, I watched as the scene unfolded, pulling my Trabzonspor scarf around my neck, unsure how I'd walk back to the hotel through the sea of fans. 'It's normal here. It's like the Black Sea, it will roar but it will then calm down,' the barman told me, putting down another frosty Efes.

Since the mid-1960s, Trabzon has been a city obsessed with football. Rival Turkish teams often get beaten at Trabzonspor's home stadium, Şenol Güneş, the fans' spiritual home. If it's a good win, the team might dance the kolbasti – a crazed jig of flailing arms and legs inspired by the moves of line-throwing fishermen. Trabzon's football mania, central to the city's identity, means cafés, taxi cabs and barbershops are decorated in the club colours of claret and blue. The fans, full of fiery, deep-rooted passion, are famous throughout Turkey for being hot-tempered, and for nurturing a strong nationalist instinct. But then Trabzon – founded as a Greek colony in the 8th century BC and historically known as Trapezus and Trebizond – is a nationalist city, with an underdog spirit. Posted like a sentinel in the northeast corner of Turkey, looking out to sea, it can, at first glance, appear a deeply introverted, and slightly unlucky place, one of dowdy streets, grey façades and traffic rages. But there are benefits for the visitor, too. Largely unused to catering to travellers, this provincial capital has hung onto an air of mystery and adventure that Istanbul, 660 miles away, has, in large parts, lost.

THE EMPIRE OF TREBIZOND

The historian, William Miller, singled out two key periods in Trabzon's history. The reign of King Mithradates of Pontus – who, born in Sinop and buried in Amasya, challenged the power of Rome – and the medieval empire of Trebizond, characterised by Miller as 'one of the curiosities of history'. Following the sack of Constantinople by the Crusaders in 1204, a separate branch of the Byzantine Empire was set up at Trapezus, with its leader, the Grand Comneni, forming large-scale coalitions with foreign rulers. Controlling southern Crimea, it was a Greek Emirate, both proclaiming its legacy of Byzantine power, while simultaneously distancing itself from it. When Constantinople fell to the Ottoman Turks in 1453, after forces barraged its walls for 40 days, the empire of Trebizond remained unconquered for another eight years. Born here, too, was the longest-reigning sultan of the Ottoman Empire, Suleiman I (1494–1566), better known to us as Suleiman the Magnificent, and it was from Trabzon that Selim I, known as Selim the Grim because of his wild temper tantrums, left to expand Ottoman power throughout Anatolia and into the Middle East.

Much later, when the Turkish Republic was realised and the exchange of populations took place between Greece and Turkey in 1923, Trabzon changed again. During this trade of populations, one and a half million Christians, including the Pontic Greeks, left Turkey to go west to Greece, and around a million Muslims were sent from Greece to Anatolia. Trabzon, and wider Pontos on the southern coast of the Black Sea, had been home to thousands of Armenians and Pontic Greeks for nearly 3000 years. They spoke an ancient dialect of Greek – not understood by those in Athens – and lived fully detached from the country we know as Greece. To them, this was not an 'exchange' at all. The Greeks called it the 'Katastrofe'. The concept that these people could no longer exist together, as they had done for centuries, has caused anguish to families for generations. Monasteries, banks and mansions with Rococo interiors, once belonging to Greeks, were left behind and Trabzon slowly became more and more Turkish, and considerably less worldly.

Odd, less reported upon, pockets of micro-trade in Trabzon have at times flourished here. In the late 1980s, following the free-fall of Mikhail Gorbachev's glasnost (openness) and perestroika (restructuring) policies and programmes, Soviet authorities opened the Georgian border crossing at Sarpi, 120 miles east, straight up the coast from Trabzon, allowing in 'trader tourists', mainly Georgians, Armenians and Russians who came across the border to sell whatever they could and to buy trainers, tracksuits and goods hard to find back home. Seizing the opportunity, Turks assembled 'Rus bazaars' in towns along the Turkish Black Sea coastline where people could buy and sell. Immediately, there was a spike in crime and disorder. Returning with their hauls and bundles of cash, these trader tourists, often travelling solo, carrying just a suitcase or two, fell prey to the Georgian mafia who'd hang around the border, shaking them down, demanding protection money and stealing goods. In Trabzon, some of the more desperate stayed on in the grotty 'Rus Bazaar' on the gritty waterfront, working as prostitutes and collectively labelled by locals as 'Natashas'.

GROTTOS AND CHAPELS

Today in Trabzon, Slavic and western faces are a rare sight. Just like elsewhere in the country, political turmoil and terrorism have slashed visitor numbers. Unlike Istanbul and the southern coastal resorts, Trabzon never did host many visiting foreigners, but the small gap left has been partly filled by a different type of visitor – Saudi, Bahraini and Kuwaiti families looking to escape the scorching summer temperatures of home. In July and August large families arrive, seeking out the exact same things that turn sun-starved westerners off: wet misty hills, rainy coastlines and alcohol-free restaurants. Much like all visitors here, they are viewed by locals with a polite suspicion.

Rather than stopping, the few westerners who do arrive in Trabzon tend to zoom through the city. They are eager to get to the Greek Orthodox Monastery of the Virgin Mary, otherwise known as Sumela, 20 miles away to the east. Built in the 4th century AD, and abandoned in 1923 when the Greek monks departed, it is a labyrinth of corridors, chapels and smoke-blackened grottos, all stacked on shapeless overhanging crags, 3900 dizzying feet up. Often veiled by shifting mists that hang heavy in the surrounding evergreen forests, it is a sight that is guaranteed to refresh the interests of even the most jaded traveller. In past centuries the surrounding forests were believed to have been savage and untamed, as described in the 14th-century *Book of Dede Korkut*, the epic stories of the Oghuz Turks: 'Twisted and tortuous will the roads be; Swamps there will be, where the horsemen will sink and never emerge; Forests there will be, where the red serpent can find no path.' That description is hard to picture today as even when restoration periods restrict access, taxis still ferry hundreds of tourists up to view the monastery from afar, stopping at waterfalls and streams along the roadside.

MAD ABOUT HONEY

The following day, with football fans dispersed, I walked towards Trabzon's bazaar, passing restaurants that, come winter, will focus on one thing only: *hamsi* (Black Sea anchovies). Grilled over charcoal and eaten with bread, and put into pilafs and even jams, they are a cheap and healthy fast-food. No other fish is as loved as *hamsi*. Magazines were published in Trabzon back in the 1940s with anchovies making up their headlines and covers, songs are sung about them and they have been the subject of countless poems. Ottoman traveller Evliya Çelebi wrote of their being bought and sold in Trabzon in the mid-17th century in his travel notes, *Seyahatname*:

> At this season boats loaded with these fish arrive in the harbor, and the dealers in fish cry them in a peculiar manner, and at the same time sounding a horn or trumpet; as soon as this sounding is heard, the whole town is in an uproar, and people who hear it, even when at prayer, instantly cease, and run like mad men after it.

But winter, not summer, is *hamsi* season so instead I went after a special pilaf, served in the bazaar, that I had heard about in Istanbul. I jostled through the thin lanes, along with hundreds of female shoppers, and noticeably few men. Holidaying Arabs dressed in niqabs bargained for perfume, and Turkish women in colourful headscarves rolled out fabrics, holding them up and debating their quality. Children peered into glass cases lining the alleys, filled with huge blocks of brown and white marbled *beton* (concrete) halva and giant tubs of olives, fat buttery yellow ones, wrinkly black ones and others brown as tar, stood begging to be plucked at. Queues snaked outside bakeries, their ovens turning out wood-fired *vakfıkebir* bread, the local Trabzon loaves, round and heavy-looking, weighty as bowling balls. Delis displayed their yellow balls of 'Tonya' butter from the *yaylas* (mountain pastures), bulbous and round, almost football-sized. It is extraordinarily good – grassy, rich and clean tasting – coming mainly from Yakçukur near Tonya, not far from Trabzon, where locals still speak a Greek dialect. All of this is food for Black Sea people, as rugged as the lands they live in.

Harder to find in Trabzon's delis is the Black Sea's infamous mad honey, known as *desi bal*, made from the rhododendron flowers that flourish in the damp Black Sea climate. In early summer, capable beekeepers set off to higher altitudes with their hives, releasing their bees and encouraging them to harvest the short-lived rhododendron blossoms. Their nectar contains andromedotoxin, a substance that is fine, even beneficial, in moderation, but lethal in large quantities. Ingesting too much is said to cause everything from blurred vision and respiratory problems to muscle paralysis, severe arterial hypotension, and even death. Trabzon locals insist that thick Turkish yogurt can cancel out the toxins, and that there are perks – increased energy and a better libido – to ingesting tiny amounts boiled in milk, upon waking.

Legend has it that historically, this honey has been used to slay armies. William John Hamilton, English geologist and President of the Royal Geographical Society, researched desi bal in the 1840s, pointing out that Strabo, the ancient geographer born in Amasya (ancient Amaseia), had warned of it: 'The Heptacometae, the wildest of the tribes who inhabit the mountains to the east of Themiscyra [near modern day Samsun on the Turkish Black Sea], destroyed three squadrons of Pompey's troops, by placing on the road cups of maddening honey, produced on the highest branches ...' And, Pliny had advised on how to identify it, describing it as 'more liquid, having a redder colour, an extraordinary smell' and cautioned that it can produce violent sneezing fits, with the eater throwing themselves down on the ground, in a fierce sweat, if too much is ingested.

It is legal to buy desi bal in Turkey, but it isn't widely advertised. Shopkeepers tend to sell it to those they know, as less than a teaspoon is the suggested amount, and even that is said to be tongue numbing. I tried in vain to buy it, but was told that last year's supply had long sold out and that to try the new batch, I'd have to come back another time. The option of trying this elusive, heady honey had been taken out of my hands, maybe for the best.

In the end, despite being deep within the maze-like bazaar, I couldn't have failed to find Tarihi Kalkanoglu Pilavi – the celebrated restaurant. Out the front, under huge signs, are newspaper cutouts of reviews stuck in the windows and family portraits of five generations, all descendants of Suleyman Aga, who founded the business in 1856. During the Crimean War Trabzon was a vital centre for providing the Ottoman armies in the Crimea and in eastern Ottoman frontlines. The governor of Trabzon, Osman Efendi, charged Suleyman Aga, the Sultan's chief pilaf cook, to make rice, *hosaf* and bread for the soldiers on the frontline between north-eastern Turkey and Batumi (on the Black Sea in Georgia). When the war was over, the tradition of selling the pilaf in massive quantities, weighed out on scales in kilos, continued in Trabzon, under the name of Tarihi Kalkanoglu Pilavi in the same district, Pazarkapi. Inside today, things haven't changed a great deal.

Ancient creaking scales sit on the counter, where the pilaf is weighed out before being dished up. Cooked with rich beef bone marrow broth, it is formidably buttery, topped only with a little beef. Compared with the complex *plovs* found in Central Asia and the Caucasus, filled with everything from quince to quail's eggs, this pilaf wins on account of its simplicity and depth of flavour. While I ate, behind me the scales constantly bobbed up and down with new orders. Finishing with a bowl of apricot *hosaf*, I then lost myself again in the bazaar amidst the hammering noise of the blacksmith's market, and the cobbled lanes above the sea. At sunset, I joined families in strolling down to the unassuming boulevard along the coast. Unlike so many others on this trip, much of Trabzon's central seafront offers little. Just a few huts, some scrubland and rocks. This is not helped by the busy east–west Black Sea Coastal Road, or D010, which has cruelly divorced Trabzon, and its citizens, from the sea.

Turning my back to the humming road, I stood by the rocks and watched little ships slowly returning to shore, tugging frothy white cables of bubbles behind them, jogged by land and sea winds. On nearby boulders solitary women, lost in problems, love and thought, looked out to sea, and pairs of young boys lolled like seals on the smooth rocks, resting and chatting in the last of the sun. Then, in the final moments of light, the air changed, becoming cooler and charged with energy. The waves transformed, turning from slate-ash grey to a glowing metallic silver, rolling over rocks and gently flaying the coast. Hypnotic with pale light, suddenly the Black Sea looked from a different world, capable of silently cutting all of us down to size.

Frontline Pilaf

It is impossible to recreate the pilaf that is weighed out in Tarihi Kalkanoglu Pilavi, because of the exceptional *yayla* (mountain pasture) butter used and the atmosphere in which it is served. Therefore this is a riff on it, recreated for the home kitchen. Unlike many other pilafs, the key to this one is its simplicity; it is quite a plain dish. To liven it up a little, it is often served with kuru fasülye (see page 130) and *hosaf* (see page 228).

SERVES 4

250g/scant 1½ cups basmati rice

350g/12¼oz braising steak, diced into chunky pieces

4 tablespoons olive oil

¼ teaspoon salt

a good few grinds of black pepper

35g/2½ tablespoons salted butter

1 large onion, finely grated (the aim is to taste it but not see it)

small handful of pine nuts, lightly toasted

1 cinnamon stick

400ml/1⅔ cups beef stock

salt and freshly ground black pepper

Put the rice in a bowl of water and leave to soak. Preheat the oven to 180°C/350°F/gas mark 4. Place the beef in an ovenproof dish and rub it well with 2 tablespoons of the olive oil, adding the salt and pepper. Cook in the oven for 20–30 minutes, until cooked through but still juicy and not dried out. Remove and set aside, tenting the beef in foil so it doesn't cool too much.

In the meantime, make the pilaf. Pour the remaining oil into a large flameproof casserole, add the butter and sauté the grated onion until translucent. Add the toasted pine nuts and the rice (drained and rinsed until the water runs clear) and the cinnamon stick, and pour over the stock.

Bring to a boil, then turn the heat down low, put on a lid and cook for around 10 minutes until the rice is soft but with a little bite – don't stir it. When it's ready, remove from the heat and discard the cinnamon stick. If it needs a little longer at this stage, poke some holes in it, put the lid back on and let it steam, off the heat, for a few minutes.

Roughly chop the beef, scatter it over the top of the rice and serve with Apricot and Cinnamon Hosaf (see page 228) and possibly some Black Sea Beans (see page 130).

Apricot and Cinnamon Hosaf

The perfect partner for buttery Frontline Pilaf on page 227, as served at
Tarihi Kalkanoglu.

SERVES 2

100g/3½oz dried apricots

1 cinnamon stick

1 tablespoon caster (superfine) sugar

1 tablespoon honey

300ml/1¼ cups water

Put all the ingredients into a small pan and heat gently, melting the sugar and
honey into a syrup, then simmer for 10 minutes, just enough to soften
the fruit. Leave to cool and steep for half a day at room temperature. Discard
the cinnamon stick from the fruit and syrup, and serve, unchilled, in bowls.

Trabzon Kaygana with Anchovies and Herbs

This is a Black Sea egg dish which is a cross between a fritter and an omelette, brightened up with slithers of silvery anchovies. I ate a version of it, without the anchovies as they weren't in season, for brunch in Trabzon. The hint of mint really makes this dish.

SERVES 2

2–4 tablespoons olive or sunflower oil

small handful of chard, washed, stems cut into matchsticks and leaves into ribbons

1 small onion, finely chopped

3 large eggs

5 or so anchovies in oil (according to taste), sliced into long slivers

2 mint leaves, cut into thin strips

2 tablespoons chopped parsley

2 tablespoons coarse cornmeal

1 teaspoon pul biber (Turkish pepper flakes), optional

salt and freshly ground black pepper

Heat 2 tablespoons of the oil in a frying pan, add a good pinch of salt and fry the chard stems (not the leaves at this stage) and the onion for a few minutes until soft, then add the chard leaves and cook until wilted. Remove from the heat, keeping the pan as you'll be frying in it later, and tip the chard and onion into a bowl to cool slightly.

In another bowl, whisk the eggs and anchovies together, adding a few pinches of black pepper, then whisk in the mint, parsley and cornmeal. Add the cooked onions and chard to the mixture and stir through.

Heat another glug of oil in the frying pan, and when hot, using a ladle, drop in saucer-sized portions of the mixture and fry – using a spatula to keep the circular shape – just for a minute or so, turning once. Repeat until the mixture is used up; you should end up with 5 or so fritters. Serve with pul biber sprinkled on top, if you like, and some cornbread.

A NOTE ON TURKEY'S OTHER HAGIA SOPHIA

'During all my winter walks I always had a wish in my soul to go to Trebizond in the approaching spring.'

— Julien Bordier, squire to Baron de Salignac,
  French Ambassador in Constantinople

On the western margins of Trabzon, by the buzzing Black Sea highway, is the Hagia Sophia. It is far smaller, and far less famous than its namesake in Istanbul. But what it lacks in architectural splendour, it makes up for in tranquillity and beauty. Built as a church in the 13th century, then converted to a mosque during the Ottoman Empire, it had a spell as a cholera hospital before opening as a museum in 1964, and was then converted back to a mosque in 2013.

Today the domed basilica and the palm-filled garden is a place of peace, roosting birds and cool sea breezes, largely unfettered by tourists despite its being one of the Black Sea's greatest monuments. The 15th-century Byzantine cleric and writer, John Eugenikos, called Trebizond 'the apple of the eye of all of Asia'. Yet, while it was a centre of Christian life in the Middle Ages, Trebizond's history and empire was largely ignored and forgotten by thinkers and historians until the arrival in the 19th century of the French scholar Gabriel Millet, in 1893, and the Russian Byzantinist, Fyodor Uspenskii, in 1917.

The spectacular reliefs on the south porch, clearly viewed in good sunlight, make up a frieze representing the story of Genesis, and above that is a Byzantine imperial eagle, the symbol of the dynasty that led the Empire of Trebizond. But these act as a mere aperitif for the majestic frescoes inside the thick walls that, having been whitewashed over for hundreds of years, were revealed by a British team in the 1950s.

Byzantine expert and art historian David Talbot Rice first travelled to Trabzon in 1928, setting off to explore deserted Pontic Greek villages on horseback, and it was he who secured permission from the governor of Trabzon in the 1950s to begin restoration work on the painted church. Born a country gentleman in Gloucestershire, Talbot Rice regularly travelled to the Near East and went on to open the world of Byzantine and Medieval art to generations of students during his teaching posts as Professor at Edinburgh University and at the Courtauld Institute in London. His first major book,

The Birth of Western Painting (1930), was written in collaboration with Robert Byron who wrote about his journeys with Talbot Rice in *The Station* (1928), published nine years before his classic *The Road to Oxiana*.

Joining Talbot Rice were the Winfields, David and June, who worked on restoring the church, starting in 1959. David Winfield's gradual journey towards his work on the Hagia Sophia as field director was no less intriguing than Talbot Rice's. His desire to preserve Byzantine churches began with a motorbike adventure from Oxford to Istanbul, via Serbia, in 1951. En route, he visited painted churches, stopping at the monasteries of Mount Athos and training with art historians at Belgrade University, where he learned wall painting conservation skills.

Only pausing work for Friday prayers, the team at Hagia Sophia slowly revealed the frescoes that are the building's calling card. Their work uncovered saints, a scene of the Last Supper, evangelists and soaring angels. Living in Trabzon for half the year, the Winfields became well known around town, hosting many writers, travellers and Byzantinists, including Rose Macaulay and Freya Stark. They completed the project five years later and persuaded the authorities to open the building as a museum.

A spotlight has recently been cast again on these great frescoes, with the Hagia Sophia reverting back to a mosque, but while some floor mosaics are covered, and a false ceiling hides the figurative Christian dome art in the main prayer room, only a fraction of them are out of sight.

Sumela Brunch

'Trebizond had a name for art and luxury. The monastery at Sumela, whatever the date of its exterior frescoes, is more nearly related than any other building to the painted churches of the Bucovina … There is some definite connection,' wrote Sacheverell Sitwell, drawing parallels between the painted churches of his beloved Romania and the Black Sea's most famous monastery, Sumela, which hugs a cliff-face an hour's drive from Trabzon. On a recent visit to Sumela, I stopped en route at a small café on a trout river. The river was low, paddling depth, and the stones had been washed smooth. Even though it was summer, the leaves had started to fall and the tops of the surrounding firs were hidden by thick mist. My brunch came served in a copper pan and seemed to me to be a Black Sea version of the classic Turkish breakfast, menemen. Chard, stalks and all, were mixed with white cheese, butter and egg whites, served with cornbread on the side. The chef, Mursel, kindly gave me the recipe.

SERVES 2

2 tablespoons olive oil

knob of butter

1 small onion, diced

pinch of sea salt

1 garlic clove, thinly sliced

6 Swiss chard leaves, roughly chopped (kale is a good substitute)

2 tablespoons chopped flat-leaf parsley leaves and stems

4 egg whites

150g/5¼oz feta, crumbled

50g/1¾oz Parmesan, grated

1 tablespoon pul biber (Turkish pepper flakes)

½ teaspoon freshly ground black pepper

Heat the olive oil and butter in a medium skillet over a gentle heat. Gently sauté the onion with the salt for 5 minutes, then add the garlic and cook for another 2 minutes, taking care that the garlic doesn't burn. Add the chard and parsley and sauté until wilted; this shouldn't take more than a couple of minutes. Next, whisk the egg whites in a bowl until they are frothy then pour into the skillet, adding the cheeses, pul biber and black pepper. You are aiming for a scrambled egg variation, so stir until the eggs are cooked as you like them. Serve in the pan, with a side of cornbread (see page 133 for homemade) or sourdough toast.

A CRIMEAN PALACE IN THE TEA BUSHES

'The harem of the sky

Glows soft with stars, eternal lamps that play

Upon a cloud that swanlike on the bay

Of heaven sleeps, bright-stained with sunset dye'

— Adam Mickiewicz, *Crimean Sonnets*

Waist-deep in a sea of tea bushes, I had forgotten what it was to be cool and dry. Jungle-like air, steamy hot and fit to burst, mixed with the comforting smell of freshly brewed tea. The stepped plantations of Rize, 50 miles east of Trabzon, pressed down to the sea, their rolling, curvy chartreuse humps reminiscent of Sri Lankan tea fields, green as spring, a hundred shades of green or more, broken only by oxblood-red tea huts.

Certain I was alone in the pin-drop silent plantation, movement in the field across suggested I was not. A trio of hessian sacks, carried on the backs of two men and one woman, moved through the sticky shrubs. All three, seasonal migrant Black Sea workers, were Georgians who'd travelled for temporary tea-clipping work during the summer months. Dressed in Wellington boots and camouflage fatigues, juggling cigarettes between the corners of their mouths, their faces told me that they were hot and tired, as they explained that there was 'no work in Georgia'. Then their Turkish boss arrived and they hushed, bundling themselves up onto the back of a pick-up truck and flopping down onto the brown tea sacks. They drove off, then U-turned back, waving and singing in Georgian, their wooden crucifixes swinging around their necks, happy the working day was over. They were headed to the Black Sea highway, a busy road lined by the chimneys of tea factories and posters for the local football side, Çaykur Rizespor, and humming with lorries transporting tea, tobacco and hazelnuts, this region's three main industries, east to the Caucasus, and west to Istanbul.

BLOOD OF THE RABBIT

The father of Turkish tea, Hulusi Karadeniz, started Turkey's tea story in the 1920s when he carried seeds from the Caucasus to grow in his garden. By 1939 the first tea crop, of several hundred pounds, was collected here, in Rize. The climate, humid, wet and almost monsoonal, a result of hot air rising in Central Asia and then cooling with damp Black Sea winds, is ideal for tea. Today Turkey is the fifth-largest tea-growing region after India, China, Kenya and Sri Lanka, and all of it comes from here, around the northeast Black Sea region, and especially around Rize. Steeped for ten minutes or so in a *çaydanlik* — a double-kettle — it is then poured into tulip-shaped glasses, wider at the top to cool the tea with a thinner waist helping to keep the lower part hot. When the tea is ready, Turks will say the colour is tavşan kani, roughly translating as 'rabbit's blood'. Turks drink tea without milk and if it is good, it is exceptionally clean, amber-hued and fresh tasting. These tulip glasses of tea fuel Turkey. It's not unusual for a thirsty Turk to drink seven, or even ten, glasses in a sitting, and it comes as no surprise that Turks consume the most tea per capita in the world. No doubt Ernest Hemingway would have celebrated this fact, and the Turkish conversion from coffee to tea. Arriving in Constantinople to cover the Greco-Turkish War (1919–1922) for the *Toronto Star* newspaper, he described Turkish coffee as 'a tremendously poisonous, stomach rotting drink that has a greater kick than absinthe'.

The sun began to set over the tea fields, turning both the sky and the sea candyfloss pink, melding the horizon and transforming the identical, skinny dirt tracks into mazes. Male stag beetles, enormous with hard bodies of black armour and flying only a few months of the year when they look to mate, dive-bombed me as I tried to navigate my way back to the hotel. In surrounding huts, Turkish tea workers relaxed, sitting under bare bulbs, reading newspapers, batting away mosquitoes and drinking tea. One came out to greet me, holding his palms open, insisting I smell the dried tea leaves from a packet labelled 'treasure' in Turkish.

Finally back, I sat out at the hotel's garden terrace, level with the tea bushes once more. Kaf Dağı is a hotel with a distinct whiff, not only of tea, but also the Ottoman era and, more curiously, Crimea, which when you understand the owner's vision, makes sense. Ahmet Oflu is a local man and antique collector, who built this small hotel as a love letter to the 16th-century Bakhchysarai, or Hansaray, palace in Crimea, once a protectorate of the Ottoman empire across the Black Sea, and a remarkable building with Gothic arches and stained glass windows. 'We could not copy all of Hansaray but the entrance of our hotel is an identical replica,' said Oflu, over another glass of tea, pointing to the entrance at Kaf Dağı, with its huge wooden door, archway and ornate carvings. The rest of the architecture co-exists with more traditional Ottoman features, with selamlık cabinets, ornate wooden balconies and latticed screens. Hansaray, beloved and venerated by Pushkin, who wrote a poem about its fountain, was home to generations of Crimean Khans with a design channelling Istanbul's Topkapi Palace and the Alhambra in Spain.

A çaydanlık bubbling before me, I watched as tiny white moths, no bigger than ladybirds but with exceptionally fluffy bottoms, flocked to the twinkling garden lamps while Orhan, the hotel's Kurdish baker, brought out the best bread I have ever tasted. Pillowy, soft white discs, similar to pitta but far, far lighter. I dipped the bread into a saucer of *pekmez*, a molasses-like grape syrup, and tahini – the best sort of very late afternoon tea there is. Below, as night fell, ships' lights glimmered on a navy-blue sea, as still as glass.

John Murray's early guidebook to Turkey (with 'maxims and hints for travellers in the East'), published in 1840, suggests that travellers arriving in this part of Turkey should be on their guard against bandits and should 'pack gunpowder as gifts'. I didn't see any guns, except for the splendid rifles on display in nearby Ottoman mansions, but I did hear the crackle and pop of gunfire in the distance that night – maybe a wedding, or maybe some tea pickers letting off steam after a long day's work in the jungly-green hills.

Pekmez and Tahini

Pekmez is a centuries-old fruit syrup made by pressing, stirring and boiling fruit until it thickens into sweet molasses. It is a staple at Turkish breakfasts and, while grapes are most commonly used, *pekmez* is also made from mulberries, plums, apples, pears and pomegranates. Rich in vitamins, Turks swear by its health-giving properties, especially relying on it in winter. I have heard it called 'the healing syrup of Anatolia'.

SERVES 4

150ml/10 tablespoons pekmez
100ml/generous 6 tablespoons tahini

On a side plate, pour the *pekmez* first then and slowly add the tahini in the middle. Serve with thick, warm pitta bread.

THE HOUSES THAT TSARIST CAKES BUILT

'Not for food; to pray was to know

Waking from a dark dream to find

The white loaf on the white snow;'

— R.S. Thomas, *Collected Poems: 1945–1990*

East of Trabzon, it rarely stops raining. Spongy moss blankets the stone walls surrounding the small town of Çamlihemşin, and the bridges are humped unusually high to allow clear passage for the thundering white-water Storm River, which rushes its course through here. The little town, crowded with holidaying Turks at the weekend, is bundled around the river surrounded by steep, green vertical valleys. Up there, pulleys, running along steel cables, zip goods between plateaus and houses and men yodel to one another across the hills. Local Hemşinli people stash their beehives up high, saving them from honey-stealing bears who plague hillsides and raid orchards, their mulberry-laden scat littering forest paths. Çamlihemşin is a trailhead for hikes to the Kaçkar Mountains, an extension of the Caucasus Mountains and the central stretch of the Pontic Alps. Up there, in the *yaylas*, the high mountain pastures, nomadic herders move with their animals during summer, and produce cheese, yogurt and honey. Dense mists regularly come in from the Black Sea and, trapped by the mountains, shroud the wooded hills in thick haze. Trabzon, the major gateway city for this wild region, may only be 100 miles away, but psychologically it felt much further than that.

This remote landscape — of double-dipper valleys and fig trees — is as idyllic as it is hopeless. Only corn and livestock thrive here, meaning a hard life of poverty for most. It is surprising, therefore, to look up and see grand wooden Ottoman konaks, some with 16 bedrooms, dotting the jade-coloured slopes, their distinctive chequerboard facades decorated with wooden frames. Dating back to the 19th century, inside there are huge wooden window seats filled with comfy divans with sweeping forest views, medieval-looking hearths for cooking and hidden hatches leading to livestock barns tucked under the house. Hanging on the walls are *nazarliks*, the beaded 'evil eye' charms that can thwart bad luck, turquoise beaded cowbells and keys for mountain houses high up in the *yayla*. One I later read about has a guest room painted claret and blue, the colours of Trabzonspor football team. There are also a few clues to the life stories, fortunes and histories belonging to these houses: a decorated Russian shotgun here, a Russian bread oven there, a stained glass panel above a door.

In one of the largest mansions, Yunus Tarakçi ran a hand through his spiky grey hair and took another sip of tea, the little glass tulip cup glittering as sunshine poured through a break in the clouds and into the wood-panelled sitting room. 'For my great-grandfather, it wasn't a case of wishing to go to Russia, it was a matter of survival. They were poor and his family was hungry. He'd heard of the Tsar and thought he was like a Sultan. The Tsar was a sure sign that in Russia, there was money.' Setting my questions aside, I settled into the divan, and let Tarakçi tell his story.

Leaving on a cargo ship, his great-grandfather had gone to Russia in the 1830s with five friends, sailing for weeks on board a ship that called at ports across the Black Sea before arriving in Yalta. 'Hungry and keen to work, they did a job that could feed them. They learned how to bake bread.' Tarakçi explained. Practising the art of baking costs time, rather than money, and so for weeks Tarakçi's great-grandfather didn't sleep. Deciding that time would be his magic ingredient, he used it to perfect techniques and to gradually knock out local competition. Word travelled back to Çamlihemşin that Tarakçi and his friends were doing well, and earning a living, and so more men left, joining them across the Black Sea. From bread, the bakers graduated to cakes, learning from highly skilled French and Austrian bakers that were living in Russia at the time. 'Before long, they ran the smartest patisserie in Yalta. It was called Dilbert,' Tarakçi said in a French accent. Massaging his temples, he recalled the names of the cakes made there. 'Napoleon cake, éclairs, apple cakes, coconut cookies. All kinds of cakes they made.'

Tarakçi remembers his relatives speaking affectionately about their Russian customers. They were noble and friendly and the women were civilised, cultured and respectful, with a sense of humour. Back home in Çamlihemşin, men were not friends with women outside of their villages and immediate families, the community protecting their long-standing Hemşinli traditions (some say the Hemşin are descended from an 8th-century Armenian prince, only converting to Islam in the 16th century) but in Yalta, the bakers and chefs mixed, going on picnics, and drinking tea with Russian women. It was another world, for both parties.

In 1912, Tarakçi's father too left the village, aged just 12, to learn the ropes and work with his family. His gamble paid off, and before long he found himself serving the Tsar at his summer palace in Yalta. The bravery and enterprising attitudes of these men was to serve them well, as for the next few decades major world events — including World War I and the Russian Revolution — would push them into danger and in different directions from other countries.

Tarakçi clearly remembers his father telling him tales of the Black Sea Raid, when an Ottoman naval sortie, supported by Germany, attacked Russian ports in 1914. 'The Germans attacked Yalta wearing fez hats, as though they were Ottomans, in disguise. My father, aged just 13, saw the bombardment of Yalta and a Russian commander told him to get lost, to disappear. This was war between Russia and the Ottomans, and he was a Turk in Russia.' The older Tarakçis were rounded up and sent to gulags, while, remarkably, his young teenage father ran the bakery alone for a year until he too was exiled, to Austria by train.

ESCAPE TO YALTA

Tarakçi's father moved from one train to the next, searching out Turks when he could. 'He wrote letters, in the Ottoman alphabet, passing them from one Turk to another. Trying to find his friends and family with these little pieces of paper. If you are a minority, you find each other,' Tarakçi said with a shrug. Other Turkish bakers, along with tea servers and hotel workers who, like the Tarakçis, had all gone to Russia to work, passed the notes along. Taking advantage of the confusion, displaced hierarchy and ambiguity that World War I created, some Tarakçis escaped from the gulags, not returning to Turkey, but regrouping in Yalta. 'They still were not secure financially, so coming back to Turkey at that stage was not an option.'

But Communism and, later, famine, made making a living impossible in Russia ('people were stealing flour'), so they switched tack again, travelling this time to Iran via Sinop from Yalta, by ship. In Tehran, they opened an 'elite' restaurant called Café Jale, while others returned to Turkey, to Izmir and Istanbul, carrying with them skills that no one had seen before. 'Those who came back couldn't make money here in Turkey at that time. The technology wasn't here to bake in the way they knew, and who wanted mille-feuille here back then? No one.' Tarakçi said, eyes wide, laying his palms open on his lap.

Eventually the Tarakçis re-gathered on the Turkish Black Sea coast, in the city of Samsun, where they opened a patisserie café, first called 'Moscow', shortly afterwards renamed 'Nation' in honour of Atatürk's new Republic. The kitchen made a spectacular 'Bébé' cake, with hazelnut, dried fruit and chocolate, and wildly popular Napoleon cakes. The baker next door, amazed by what the new competition was up to, finally plucked up the courage to pay these worldly pastry chefs a visit. 'He wanted to try the special cream cakes, but had no idea. He put a piece of cake between two slices of bread and tried to eat it that way. He had no clue!'

Naturally enough, relationships developed overseas, causing culture clashes and divided loyalties. 'Of course, the end result of all this, other than these houses that the families built with the money made, was ignored Turkish wives, new Russian wives, and more children. The first time I really met my father, I was eight years old. He didn't know who I was. I think all together he was away for 40 years.' Tarakçi said, adding that as well as the two Turkish wives that his father had, there was a third woman in his life, a Russian. 'I never met her but I saw a photograph. She was very beautiful but very sad as they could never be together. Her parents warned her to stop the love affair, they said my father would return to Turkey. And, he did. Heartbroken, she killed herself.'

Today, wherever you go in Turkey, you can find a well-stocked *pastane* (pastry shop) with glass counters filled with fancy iced cakes, trays of cookies and fondants. And the story of many Turkish pastry shops can be traced back here, to tiny Çamlihemşin, where bears roam and the Storm River rages, running below the grand hillside mansions that Tsarist gold, Crimean bread and Russian cakes built.

Bébé Cake

Going on the interview with Yunus Tarakçı, I have attempted to recreate the kind of Bébé cake that may have been served at Dilbert in Yalta. A chocolate cake, it is, if anything, in honour of the resourceful men of Çamlihemşin who left their village and sailed across the Black Sea to work and send money home to their families.

FOR THE SPONGE

350g/1½ cups plus 2 teaspoons unsalted butter, softened, plus extra for greasing

350g/1¾ cups golden caster (superfine) sugar

6 medium eggs

200g/1½ cups self-raising flour

100g/1 cup cocoa powder

120g/4¼oz dried cranberries or sour cherries

80g/3oz mixed peel

FOR THE FILLING

50g/1¾oz dark chocolate (70% cocoa solids), chopped

120g/½ cup unsalted butter, softened

200g/1½ cups icing (confectioners') sugar

½ teaspoon vanilla extract

1 tablespoon milk

FOR THE GANACHE

150ml/10 tablespoons double (heavy) cream

250g/8¾oz dark chocolate (70% cocoa solids), chopped

FOR THE HAZELNUT TOPPING

50ml/3½ tablespoons water

120g/⅔ cup caster (superfine) sugar

100g/¾ cup blanched hazelnuts

Preheat the oven to 180°C/350°F/gas mark 4. Butter two 23cm/9-in round cake tins. Cream the butter, adding the sugar gradually, until fluffy. Then stir in the eggs, flour and cocoa powder with a metal spoon, and add the dried fruit and peel. Divide the batter between the tins, smooth the tops and bake for around 30 minutes, until risen and springy but firm to the touch. Remove from the oven and allow to cool before turning out onto a wire rack.

Now for the filling. Melt the chocolate in a heatproof bowl placed over a pan of simmering water, making sure the base of the bowl isn't touching the water. Set aside.

Then beat the butter in a bowl until soft, gradually stirring in the icing (confectioners') sugar before adding the vanilla extract and beating again. When the chocolate is cool, fold it into the mixture, adding the milk to loosen the mixture ever so slightly, and set aside.

Now to make the dark chocolate ganache. Gently heat the cream and then stir into the chopped chocolate, mixing thoroughly until you have a smooth, shiny mixture. Set aside to cool.

Finally, make the candied hazelnuts. Put the water and sugar into a pan and heat until it starts to thicken and is bubbling and sticky; this should take around 5 minutes. Then turn the heat down and swirl the pan but don't stir, for another 2 minutes, until the mixture is amber. Remove from the heat and quickly roll the hazelnuts in the thick syrup, then tip them onto a china plate to cool.

To assemble the cake, work on a plate or stand. First put down one of the sponges, then thickly and evenly spread over the filling, then put the other sponge on top. Spread the ganache over the top with a spatula and allow to set. Then dot the caramelised hazelnuts over, sticking them gently into the ganache. Chill for 3 or so hours, which will make it easier to slice. Serve from the cake stand.

Yayla Sutlaç

Pokut is a remote village set in a glorious flower-strewn *yayla* (high mountain pasture) above Çamlihemşin. Cows, wearing turquoise beaded necklaces, graze with their golden bells ringing, while blankets of clouds, way down in the valleys, gather late afternoon. Up there, where the milk and cream is super-fresh, I met a farmer, a retired soldier, who told me that he whistles to his five cows every morning. His favourite cow, Black Rose, produces the milk for his superior *sütlaç*, a rice pudding with a golden top and a creamy middle, which we ate surrounded by goats and cows, high above the clouds. From the end of August, it is hazelnut season in Turkey's Black Sea region. Seventy per cent of the world's hazelnuts come from here and some make it onto the top of creamy sütlaç, like this one.

SERVES 4

FOR THE SÜTLAÇ

570ml/scant 2½ cups full-fat milk

50g/2½ tablespoons demerara (light brown cane) sugar, plus extra for the top

1 teaspoon vanilla extract

1 cinnamon stick

2 cloves

75g/2¾oz arborio rice

70ml/4½ tablespoons double (heavy) cream

TO SERVE

½ teaspoon ground cinnamon

20g/¾oz hazelnuts, roasted and roughly chopped

In a medium pan, gently heat the milk, sugar, vanilla, cinnamon and cloves. Simmer just for 2 minutes, then take off the heat and set aside to infuse for 20 minutes. Then strain the infused milk into a pan, add the rice and cook, regularly stirring, until the rice is cooked and soft, with a little bite.

Remove from the heat and, once cool, gently stir through the cream. Transfer to 2 ovenproof ramekins and heat your grill as high as possible. Sprinkle over some demerara (light brown cane) sugar and grill until caramelised. Once cool, sift over the ground cinnamon and sprinkle over the chopped hazelnuts.

A Storm River Salad

At the Puli hotel in Çamlıhemşin, I ate an exceptional salad, cooked by a Turk and served by a Georgian. This is a sweet salad, so it goes well with meaty kebabs.

SERVES 6 AS A SIDE

1 red (bell) pepper

70g/2½oz sultanas

½ red cabbage, tough core removed, finely shredded

¼ teaspoon fine salt

2 tablespoons olive oil

2 tablespoons sherry vinegar or red wine vinegar

freshly ground black pepper

Heat the grill to its highest setting. Slice the pepper in half from top to bottom and set it on a tray, skin side up. Grill until the skin is peeling and blackened, then place the halves in a bowl with cling film (plastic wrap) over the top. Leave to cool and steam slightly (which will make them easier to peel) while you get the sultanas ready.

Place the sultanas in a heatproof bowl and pour over enough boiling water to cover them, then cover the bowl with cling film. Let them sit like that for 10 minutes, during which time the peppers should have cooled, then drain the sultanas and set aside.

Once the peppers are cool to touch, peel them and thinly slice them lengthways. Place the shredded cabbage in a large bowl and toss through the salt. Then stir the oil and vinegar through, followed by the sliced pepper, sultanas and some black pepper.

Cover and leave the salad in the fridge for at least 6 hours to let the flavours develop, then taste and adjust the seasoning as necessary. Serve at room temperature, adding another splash of vinegar, to refresh it.

THE BLACK SEA OF THE MIND

Airport shuttle buses gathered outside Trabzon's Hotel Usta Park. Saudi Arabian holidaymakers filed out and into the lobby, handing their green passports, decorated with crossed swords and a golden palm tree, to receptionists. With courtesies exchanged and suitcases delivered back to them, the families slumped down onto leather sofas, travel-tired. The women – daughters, mothers, wives and sisters – chatted and sipped tea from under niqabs. In their black-gloved hands, they held brightly coloured handbags and glittery mobile phones. They were the latest group of tourists to arrive looking to escape the heat of the Gulf. I finished my coffee in the lobby and made my way up to the sixth floor, where the breakfast buffet was drawing to a close.

Among the debris of half-eaten *simit* rings, olive stones and yogurt cartons, polite staff dusted and tidied, staring out of the large curved windows that offered slices of the Black Sea across the rooftops. Shortly, I'd be leaving Trabzon, flying home via Istanbul. I sat, watching the ships in the distance, and considered the previous evening.

In Trabzon's main square, just before midnight, a group of 20 or so Turks had gathered by the statue of Atatürk. An elderly man, wearing a too-big black blazer, brought out a *kemençe*, the sorrowful-sounding box-fiddle found in these parts, propped it onto his shoulder and began drawing his bow quickly across the steel strings. A group formed a circle and slowly, the men began to dance the *horon*, the circular folk dance of the long-departed Pontic Greeks. The music caught the attention of holidaying Arab tourists and they gathered, edging forward, filming the dance on their phones. Trabzonlus walked by, having seen it all before. Not a single Western tourist could be seen in the busy square. The pace picked up and the dancers leaped and skipped and stamped the ground. Some yodelled into the night sky as they do in the surrounding villages of the Black Sea Mountains. This cavorting dance is said to channel the movement of the shimmying silver *hamsi* (anchovies), so abundant in the Black Sea. Something of Trabzon's essence was clumsily captured in that moment: the city's lost multiculturalism, its long-standing traditions and spirit, the new face of tourism and even its affection for *hamsi*.

Clues, mysteries and the unforeseen had been strong and constant running themes as I'd travelled from Odessa to Trabzon via Istanbul, the three central cities in this book. With its tempestuous reputation, waves of migration and dense history, I had always expected to be surprised by the Black Sea, but I could never have predicted much of what I'd felt and uncovered.

It was the human stories by which I was most taken most aback. Given the scale of the White Russian exodus into Istanbul (then Constantinople), with tens of thousands arriving, it was strange to discover how very little remains of their history in the city today. The same could be said of the Jews in Odessa, although, if you know where to look, traces do linger, and there is an excellent small museum dedicated to them. Equally surprising was the degree of bravery and determination shown by the Turkish bakers from Çamlihemşin, who shortly after crossing the Black Sea and serving the Tsar tea, survived wars, gulags and revolutions. St Honoré, the patron saint of bakers and pastry chefs, must have been looking over them.

Obscure communities appeared in my historical research where I'd not predicted them at all: the Swiss winemaking immigrants of Bessarabia and the surviving Russian Old Believer cultures in the Black Sea wetlands of Bulgaria. Cities, too, surprised. Odessa I knew from books and study, but it wasn't until I went there that I truly believed the writers before me who wrote so lyrically of the city's literary atmosphere. Pleasingly, I found it: in the *dvoriki* (courtyards), in the cafés and in the peeling architecture. It is possible, with just a dash of imagination and the right light bouncing off the Black Sea, to still feel something of Isaac Babel's long-lost world. There, too, is the strongest sense of hangover and melancholy, the 'imaginative grip', as I described it. This followed my journeys further south and eastwards, trailing me.

Between my starting point of Odessa, and my end point in Trabzon, 1400 miles away, there was little that the region didn't offer: rushing rivers, castles, ruined churches and, often, cuisine as sublime as the music, architecture and hospitality. Shared flavours and ingredients played out in a fondness for herbs, polenta, kebabs, dolma, tea, nuts, *pekmez*, mastic, olives, fermented dairy, honey, anchovies and meze traditions. All the results of centuries of migration and trade winds around the Black Sea.

But as there is light, there is darkness. In the middle of my research, I travelled to Istanbul several times, staying at the Pera Palace as I usually do, and eating, drinking, exploring and walking as normal. But times were not normal in Istanbul and I was shocked at just how abandoned the city felt. So regularly pitched as a top destination in glossy travel magazines and supplements, it had fallen completely and utterly out of favour. Terrorism and the failed coup attempt in 2016 had succeeded in slaying tourism. One cold, snowy Friday in January 2017, I bundled up and went to the Grand Bazaar. Inside, it was eerily quiet, with virtually no other foreign visitors. And, as men knelt in between their shops for the call to prayer, I was almost the only person left standing. Given the usual buzz of crowds and trade found at this major tourist attraction, it was a disconcerting experience.

Power, both physical and psychological, was another recurring theme. It shifts, rides and falls around the Black Sea. Today it displays its might at Constanta's Navy Day celebrations, in the nationalism of Trabzon and in the clout of Putin's warships cruising on the Bosphorus. The Black Sea, overflowing with intrigue, often feels as though it is the pivot of the geopolitical world. But its strength lies in less obvious places, too.

It is under the water, invisible to us above the waves. Down there are sunken shipwrecks, preserved by the sea's un-oxygenated layer. A fascinating, salty stockpile of dead civilisations – Venetian, Byzantine and Ottoman. It can be felt, too, in the world's oldest worked gold in Varna, a result of riches made by salt mining in Europe's 'oldest prehistoric town', close to the Bulgarian Black Sea. And, too, in the small historic empire of Trebizond which expanded across the Black Sea from the northeast corner of Anatolia to what is now southern Crimea.

But there was more. The Black Sea's spirit, undeniably magnetic, was at times, intense. I saw it in the eyes of the fishermen and the fisherwoman that I met and I heard it in their voices. They lived by it, longed for it and respected the sea more than anything else. I felt the sea's power most acutely when it was lit by a movie-light, not imagined, but real, intensified by stillness and sunsets and the thunder-flash of storms. Its appearance constantly changed from savage to still, jet black to silver, from different country to different shoreline. I know that the notebooks, photographs and voice recordings I have collected, containing interviews, observations and port and sea sounds, will all have the capability of sending me drifting back to the Black Sea.

It might indeed look like a lake on the map, but in the mind the Black Sea is as intoxicating as it is frontierless. Its rich atmosphere and layer-cake history much more than physical maps and borders. And for Odessa, Istanbul and Trabzon, the Black Sea is more than a backdrop, physical and mental. It is a stage for people to play out their lives on; a source of life, some despair and, often, hope.

SOURCES AND BOOKS CONSULTED

Research for this book has involved a range of books, newspapers, journals, websites and magazines. Anyone familiar with two writers and historians in particular, Neal Ascherson and Charles King, will recognise my principal debt. Also, in Turkey, *Cornucopia* magazine has provided much inspiration. Every issue is an absolute joy and I heartily recommend it to anyone with even a passing interest in Turkey (www.cornucopia.net).

ODESSA

A SKETCH OF ODESSA: STEVEDORES, STOWAWAYS AND FABERGÉ EGGS

Ascherson, Neal, *Black Sea: Coasts and Conquests: From Pericles to Putin* (Vintage, 2015)

King, Charles, *The Black Sea: A History* (Oxford University Press, 2005)

Buckler, Julie and Johnson, Emily D., *Rites of place: public commemoration in Russia and Eastern Europe* (Northwestern University Press, 2013)

Tanny, Jarrod, *City of Rogues and Schnorrers* (Indiana University Press, 2011)

Kuprin, A. I. Granatovyi brasle: Povesti i rasskazy. Ed. I. Parina. Moscow, 1984 (Taken from: Bethea, David M.,'Underground' to 'In the Basement': How Odessa Replaced Petersburg as Capital of the Russian Literary Imagination, *American Contributions to the 14th International Congress of Slavists* Vol. 2, Slavica, 2008

The Mystery Of Odessa's Mascarons, odessareview.com, http://odessareview.com/mystery-odessas-mascarons

BABYLON ON THE BLACK SEA – ODESSA'S JEWISH ROOTS

Sefarim, Mendele Mocher, *Tales of Mendele the Book Peddler* (Schocken, 1996)

Tanny, Jarrod, *City of Rogues and Schnorrers* (Indiana University Press, 2011)

Babel, Isaac, *Odessa Stories* (Pushkin Press, 2016)

AN ICE-CREAM DEBAUCH AND OTHER LITERARY FEASTINGS

Nabokov, Vladimir, *Nikolai Gogol* (New Directions, 1961)

Gogol, Nikolai, *The Collected Tales* (London, Everyman, 2008)

Greenleaf, Monika, Moeller-Sally, Stephen, *Russian Subjects: Empire, Nation, and the Culture of the Golden Age* (Northwestern University Press, 1998)

Klekh, Igor, *Adventures in the Slavic Kitchen: A Book of Essays with Recipes* (Glagoslav Publications, 2016)

Rayfield, Donald, *Anton Chekhov: A Life* (Northwestern University Press, 1998)

Twain, Mark, *The Innocents Abroad* (Wordsworth Editions, 2010)

Odessa: City of Writerly Love, www.newyorker.com, https://www.newyorker.com/books/page-turner/odessa-city-of-writerly-love

The Odessaphiles, 1843magazine.com, https://www.1843magazine.com/content/arts/odessaphiles

Akhmatova, Anna, *Selected Poems* (Bloodaxe Books, 1989)

de Balzac, Honoré, *Complete Works of Honoré de Balzac* (Delphi Classics, 2013)

Shirley Brooks, Charles, *The Russians of the South* (Longman, 1854)

Moore, John, *A Journey from London to Odessa* (Printed for the author, 1833)

Ilf, Ilya and Petrov, Yevgeny, *The Twelve Chairs* (Northwestern University Press, 1961)

A BORSCHT REBELLION –
A SHORT MEDITATION ON THE BATTLESHIP POTEMKIN

Potemkin: the mutiny, the movie and the myth, www.independent.co.uk, http://www.independent.co.uk/news/world/europe/potemkin-the-mutiny-the-movie-and-the-myth-225737.html

16 November 1929: Film review of *Potemkin*, www.theguardian.com, https://www.theguardian.com/media/from-the-archive-blog/2011/may/24/sergei-eisenstein-potemkin-1929

A Monstrous Staircase: Inscribing the 1905 Revolution on Odessa, www.columbia.edu,http://www.columbia.edu/~rjs19/Stanton%20(2013a)%20A%20Monstrous%20Staircase.pdf

PORTO-FRANCO – ODESSA'S ITALIAN CONNECTION

Pushkin Alexander, *Eugene Onegin* (Penguin Classics, 2003)

Shipwrecks of the Black Sea: Finding an Underwater Graveyard, www.nationalgeographic.com, https://www.nationalgeographic.com/archaeology-and-history/magazine/2017/03-04/black-sea-ancient-shipwrecks-bulgaria/

Centuries of Preserved Shipwrecks Found in the Black Sea, www.news.nationalgeographic.com, https://news.nationalgeographic.com/2016/10/black-sea-shipwreck-discovery/

BESSARABIA

A WAGON, A BIBLE AND A RIFLE

Black, François-David, *Journal de voyage Lausanne–Chabag–Odessa* (CABEDITA, 2016)

History of Shabo, www.shabo.ua, http://shabo.ua/en/sp/history

A living history since 1820, http://www.cavebessarabie.ch/

The Tardent Family from Ormont-Dessous, Vaud, Switzerland, www.tardent-history.info http://www.tardent-history.info/Swiss%20 Colony%20Chabag.htm

Once a Swiss Winegrower Colony CHABAG in Russia, Now a Modern Wine-Culture Center, www.chabag.ch, https://www.chabag.ch/Once%20a%20 swiss%20winegrower%20colony%20named%20Chabag%20in%20Russia.pdf

Rhinelander, Anthony L.H., *Prince Michael Vorontsov: Viceroy to the Tsar* (McGill-Queen's Press, 1990)

How Churchill, Roosevelt and Stalin Planned to End the Second World War, www.iwm.org.uk, https://www.iwm.org.uk/history/how-churchill-roosevelt-and-stalin-planned-to-end-the-second-world-war

ROMANIA

NAVY DAY

Turks and Tatars in Bulgaria and the Balkans, www.academia.edu, http://www.academia.edu/3759955/Turks_and_Tatars_in_Bulgaria_and_the_Balkans

Forwood, William, *Romanian Invitation* (Garnstone, 1968)

BLACK SEA SUPPER FOR THE TSAR

National History Museum of Romania Hosts Exhibit Dedicated to 1914 Visit of Nicholas II to Constanta, http://www.angelfire.com/pa/ImperialRussian/blog/index.blog/1455160/national-history-museum-of-romania-hosts-exhibit-dedicated-to-1914-visit-of-nicholas-ii-to-constanta/

The Russian Queen of Romania That Almost Was, www.kingofromania.com https://kingofromania.com/2017/08/10/the-russian-queen-of-romania-that-almost-was/

Visit of the Russian Imperial Family in Constanta, 1914, www.net-film.eu https://www.net-film.eu/film-65298/

SEA COSSACKS AND SHERBET – ROMANIA THROUGH TRAVELLERS' EYES

Sitwell, Sacheverell, *Roumanian Journey* (Bloomsbury Reader, 2012)

Leigh Fermor, Patrick, *Words of Mercury* (John Murray, 2004)

Leigh Fermor, Patrick, *The Broken Road* (John Murray, 2013)

Blacker, William, *Along the Enchanted Way* (John Murray, 2010)

von Hardenberg, Wilko Graf, *The Nature State: Rethinking the History of Conservation* (Didcot, Taylor & Francis, 2017)

BULGARIA

OLD GOLD AND DEEP PURPLE

Mystery of the Varna Gold: What Caused These Ancient Societies to Disappear? www.smithsonianmag.com www.smithsonianmag.com/travel/varna-bulgaria-gold-graves-social-hierarchy-prehistoric-archaelogy-smithsonian-journeys-travel-quarterly-180958733/

Europe's 'oldest prehistoric town' unearthed in Bulgaria, www.bbc.co.uk, www.bbc.co.uk/news/world-europe-20156681

http://www.atimes.com/article/brief-history-chinese-salt-worlds-oldest-monopoly/

Kurlansky, Mark, *Salt* (Vintage, 2003)

Johnson, Stowers, *Gay Bulgaria* (Robert Hale, 1964)

Walker, Harlan, *Food on the Move: Proceedings of the Oxford Symposium on Food and Cookery*, 1996

Bulgaria's 'Rock 'n Roll' Capital Falls Silent, www.balkaninsight.com http://www.balkaninsight.com/en/article/bulgarian-town-s-rock-story-faces-bitter-end-05-31-2017

TRAVELS WITH THE BARD OF POLAND

Food and drink in Pan Tadeusz, wikiquote.org, https://en.wikiquote.org/wiki/Food_and_drink_in_Pan_Tadeusz

Orientalism in Adam Mickiewicz's Crimean Sonnets, slavic.ucla.edu, http://slavic.ucla.edu/wp-content/uploads/2016/09/roman_1100.pdf

Kassabova, Kapka, *Bulgaria* (New Holland Publishers, 2008)

STRANDJA – TO THE TURKISH BORDER

History Strandja Mountains Bulgaria, www.visitstrandja.com
http://www.visitstrandja.com/history-Strandja-Mountains-Bulgaria.php

Thousands Remember Bulgaria's 1903 Ilinden-Preobrazhenie Uprising,
www.novinite.com, http://www.novinite.com/articles/107060/Thousands+Re
member+Bulgaria%27s+1903+Ilinden-Preobrazhenie+Uprising

Kay, Annie, *Bulgaria: The Bradt Travel Guide* (Chalfont St Peter, Bradt, 2008)

ISTANBUL

ISTANBUL – THE SEA COMES TO THE CITY

Üner, Turgay, A., *Trabzon: Port-Cities of the Eastern Mediterranean 1800-1914*, Review
(New York, Fernand Braudel Center, 1993)

Freely, John, *The Black Sea Coast of Turkey* (Redhouse Press, 1996)

Kazım Koyuncu: Pride of Lazuri, www.dailysabah.com,
https://www.dailysabah.com/portrait/2015/10/31/kazim-koyuncu-pride-of-
lazuri

Fortna, Benjamin C., *The Circassian: A Life of Eref Bey, Late Ottoman Insurgent and Special
Agent* (OUP, 2016)

'The Compass: On The Black Sea' www.bbc.co.uk, http://www.bbc.co.uk/
programmes/p058fnwr

http://www.argonauts-book.com/symplegades.html

Oktem, Emre, *Secret Istanbul* (Jonglez Publishing, 2016)

Taylor, Jane, *Imperial Istanbul: A Traveller's Guide: Includes Iznik, Bursa and Edirne*
(I.B.Tauris, 2007)

Byron, Lord, *Selected Poems of Lord Byron: Including Don Juan and Other Poems*
(Wordsworth Poetry Library, 1994)

Tillinghast, Richard, *An Armchair Traveller's History of Istanbul: City of Remembering and
Forgetting* (BookHaus, 2012)

Kinglake, Alexander, *Eothen* (J. Ollivier, 1844)

TEA AND LONGING IN TSARIGRAD

Bulgakov, Mikhail, *Flight* (lulu.com, 2014)

Istanbul's Russian history is fast fading into distant memory, platform24.org,
http://platform24.org/en/articles/307/istanbul-s-russian-history-is-fast-
fading-into-distant-memory

Deleon, Jak, *The White Russians in Istanbul* (Istanbul, Remzi Kitabevi Publications,
1995)

Aya Panteleymon Russian Orthodox Church, www.cornucopia.net, http://www.cornucopia.net/guide/listings/sights/aya-panteleymon-russian-orthodox-church/

King, Charles, *Midnight at the Pera Palace: The Birth of Modern Istanbul* (W.W. Norton & Company, 2015)

About Smirnoff, www.smirnoff.com, http://www.smirnoff.com/en-gb/about/

Beyoğlu in the Jazz Age: Dancing Until Daybreak, www.cornucopia.net, http://www.cornucopia.net/magazine/articles/dancing-until-daybreak/

TURKEY'S BLACK SEA REGION

MOON CHORUSES IN THE CITY OF SAFFRON

Mansions & Secret Garden, www.gulevisafranbolu.com.tr, http://www.gulevisafranbolu.com.tr/en/mansion

Safranbolu and Its Neighbouring Provinces, www.kultur.gov.tr, http://www.kultur.gov.tr/EN,113772/safranbolu-houses.html

Freely, John, *The Black Sea Coast of Turkey* (Redhouse Press, 1996)

A REVOLUTION ON THE HEAD

Turkey's Glorious Hat Revolution, www.lareviewofbooks.org, https://lareviewofbooks.org/article/turkeys-glorious-hat-revolution/#!

RAIDERS AND AMAZONS ON THE EUXINE

Ostapchuk, Victor, *The Human Landscape of the Ottoman Black Sea in the Face of the Cossack Naval Raids* (Oriente Moderno Journal, 2001)

The Real Amazons, www.newyorker.com, https://www.newyorker.com/books/joshua-rothman/real-amazons

Prison Song, turkishpoetic.wordpress.com, https://turkishpoetic.wordpress.com/2015/03/12/prison-song-v-sabahattin-ali/

ROCK TOMBS AND A BACKWARDS RUNNING RIVER

Secret Tunnel Helped to Baffle Tamerlane (Times, 27 Nov. 1965)

Mount Harşena and the Rrock-tombs of the Pontic Kings, unesco.org, http://whc.unesco.org/en/tentativelists/6039/

Darke, Diana, *Eastern Turkey* (Chalfont St Peter, Bradt, 2011)

Championed by the Cavalry, www.cornucopia.net, http://www.cornucopia.net/magazine/articles/championed-by-the-cavalry/

TRABZON

TRABZON – FROM PORT OF PERSIA TO TRADER TOURISTS
Bryer, Anthony, *The Empire of Trebizond and the Pontos* (Variorum Reprints, 1980)

The Strange History of 'Mad Honey', www.modernfarmer.com, https://modernfarmer.com/2014/09/strange-history-hallucinogenic-mad-honey/

Hamilton, William John, *Researches in Asia Minor, Pontus, and Armenia* (John Murray, 1842)

A NOTE ON TURKEY'S OTHER HAGIA SOPHIA
Turkey's other Hagia Sophia – in Trabzon, www.theguardian.com https://www.theguardian.com/travel/2017/oct/25/turkey-other-hagia-sophia-trabzon-church-mosque

Obituary: Professor David Talbot Rice (London, Times, 20 March 1972)

Runciman, Steven, David Talbot Rice (London, The Burlington Magazine, 1972)

A CRIMEAN PALACE IN THE TEA BUSHES
Our Ankara Correspondent: For All the Tea in Turkey (London, Times, 9 June 1962)

Boreth, Craig, *The Hemingway Cookbook* (Chicago Review Press, 2012)

A Handbook for Travellers in the Ionian Islands, Greece, Turkey, Asia Minor and Constantinople (John Murray, 1840)

THE HOUSES THAT TSARIST CAKES BUILT
Daunt, Patricia, The Country Houses that Ride 'the Storm' (Istanbul, Cornucopia, Issue 12, 1997)

Film: *Gurbet Pastası* by Uğur Biryol (Istanbul, 2013)

GENERAL RECOMMENDED READING LIST

BLACK SEA

Applebaum, Anne, Between East & West (Penguin, 2015)
A travel and history book, with insights on Adam Mickiewicz and Odessa.

Ascherson, Neal, Black Sea: Coasts and Conquests: From Pericles to Putin (Vintage, 2015)
A marvellous book, and the modern classic on history and culture of the region. It is soul-stirring, impeccably researched and sweeping in its scope. My copy is falling apart, not having left my side since I began my Black Sea adventuring.

Freely, John, The Black Sea Coast of Turkey (Redhouse Press, 1996)
A scholarly guide containing many insights from writers including William Hamilton, a 19th-century English traveller.

Kassabova, Kapka, Border: A Journey to the Edge of Europe (Granta, 2017)
Kassabova's celebrated book provides a lyrical look at the borderlands where Bulgaria, Greece and Turkey meet.

King, Charles, The Black Sea: A History (Oxford University Press, 2005)
Researched in many languages and a must-read.

ODESSA

Babel, Isaac, Odessa Stories (Pushkin Press, 2016)
This edition, newly translated by the masterful Boris Dralyuk, is a collection of all the stories Babel set in the city.

Kaminsky, Ilya, Dancing in Odessa (Arc Publications, 2014)
An unusual, captivating and award-winning poetry collection.

King, Charles, Odessa (W. W. Norton & Company, 2011)
A masterful and brilliant history book, written with such ease that it reads like a novel.

Halkin, Hillel, Jabotinsky, A Life (Yale, 2014)
A fascinating insight into Ze'ev Jabotinsky. Son of Odessa, first-rate writer and Russian journalist, and Revisionist Zionist leader.

Hercules, Olia, Mamushka: Recipes from Ukraine & beyond (Mitchell Beazley, 2015)
A unique book, *Mamushka* showcases Hercules's personal stories and recipes.

Tanny, Jarrod, City of Rogues and Schnorrers (Indiana University Press, 2011)
A look at the Judeo-Russian culture that emerged in Odessa in the 19th century. If you want to know more about the city's historic swindlers, Jewish gangsters and jokers, real and imagined, this is the book to buy.

ROMANIA

Blacker, William, Along the Enchanted Way (John Murray, 2010)
A bucolic memoir set in rural Romania, elegant writing and capturing a place and time now almost gone.

Leigh Fermor, Patrick, The Broken Road (John Murray, 2013)
Published posthumously by John Murray, this is the final section of Leigh Fermor's journey across Europe from the Hook of Holland to Constantinople in the 1930s.

Sitwell, Sacheverell, Roumanian Journey (Bloomsbury Reader, 2012)
First published in 1938, this is a book of its time, but it captures the joy of travel, and contains vivid descriptions and poetic passages.

BULGARIA

Johnson, Stowers, Gay Bulgaria (Hale, 1964)
Old-school travel writing.

Kaneva, Johnson, Balkan Food and Cookery (Prospect Books, 1995)
An excellent resource on Balkan food with lots of lively anecdotes.

Nicoloff, Assen, Bulgarian Folklore (Privately Published, 1983)
A collection of obscure and wonderful Bulgarian folklore facts.

TURKEY

Clark, Peter, Istanbul: A Cultural and Literary History (Signal Books Ltd, 2010)
In-depth cultural, historical and literary guide to Istanbul.

Clow, Kate, The Kaçkar – Trekking in Turkey's Black Sea Mountains (Upcountry Turkey Ltd, 2012)
Unique guide to Turkey's Black Sea Mountains featuring in-depth trekking routes and cultural insights. A must-have if you go trekking in the region.

Darke, Diana, Eastern Turkey (Bradt, 2011)
Excellent primer and guidebook featuring plenty of history, culture and context.

Finkel, Andrew, Turkey: What Everyone Needs to Know (Oxford University Press, 2012)
Finkel is a widely respected senior journalist based in Turkey, and is restaurant critic for *Cornucopia* magazine.

Genç, Kaya (Ed.), An Istanbul Anthology (The American University in Cairo Press, 2015)
Pocket-sized collection of writings and observations of travel writers and diarists through the centuries.

Işın, Mary, Sherbet & Spice (I.B. Tauris, 2013)
A magnificently researched book about Turkey's love affair with sugar, sweets and spice.

King, Charles, Midnight at the Pera Palace (W.W. Norton & Company, 2015)
Focusing on Istanbul and its decadent jazz age – this is essential reading if you want to know more about 20th-century Turkish history, White Russians and Istanbul's iconic hotel, the Pera Palace.

Kitchen, Leanne, Turkey – Recipes and Tales from the Road (Murdoch Books, 2011)
A wide-ranging Turkish cookbook with achievable recipes.

Macaulay, Rose, The Towers of Trebizond (Collins, 1956)
Winner of the James Tait Black Memorial Prize for fiction, the account of a trip to Turkey by narrator Laurie, who is accompanying her Aunt Dot (and camel).

Oktem, Emre, Secret Istanbul (Jonglez Publishing, 2016)
A quirky guidebook for those who want to peel the city back further.

Orga, Ates (Ed.), Istanbul: Poetry of Place (Eland Publishing Ltd., 2007)
Beautiful collection of poetry in a miniature format, perfect reading for the upper deck of a Bosphorus ferry.

Seal, Jeremy, A Fez of the Heart (Picador, 1995)
Jeremy Seal uses the fez as a central theme for his journey to understand contemporary Turkey. A funny, wise and engaging piece of travel writing. Jeremy's other books on Turkey are perfect travel companions, too. If you haven't yet, read him and see.

MAGAZINES AND JOURNALS

Cornucopia

Slavic Review

The Odessa Review

RADIO

BBC reporter Tim Whewell's brilliant series 'The Compass: On The Black Sea', BBC World Service (available as a podcast)

ACKNOWLEDGEMENTS

Thanks must go first to my agent Jessica Woollard and my publisher Sarah Lavelle. I owe you both more than I can articulate here. I'd also like to thank Susannah Otter for her exceptional editorial guidance.

Thanks also to Theodore Kaye (Teo), not only for his peerless location photography but also for always going the extra mile(s). Thank you also to Huseyin Ozpehlivan for assistance in Turkey. In London, it was a blessing to have such a strong, good-humoured and utterly charming team working on the food photography and design of the book. Thank you to Claire Rochford, Ola O. Smit, Dave Brown, Pip Spence, Amy Stephenson, Ivana Zorn and to Tabitha Hawkins.

Many Odessans, in Ukraine and in the USA, have extended welcoming hands. I'd especially like to thank my friend and literary translator Boris Dralyuk for his on-going humour and support and especially for generously offering his translation of Bagritsky's 'Smugglers' poem for this book. Also, many thanks to Vladislav Davidzon, Ilya Kaminsky, and to Andrei Malaev-Babel. Thank you to those who helped me in Odessa on assignments and research trips, including the wonderful Julia Gorodetskaya, Katya Michaels, Dmytro Sikorsky, Nika Lozovska, Tatiana Zagnitnaya and all the helpful and kind staff at the Frederic Koklen boutique hotel who have looked after me so well during my stays in the 'city of dreams'.

For ideas and assistance in Bulgaria, thank you to the author of the Bradt guide to Bulgaria, Annie Kay, and to my patient translator, fixer and hard rock enthusiast, Todor Kenov.

In Bucharest, at the National Museum of Romanian History, thank you to the documentalist Alexandra Mărăşoiu, for her help with research into Constanta's Casino.

In Istanbul and Turkey's Black Sea region, I'd like to thank Pinar Timer, Nessi Behar, Uğur Ildiz and Yigal Schleifer. A hug to you, Demet Akay, I hope we will go into the Kaçkar Mountains again one day. Thank you also, to Nurfer Tosun, Mehmet Gurbuz, the team at Tarihi Kalkanoglu Pilavi, Harun Can Biryol, and Yunus Tarakçı. To my dear friends Ibrahim and Gul Canbulat, I am forever in your debt. Also, Ayiln Tan: teşekkür ederim.

To writers whose work on the region I have read, drawn upon and enjoyed, thank you to: Charles King, Orhan Pamuk, Anna Reid, Simon Sebag Montefiore, Neal Ascherson, Shaun Walker, Jeremy Seal, Thomas de Waal, Edmund de Waal and Anne Applebaum.

Closer to home, a special thanks to two of my editors — Jane Dunford at the *Guardian* and Joe Kent at the BBC — who have commissioned recent stories about Ukraine and Turkey.

In the food-writing world, I'd like to thank Diana Henry, Olia Hercules and Sabrina Ghayour for their kind words and interest in my travels and projects. Giverny Tattersfield, thank you for your good humour and generosity. I am also grateful and indebted to Sally Somers for her guidance.

I'd like to say sorry to my dear friends (especially to you, Helen) and my patient in laws (Linda and Daddy K, Annabel, Charles and Di) for my usual disappearing acts, general hopelessness and prolonged silences. Also, thank you to Judith and Duncan at Langcliffe.

The greatest debt is to my beloved husband, fellow-journalist and the finest travel companion one could hope for, James Kilner; thank you for your guidance, comments and for everything else.

Finally, I thank my Dad, David Pink, for his humour, encouragement and moral support. This book is for him.

INDEX

Caroline Eden is a journalist and writer specialising in the
former Soviet Union. Her writing has appeared in the travel,
food and arts pages of the *Guardian*, *Daily Telegraph* and *Financial
Times* and over the past decade she has filed stories from
Uzbekistan, Ukraine, Russia, Kyrgyzstan, Kazakhstan and
Azerbaijan for BBC Radio 4's *From Our Own Correspondent*. As
well as leading occasional private tours to Central Asia, she
has also spoken about her work to audiences at the Frontline
Club, RGS and Asia House. Caroline's first book, *Samarkand*,
was a *Guardian* book of the year 2016 and went on to win the
Guild of Food Writers Award for best food and travel book
in 2017. She lives in Edinburgh.
Twitter and Instagram: @edentravel

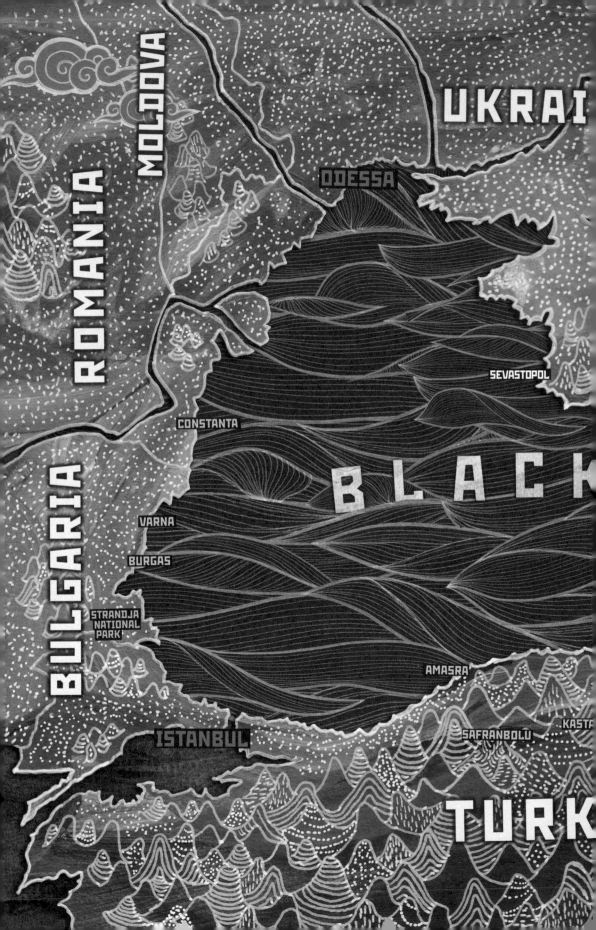